D1756955

The informal economy and connections with organised crime

The informal economy and connections with organised crime: the impact of national social and economic policies

Joanna Shapland
Paul Ponsaers
(eds.)

BJu Legal Publishers
The Hague
2009

ISBN 978-90-8974-164-6
NUR 741

www.bju.nl

CONTENTS

Introduction

Joanna Shapland and Paul Ponsaers

The informal economy is a constantly present undercurrent in the cities and countryside of Europe. Sometimes it becomes suddenly visible: groups of men standing around on certain streets waiting for someone to offer them a day's work; trinket sellers on beaches and rose sellers in restaurants; a newspaper revealing dire conditions of overcrowding for agricultural workers or factory workers; the collapse of a building built with substandard materials or inadequately trained employees who were not on the official payroll. But generally the informal economy tries to remain hidden – it depends upon not being noticed. These conditions tend also to attract the attention of organised crime. Where trade is being carried out under cover, then illegal substances and even people may be able to be trafficked as well. Those who are working illegally can be susceptible to other forms of scams and forceful treatment.

In this volume, we explore the connections between the informal economy and organised crime – and pose the question of whether countries' national social and economic policies affect the form and extent of their informal economies and the extent and nature of connections with organised crime. At the level of the nation state, there is of course one definitional connection between the informal economy and national policy. Formally, the informal economy is defined by what is not the formal economy – what is not within the Gross Domestic Product (GDP) of that country. Hence policies which impact directly on that definitional boundary will necessarily affect the nature of the informal economy in that country. If, for example, in one country prostitution is legalised and prostitutes pay taxes, then prostitution is part of the formal economy – whereas in another it will be part of the informal economy (not legal, not paying taxes).

We, however, are interested primarily in the inadvertent or more indirect consequences of national policies. If, for example, a country decides to have very high tax rates for service taxes (such as VAT), then tradesmen and service providers may decide to undercut those in the formal economy and take the consequences of offering their services in the informal economy (such as not being able to pursue defaulters through the courts). If few resources are put into enforcement, then the informal economy may boom. If wages in the formal economy are very low (as for example in the former Soviet Union countries), then those who can sell some of their products or services 'on the side' may do so, using their employers' tools and materials. If national borders are porous, economic differentials are high between countries, but there are few legitimate opportunities for migrants in the formal economy (i.e. residence permits are needed to work legitimately), it may encourage 'slave labour' and sometimes human trafficking. If countries are in transition, democratic traditions weak and economic opportunities beckon, then bribery may flourish, not just in professional services or law enforcement, but even to sway votes in parliament – so-called 'state capture'.

This is a new field of research in relation to the informal economy. It needs to bring together those interested in social policy, crime, the sociology of work, regulatory enforcement and economics. Because it is interested in differences in national criminal, fiscal and social policies, it has to work flexibly across economic and legal definitions of the informal economy, incorporating both what is often called the 'grey' economy (not complying with work regulations) and what is called the 'black' economy (provision of goods or services which is against the criminal law).

The volume stems from a series of European seminars funded by the European Commission under the auspices of the co-ordination action CRIMPREV, funded under the 6th Framework and co-ordinated by GERN (the Groupe Européen de Recherche sur les Normativités) and, more concretely, by Rene Levy. One of the workpackages of CRIMPREV was on the informal economy and its connections with organised crime and was directed by ourselves.

The first seminars focused on the nature and extent of the informal economy in different European cities and countries and was published as Ponsaers et al. (2008) *The informal economy and its links to organised crime*. Having considered the wide differences in the forms the informal economy takes in different countries, we then moved on to look at factors influencing its nature and extent and the extent to which these related to national legislation and enforcement practices. We looked first at migration, migration law and labour practices in a seminar held in Bologna, organised by Professor Dario Melossi. We then focused on countries in transition and their economies at a seminar in Ljubljana, organised by Professor Bojan Dobovsek. Finally, we met together with practitioners and local and national policy makers at a seminar held in Rotterdam, organised by Professor Henk van de Bunt. We are very grateful to all the seminar organisers, together with Rene Levy and Daniel Ventre of GERN, for facilitating this continuing discussion over a period of 18 months which permitted us to move beyond the city and national boundaries of looking at what is the informal economy, to consider how it is shaped and moulded by national policies.

The first paper in this volume, by **Shapland and Ponsaers**, provides an overview, derived from the discussions during all the seminars, of ways in which national policies in the social, fiscal, economic and immigration fields, may impact on the informal economy and make it more or less susceptible to infiltration by organised crime. **Aden** tackles the dilemmas national governments face when confronted with a burgeoning informal economy in the service and construction sectors, related to regulation and enforcement practices, using the case of Germany. The theme of work and of what one does when one does not have a legal status to work is then taken up by **Ferraris** in relation to Italy's migration laws and how they interact with requirements for residence permits and work permits. The ways in which migrants have to work illegally in order to remain long enough to obtain a legal status or benefit from measures designed to deal with employers' shortages of labour are discussed. **Saitta** concludes this section focusing on the nature of work by examining how two migrant groups have fared in two different areas of Sicily, re-examining the almost taken for granted theory that work provides a route to assimilation within the host nation. He finds that, due to cultural and linguistic barriers and stereotyping of migrants, there is minimal integration within the workforce, even in occupations which depend heavily on migrant and temporary labour.

The second group of papers in the volume focus on the business community and explore the porous and uncertain boundaries between legal and illegal practices in normal business circumstances and their interaction with modes of regulation. **Verhage** looks at the financial sector in Belgium and specifically at how banks operate their legal responsibilities to report and police money laundering, examining the interactions between bank compliance officers, regulators and the criminal authorities (police and prosecutor). She finds tensions between roles and sometimes inadequate communication stress banks' ability to detect and take action against those operating in the informal economy, particularly given the ambiguity of their simultaneous status as clients. **Dorn and Meerts** continue these themes of role tensions and fluid definitions in the corporate sector in their examination of corporate security decisions in the Netherlands and Belgium on how to deal with instances of fraud or theft from the company by its employees. The informal economy has its parallels in informal enforcement practices when illegality has been discovered.

Dobovšek considers the serious field of corruption of the public sector, in his review of state capture in transition countries in central and eastern Europe. At its worst, the public sector can become the tool of private enterprise and organised crime, as public servants and members of parliament are 'bought' to secure the 'right' result in crucial votes. **Kupatadze** compares the results of the 'revolutions' in Georgia, the Ukraine and Kyrgyzstan and how effective they have been in combating such corruption, finding that political and cultural factors have contributed to the different paths and types of corruption that were in existence and the extent to which they have been tackled. Finally, **Copic and Simeunovic-Patic** explore the changing patterns of human trafficking and their routes through Serbia, relating trafficking flows to migration flows, migration policies, possibilities for illegal work and the economic status of countries of origin, transit and destination countries.

Each of these papers has drawn upon empirical work in the countries involved, often research done with some difficulty in environments where research and transparency are threats, due to the hidden nature of both the informal economy and organised crime. Together, they provide important new pointers to the ways in which states, often inadvertently, mould and shape their informal economies through their legislative, regulatory and enforcement policies.

REFERENCES

Ponsaers, P., Shapland, J. & Williams, C.C. (eds.) (2008). 'The informal economy and its links to organised crime'. *International Journal of Social Economics*, 35(9-10): 644-762.

Potential effects of national policies on the informal economy

Joanna Shapland and Paul Ponsaers[1]

INTRODUCTION

Economies can be divided into two sectors, the formal and the informal. Much of the unreported income of the informal sector is the result of a deliberate attempt to evade taxes.[2] The most recent (indirect) studies looking at the size of the informal economy, such as Schneider (2005), show that the informal sector in developing countries ranges in size from 20% to 70% of the Gross Domestic Product (GDP) and is still growing. Today half of the world's population is living in cities. The informal employment currently constitutes anywhere from 40 to 60 percent of total urban employment and will probably form an increasing proportion of urban employment (Charmes, 2000). Parallel to an increase in home work there has been an increase in street vending in towns and cities world-wide. Informal trade, most of which is street trade, constitutes anything from 30 to 50 percent of total urban informal employment (Chen et al., 2002). Existing estimates remain never the less rather inconclusive, and – as a consequence of this – evaluation of the effectiveness of national and international financial, economic and social policies is difficult (Verhage, 2009).

The term 'the informal sector' can refer to street vendors in Bogota; rickshaw pullers in Hanoi and Calcutta; garbage collectors in Cairo; home-based garment workers in Manila, Madeira, Mexico City, and Toronto; and home-based electronic workers in Leeds, Istanbul, and Kuala Lumpur. Some observers feel the sector is simply too varied or heterogeneous to be meaningful as a concept (Peattie, 1987). In this contribution we try to summarise the policy arguments which arose during the series of seminars held in relation to the workpackage on 'The informal economy and organised crime', as part of the CRIMPREV Co-ordination Action funded by the EU[3] (Shapland and Ponsaers, 2008). In essence we ask ourselves if

---

1. We are very grateful to Thierry Godefroy for a number of suggestions about an earlier version of this paper, as well as to participants in the CRIMPREV seminars.

2. There are direct and indirect methods of estimating the informal economy. *Direct* methods involve undertaking sample surveys (small in-depth samples or large questionnaire-based samples) and extrapolating to the whole economy. *Indirect* methods involve analysing the money supply data and estimating the discrepancy between income and expenditure (Schneider, 2002).

3. See http://www.gern-cnrs.com/gern/fileadmin/documents/CRIMPREV/WP1/Report_WP1/rapport WP1_final_28jan08.pdf for the original starting position of this series of seminars.

the informal economy functions in the same way everywhere? Do similar factors do affect it? We especially concentrate on the question as to how this may interact with countries' social and economic policies? Do some policies encourage the informal economy? Do some countries make (semi-deliberate) choices to have a certain amount of the informal economy or particular profile for it?[4]

It has primarily been nation states' choices as to which economic activities they have decided should be criminal (subject to the criminal law) or legal. Similarly, states' choices as to which activities should be regulated by workplace regulation or quality standards (trademarks, etc.) started primarily as national choices, driven by national political needs, though more recently much regulation has taken an international dimension, through the health and safety etc. work of the EU and the intellectual property endeavours related to the World Trade Organisation. There are still, however, substantive differences between the criminalisation and regulation of work activity in different nation states – which has allowed us to examine in these seminars the effects of different national social, economic and fiscal policies – and hence the extent to which countries are 'choosing' to have different sectors of the informal economy dominant in their country.

WHAT KIND OF INFORMAL ECONOMY: THE OPPORTUNITIES THAT ARISE

Western national economies are characterised by a high degree of state intervention. In other words, the economic structural level, which functions according to the logic of a free market economy, is to a large degree corrected and tempered by means of politico-legal measures. This correction is usually indicated with terms such as 'state intervention' or 'regulation'.

State intervention and regulation have several functions. In the first place, even the most fervent advocates of the free market model are convinced that political intervention within economics is a facilitating factor for the continuity of the economy itself. Western entrepreneurs depend on politico-legal action because the necessary industrial material infrastructure (e.g. roads, sea and airports, supply of energy, etc.) has to be provided, at least partly, by public authorities. From a historical point of view, it is striking that the early industrialisation of most of our Western economies was only possible because state intervention and regulation facilitated this evolution.

Moreover, continuity of production and trade are guaranteed by social peace, or at least the absence of major social strife, again ensured by public authorities. In most of our Western societies, relative social peace has been the result of a long process of pacification and collective bargaining, between employers and employees, or other interest groups and lobbies. Most outcomes of this social struggle

---

4. One of the most documented examples of links between the formal and informal economies, with tolerance of the informal by the formal is the position in several Soviet countries during the Cold War. Many of these practices seem still to exist (Rodgers, Williams and Round, 2008).

and industrial bargaining have resulted in social legislation and policy. In other words, a balanced industrial relation pattern and social conventions seem to be the best conditions for social peace and thus a preliminary condition for continuity of production and trade. These balances and compromises have contributed to increases in formal regulation, with attendant public controls and inspection, and often public sanctioning.[5]

Social policy in Western economies has thus often been a compromise between an unbridled free market, where all competitive means could be mobilised and used, and a mixed regulated economy, where certain of these means (those claimed to be inhumane, or defined as situations of exploitation) were excluded, or at least tempered. One example is working conditions and circumstances. The most striking historical examples in this respect are of course the abolition of child labour and the restriction of working time in Western economies.

In short, social pacification is about the exclusion of certain means of competition, or rather, is about the introduction of formal social norms and limits which should no longer be transgressed. Competition within the free market is hence limited to certain types, for example, through adjusting prices, through the introduction of advanced technology, or through marketing. An impressive amount of social policy is from this point of view focussed on labour – the human factor in production and trade. Labour is to a large extend excluded as a competitive means and is regulated, in other words equalised or 'normalised' between competing firms. It is precisely this last point that must be supervised by public regulation and government; otherwise we speak of *unfair competition*. The consequence of this evolution has been the formalisation of labour conditions and circumstances, in short within formal employment and the formal economy. As a consequence of this evolution, many researchers have subscribed to the view that the informal economy is becoming marginal or peripheral and not linked to the formal economy.

Of course the process described above is not unilateral or one dimensional. In times of economic growth, the maintenance (or even acquisition) of 'social achievements' is under less pressure than in periods of economic stagnation or crisis. Implosion of the economy brings to a certain degree again forms of informal, flexible and deregulated industrial relations – though normally without putting social peace completely at risk.

---

5. The historical situation is different in post socialist Eastern countries. Most of these countries have an economic system in which social claims and collective bargaining are still relatively absent. Employers can easily pay low wages, dismiss staff with impunity and/or pay salaries in blank envelopes, whilst employees have little legal support. It is therefore not surprisingly that employees have turned to informal practices in order to secure the future of their families (Rodgers, et al., 2008). Economic liberalisation and political decentralisation in countries in emerging democracies have had disappointing results. Economic liberalisation is only effective if accompanied by a strong state (Dobovšek, 2008). Moreover, it is clear that working conditions in developing countries are still only rarely the subject of collective bargaining.

In any case, a national, regional or city economy is never purely formal or informal. Certain segments are formal, others are informal; some are becoming more formal, whilst others are becoming more informal. The study of the informal economy is from this perspective the study of an object in evolution. Today this probably means studying a phenomenon which is becoming increasingly informal, and the corresponding retreat of the political, rather than analysing processes of formalisation (Lippens and Ponsaers, 2006). Characterising an economy will therefore always be in terms of dominance and today most segments of Western economies have (still) dominant formal contours.[6] These general processes tend to displace workers in informal economies within Western societies towards a marginal and often isolated labour position.

In short, we may argue that the informal economy is, to a greater extent than a regulated economy, the subject of (or determined by) market mechanisms, driven by supply and demand. First, it is to a great extent characterised by non-regulation, and from that point of view the difference between legality and illegality has no meaning, nor makes sense. Therefore, it is logical to infer that in the informal economy the notion of 'economic criminality' is almost non-existent. Secondly, the informal economy is accompanied by the absence or non-functioning of formal public control agencies, including the police, law-enforcement agencies, regulatory bodies and inspectorates, though regulations (and/or even criminal sanctions) of course still do exist (but are not applied).

The informal economy is in this sense a simple consequence of the absence of or the withdrawal of the state. Though what is characterised as formal and what is characterised as informal is a deliberate choice of nation states as to what activities are designated criminal or to be regulated, the informal economy is in essence not driven by formal state or local political choices about *social* struggles, compromise or workplace bargaining. We might propose that the informal economy is driven by simple and harsh economic mechanisms and by rather blind logics of supply and demand, no longer steered by social policy.

Because of the absence of public intervention in the informal economy, we are dealing with economic activities or labour conditions and circumstances (trade, production, services, trafficking, etc.) that are not (no longer) labelled as 'illegal'. The occurrence of informal market mechanisms is seldom a subject of collective action or social struggle, endangering social peace. Nevertheless, from a moral point of view, we are mostly dealing with (working) situations and conditions, characterised by dominance and exploitation, in the sphere of survival economics.

---

6. While informal segments dominate in the survival economies of developing countries (Harriss-White 2008).

If workers within the informal economy perceive themselves to have no alternative to working in that sector, because opportunities in the formal economy are not open to them, possibilities for collective action are fairly restricted and formal protest is almost impossible. There seems to exist a sphere of 'tolerance' and they are considered 'marginal' in comparison with the dominant regulated economy.[7] Therefore, we consider that a sociology of the informal economy should be translated as a sociology of informal labour and labour division.

If supply and demand (market forces) determine the extent of the informal economy, as long as most of these activities are to a large degree developing as part of survival logic, it is *not* the entrepreneur who is investing, and it is *not* the government who is setting the rules of the game. The informal economy will therefore flourish where opportunities (geographical, social contacts, etc.) *already* exist. It is these opportunities which we would suggest dictate the precise nature of the kind of informal economic activity which takes place in different locales.

The informal economy has a certain tradition and is embedded in historical networks and families, trades and trafficking routes, many of which parallel routes used for legal goods and services (Tarrius, 2003; Godefroy et al., 2003). Informal employment opportunities are based on social contacts and networks – because the public advertising which characterises seeking for employees in the formal sector is inappropriate for those who do not wish to draw the attention of the authorities to their activities. The demand side: the requirements of citizens for illegal drugs, stolen designer goods or fake branded goods seem to have a longer history in the informal economy. Indeed, demand for illegal drugs may well have saturated, with relatively easy supply everywhere, though the demand for stolen goods may well increase in times of economic recession or to keep up with the ever-changing demands of fashion (Sutton, 2003). We would also argue that the informal economy may be less able to develop rapidly and takes less advantage of new business opportunities or competitive means than the formal economy. For example, it is difficult to supply illegal goods except from seller to buyer personally: using mail order, electronic web ordering or conventional postal delivery is risky, because the electronic and postal authorities are likely to notice the supply of illegal goods. From this point of view, informal economy is *not* innovative.[8] Informal economies develop in the periphery of formal economies, according to alternative logics of survival. The pressures towards globalisation which are dominating the formal economy (manufacturing in the cheapest areas, 'just-in-time' delivery of goods because transport costs are relatively cheap) are countered by the fear of detection once the supply chain moves outside known contacts and sources in the informal economy. The informal economy, we would argue, hence

7.   See also Foucault (1979), who argued that wide margins of tolerance of informal or illegal work can serve to provide considerable space in which dominant social groups can control other groups.

8.   On the other hand, where technological developments do permit relative anonymity (as in the case of throw-away, pay-as-you-go mobile phones, or some internet auctions), they have been enthusiastically taken up by those engaged in illegal or informal work (for example, drugs smuggling or distribution of stolen goods or (normally prescribed) pharmaceuticals).

is less affected by innovative, more global responses and remains relatively historically cast, depending upon tried and sure routes and methods.

Though we need to depend upon relatively few research sources, we would also argue that the workplace for the informal economy is also likely to remain relatively static in terms of work methods and job descriptions. We would see it as an epiphenomenon of ritual behaviour, in the sense that informal workers think: 'It has always been this way, and it will never change'. Workers are relatively powerless compared to those higher up the chain: neither means nor possibilities of changing the existing situation are considered as realistic; they are convinced that power relations are so unbalanced that they don't feel able to change this disequilibrium (Verhage and Ponsaers, 2009). From this angle, the informal economy is quite similar to the organisational structure of some organised crime. Organised crime entrepreneurs, families and groups may do different things, but one element seems to be constant. They endure over quite long time periods and are remarkably stable in their dominant position and in the quasi-monopoly of the exploitation of their manpower (and victims).[9]

But also from the point of view of the informal entrepreneur (or employer) the workplace situation seems to be surprisingly stable. New investments in infrastructure seem to be unnecessary and avoidable as long as the informal workforce is willing to sell its labour for low wages in more or less inhumane circumstances. Countervailing collective power, in terms of, for instance, labour unions or interest groups/lobbies, stays absent. This is another reason why we would see the informal market as surprisingly stable, and not changing as fast as the formal economy.

We should not overdo, however, these distinctions between the formal and informal economy. As Patrick Van Calster (2006) demonstrates, focusing on the illegal informal economy and on organised crime, the microscopic study and analysis of the more mundane aspects of everyday economic life may reveal how practical concerns of and minute decisions by economic actors weave an almost inextricable pattern of practices across the formal/informal divide.

Another angle on the intertwining of formal and informal work is the extent to which participants are labelled as falling foul of official rules on criminalisation or regulation. In many circumstances, for example, informal labour is performed within illegal situations. From a pure legalistic point of view, the informal worker is commonly in these circumstances labelled as offender, as 'criminal'. Here we think for example of drugs couriers or female drug 'mules' (Seddon, 2008) or beach sellers (Nelken, 2006). Because of the striking situation of exploitation in which participants are working, however, the role of the 'offender' seems easily to shift to that of the 'victim'. Within the domain of trafficking and smuggling of

---

9. This doesn't mean of course that all informal activities are necessarily forms of exploitation by organised crime groups. We only want to stress the striking similarity.

human beings this shift is sometimes officially recognised, although it is still the subject of much debate by researchers (Sanders, 2008).

Using the same line of reasoning, Nikos Passas (2006) and Dina Siegel (2008) argue that informal money transfer systems such as *hawala* banks ought not to be over-policed or over-controlled, or driven 'underground'. In particular migrant workers put more trust in *hawala* bankers than in formal banks for transferring their money to their families abroad. Nevertheless Van de Bunt (2008) warns about the misuse of the *hawala* banking system by criminal organisations in transferring their proceeds of crime, which again is an illustration of how easily victims shift to the role of offender and vice versa.

We have seen that, though the fundamental structure of the informal economy may be relatively stable, the form and the extent of it can vary considerably (Ponsaers et al., 2008). Those activities that can be considered as belonging to the formal economy in one country, can be part of the informal economy in another. National regulation and law enforcement can vary strongly. National governments make choices in respect to this, by regulating or not, by criminalising or not, by engaging in considerable control activity (using inspectors etc.) or not. An important part of the informal economy is trade, and by necessity international trade (or trafficking). Though some trade is illegal practically everywhere (opiate drugs, endangered species of animals), for some other commodities (such as prescribed drugs, antiquities and fashion garments), we observe a constant shift in the labelling of these goods, as they travel, from informal to formal (illegal or legal) and vice versa. There seems to exist a growing interaction and interwovenness between formal and informal markets. We suggest that the combination of formal and informal economies can lead to synergetic, or to symbiotic relations, but that it can also lead to conflictual relations and even to parasitic relations (Vande Walle, 2008). As a epiphenomenon of that, even the vulnerability of certain formal sectors, such as property/real estate, for illegal activities becomes a subject of analysis (Vander Beken, 2008).

Informal economies have both a stabilising and a transforming potential. According to Henry and Sills (2006), capitalism is the unsettled outcome of relations with a plurality of economic orders, both formal and informal at the same time. The free market seems to have an endless ability to absorb, co-opt, transform and capitalise even those fragments which seem to challenge this kind of economy. As Gerald Mars (2006) argues in his anthropological analysis of shifts in workplace cultures, the 'hidden economy' seems to be growing in an age of globalisation, individualisation and technological change. The concept of the 'bazaar economy', proposed by Vincenzo Ruggiero and Nigel South (1994), questions the possibility of ever stably identifying crime zones precisely. The evocative value of the concept of the bazaar economy is that it alludes to a variety of individuals interacting in a marketplace where goods and services are bought and sold without regard for whether they are legal or illegal. The concept of a bazaar, applied to contemporary large cities, or even regions, expresses the coexistence of legality and illegality and changes in the boundaries between the two. The art market is a impressive example of these mechanisms (Massy, 2008).

Overall, despite the potential for change, particularly in markets which have only recently been the subject of international legal intervention or regulation (intellectual property matters, art), we would characterise the main emphasis within the informal economy as one of a relatively stable, but geographically diverse, set of activities. If formal regulation and social policies stay constant, and there is no war or major upheaval, there seems to be no major change.

WHO GETS INVOLVED IN THE INFORMAL ECONOMY?

Pursuing work within the informal economy is often said to be useful for migrants, youngsters or socially excluded persons, including asylum seekers. However, is this correct? Are these kind of activities only functional for marginalised groups within society?

Nelken (2006), for example, argues in his article concerning immigrant beach selling along the Italian Adriatic coast, that it concerns a 'social issue'. The problem is, according to him, how countries could regulate the flows of immigrants and to create possibilities for immigrants to find work without being forced into illegal activity (such as selling goods on the beaches). This would include either more flexibility in awarding entry licences to be used for alternative work, such as factory work, or the legalisation and regulation of selling: special places set aside for this form of selling, specific licences, seasonal permissions for work, etc. As Aden argues (2009), if employment or remunerative work can occur without any formal requirements, it cannot enter into the field of illegal work. Public policy can also reduce the market for illegal work by making legal work more attractive and salient for workers and employers. However, at the same time Nelken points to the formal – and therefore taxed – shopkeeper economy, which is vehemently opposed to particular informal selling practices, and labels these activities as forms of 'unfair competition'. Yet shopkeepers themselves are inclined towards informality if it furthers their *own* interests. In other words, informal activities are not limited to marginalised groups, although they clearly are undertaken by marginalised groups.

First, by 'marginalised', we are referring not only to those shunned by mainstream society but also the bottom stratum for employment in the legitimate economy. Here we are dealing with those without qualifications, those without a work record, and the young with no contacts (and so no social capital). Two pilot projects done in two European cities in summer 1997 show nevertheless that the informal economy – as opposed to the criminal economy – requires skills, though not the formal paper qualifications increasingly required for work in the formal economy. It particularly requires skills so that it does not come to the attention of regulatory authorities, e.g. through accidents. One of these projects was in

Aulnay, a suburb to the north of Paris, which was in fact one of the areas (ban-lieus) in which riots occurred later on, in November 2005 (Godefroy et al., 2003). The second project was in a part of Frankfurt (Smettan, 2003). Both were in resi-dential areas and did not encounter much street prostitution or other localised forms of the informal economy (Shapland, 2003).

The population of Aulnay was quite young and rapidly changing (nearly 40% had changed between 1982 and 1990), with significant numbers of migrants. The profits from all the informal activities were very small and most people involved were young, including migrants. Families might be supported by several of these activities, as well as some members of the family having casual jobs, state bene-fits or some employment. Key elements in the informal economy included: very visible car maintenance and repair workshops in the car parks, which included both legal businesses repairing people's cars and dealing in stolen vehicles and parts; trade in fashion items, primarily clothing and hi-fi, stemming from non-local commercial burglary; subcontracting of construction trades down to a level where the people doing the work had profit levels which could not sustain state regulatory activities; provision of services, such as hairdressing, cleaning etc. through unregistered businesses; a visible and large market in cannabis; and home work by women, often through ethnic networks, in the garment industry; etc.

The pilot study in Germany was in Bornheim, an old residential district of Frank-furt, with a considerable proportion of migrants and guest workers (27%). Again, the profits from the various forms of the informal economy were very low and those involved were primarily the young, unemployed, migrants, and those in debt. The locations for localised activities were well known to residents and agen-cies. The forms of the informal economy were, at that time, very much influenced by state taxation and regulation: provision of services through notices put up in the neighbourhood or adverts in local papers for personal services, tuition, gar-dening, household repairs etc., on a cash-in-hand, no-bills basis; other services, such as the catering trade, taxi driving and cleaning services, a proportion of which were unregistered and did not pay taxes; trade in stolen goods, carried out primarily in some bars, restaurants and private houses; and a visible drug market (all kinds of drugs) around the metro stations and one of the squares; etc.

In short, even though we are confronted here with marginal groups, functioning within the informal economy seems to be demanding and presupposes a certain day-to-day ability. It certainly requires skills to cover up these – rather massive – economic activities.

Secondly, there are other marginalised groups than those mentioned already. Here we focus on groups and individuals who are living in a country, but are not officially registered as citizens or legal immigrants: those without (official, for-mal) papers. They are groups which are in fact officially non-existent, and thus by definition 'informal'. They do not necessarily act illegally, they *are* themselves (labelled) illegal. Most of them have left their home country because of economic reasons. We are dealing here with persons that can have certain abilities, skills and educational qualifications, sometimes even people who have previously held professional jobs. Economic migrants often come from families with financial resources. That is mostly the reason why they had the ability to leave their original situation. They should not be seen as similar to the (indigenous) downtrodden masses left on housing estates as others sell up and move on. But social networks and ethnic ties (and common languages) are really important in respect of which groups of immigrants (legal or illegal) find themselves where in each country.

In an intriguing paper Saitta (2008) shows how a group of Roma from Kosovo, living in the area of Mazara del Vallo (Sicily) since the 1970s, have gained a livelihood through such enterprising methods as music, improvised handicrafts, and small-scale drug dealing. Their precarious situation is conditioned in large measure by the complex interplay of state regulation and the practice of local authorities. Nevertheless, these individuals have been able to exploit the ambivalence of the authorities as well as opportunities presented by the endemic informality of this southwestern Sicilian city. Although a culture of poverty perspective would suggest that they are merely reproducing poverty from generation to generation, in-depth observation shows nevertheless that the informal economy presents paradoxical means for social advancement.

Thirdly, there are those who pursue criminal opportunities. Some do so because they find it very difficult to obtain legal employment (because they have few qualifications, have been in care and so have no contacts to find work, have substance abuse problems or mental health issues, or have no stable place to live and so live on the streets). Usually part of the indigenous population – and relatively visible to the public authorities – they are another marginalised group.

Of course these different social segments who take part in the informal economy are not mutually exclusive. Migrants may undertake criminal activities as well as illegal, non-regulated work. Those who make most of their money from shop theft or drugs may also take cash in hand jobs. Many participants in the informal economy have portfolio jobs, both at the same time and over time – a bit of one and a bit of the other (Sbraccia, 2008b).

However, the precariousness of all these types of work (whether informal or criminal) seems to start preying on people's minds as they get older (Shapland, 2003). It reinforces the point of view that it is the workers' perception which determines what they are prepared to accept or the conditions they wish to tolerate. Being at least to some degree illegal, informal economic activities only continue if workers wish to continue them: coercion will only work for so long; employers and bosses (even organised crime bosses) can only continue to exist if no-one 'blows the whistle' on the business.

There is an analogy to this at the societal level. If the informal economy is very prevalent in a country (in terms of service provision or manufacturing industry), then the population itself may become accustomed to it. Once this point reached, it becomes very difficult to raise standards or impose effective regulation. This will be for example the case for the societal acceptance of corruption (Dobovšek, 2008) or the habit of not paying taxes (Smettan, 2003).

THE EFFECTS OF DIFFERENT POLICIES WHICH MAY BE 'ENCOURAGING' THE INFORMAL ECONOMY

In this section, we indicate a number of national or regional policies (especially social policies) which can have an encouraging or boost effect on the development of the informal economy. The list has been generated through discussion during the seminars which gave rise to this book, primarily through the opportunity the seminars provided for discussion of the effects of different policies in different European countries. These effects are very difficult to discern through single-country studies and indicate the value of pan-European research. Because the informal economy is often connected with the supply of labour, rather than goods, it tends to emphasise the effects of social, economic and foreign policies which affect the labour supply. The list is not in any way exhaustive.

(a) Policies which hinder desistance from criminal activity/lack of policies encouraging desistance

Within criminology there is increasing interest in desistance: the processes by which people cease criminal activity or reduce its frequency. As offenders move into early adulthood, some start to desist from the bulge of criminal activity in adolescence (Bottoms et al., 2004). However, desistance requires replacing the income obtained from criminal activity with income from more legal sources, which can be very difficult if the young person has dropped out of school or been excluded from school and so has few or no qualifications. Desistance policies have tended to emphasise changing attitudes away from criminality, but researchers have shown that support is often required from correctional or community criminal justice personnel to acquire jobs and sort out accommodation and debt issues, particularly on release from correctional establishments (Farrall and Calverley, 2005; Shapland et al., forthcoming). Desistance policies hence are designed to prevent or remedy (through adult education) school drop-out, minimise structural unemployment, alleviate social isolation, etc. In other words, desistance policies are directed to restructure the unstructured, to formalise the informal. On the contrary, policies which stop people desisting or hinder desistance in the early and late twenties may encourage those who drop out of school or who commit crime in adolescence to continue or start in the informal economy, or continue criminality.

Examples of national social policies which may be hindering desistance are: the absence of resettlement policies after being in care or after custodial sentences; requiring people to produce certificates to employers saying they do not have any criminal record to obtain a job in the formal economy; requiring formal qualifications for relatively low skilled jobs; and cartels which tend to restrict some forms of employment to certain social or ethnic groups and so reduce employment possibilities for others. These kind of policies can be considered as counterproductive, not only in terms of prevention of recidivism, but also with respect to encouraging informal forms of economic activity.

(b) Creating underclasses

It seems clear to us that creating 'ghettos' of the less skilled or poorer will stunt the aspirations of young people and either create political dissent/riots or possibly encourage criminal 'solutions'. A striking example of the creation of underclasses became clear when looking at the reasons behind the youth riots in the *banlieus* of Paris in November 2005. Body-Gendrot (2008) describes the youths engaged in these riots as very diverse. Some were college students, some had regular jobs; some were high school students, others were idle; their attitudes and age varied. Some of them disapproved of the actions that were taken by the rioters, such as arson of schools or of day-care centers, and did not want to jeopardize their future with a judicial warning on their file. Not all banlieus were poor, some were even rich. Within some banlieus very poor immigrant newcomers doubled up in impoverished housing units, while in others middle class households contributed to the gentrification process.

What was striking was that these youths asked for nothing, they merely expressed emotions during rioting. They were probably aware that there were no structures and no elaborated social proposals aimed at engaging in a dialogue with them. They were to be considered as 'institutionally disempowered' and politically ignored. Despite the political rhetoric and the media coverage, society and political parties were rather indifferent to people at the margins who hardly voted. It was ironical to observe that during the urban unrest, the Stock Exchange kept rising from 4,320 points on 28 October to 4,521 points on 8 November 2005 (Roché, 2006).

This kind of observation is far from new in criminology. Julius Wilson (1996), one of our foremost authorities on race and poverty, challenged – already years ago – decades of liberal and conservative pieties in the United States to look squarely at the devastating effects that joblessness had on urban ghettos. Marshalling a vast array of data and the personal stories of hundreds of men and women, Wilson persuasively argued that problems endemic to America's inner cities stem directly from the disappearance of blue-collar jobs. Julius Wilson's structural perspective was based in understanding the racial and economic history that developed what he termed the 'underclass' or the 'ghetto poor'. This structural perspective sites the rise of disparity in opportunity and social isolation, noting current and historic discrimination, to create minority urban communities with high rates of delinquency and areas in which the only viable economy is the illegal drug economy.

(c) High service taxes, much outsourcing and inefficient regulation

Classical economists were not able to predict the notable shifts in recent years from mass production to flexible specialised production. Neither did they predict the persistence of traditional forms of non-standard wage work (e.g. casual jobs) and self-employment (e.g. street vending or [high-tech] home-based work); or the emergence of new forms of work (e.g. temporary, interim and part-time jobs with low or hourly paid wages) and exchanges of services without even any financial transaction (barter, exchange of favours). Today, however, the labour market is under pressure, in transition, becoming more 'flexible', and forms of outsourcing and subcontracting are common (Chen et al., 2002). As a result of that, there is a remarkable convergence in insight that the informal economy is here to stay, in both new and old guises.

Again we can ask ourselves: who is avoiding regulation: informal workers, or their employers in both informal and formal businesses? This can be translated into the question we raised already, in criminological terms, as: 'Who is the victim?', or even 'Who is the offender?' The answer to this question is highly related to the perception governments have of the problem and will determine to a large extent the (tax/fiscal) policy they develop: dismissive (ignoring), punitive (eliminating), restrictive (containing) or promotive (supporting/protecting).

In analysing the likely impact of fiscal/tax policies, policy makers need to consider the impact of direct and indirect taxes on the informal workforce as both consumers and producers. There are several forms of taxes involved, including personal income tax and value added tax. Personal tax policies can be progressive or regressive, depending on whether a differential progressive rate or a flat rate is imposed. It is important to recognise that many categories of informal activities are governed by powerful economic interests in the formal economy (e.g. home-based workers). We would argue in favour of a policy that recognizes that the informal economy is linked to the formal economy, and recognizes at the same time more explicitly the distinction between informality and outright illegality. More concretely, we would argue for a policy that recognizes that street vendors often have to vend informally either because they are not incorporated in existing regulatory frameworks or because existing regulatory frameworks are too punitive or constraining. Informal workers have little (if any) bargaining power with the economic units who put out work to them.

Consequently, it seems arguable to us that in those countries where a policy of high service and manufacturing taxes exists, combined with an important amount of subcontracting or outsourcing, and where there is relatively inefficient regulation and law enforcement agencies or inspectorates, the consequence could be an expanding informal economy. It is the combination which is important, with each interacting with the other in its effects. So, a high tax rate for VAT or on businesses will not encourage the informal economy if these businesses are relatively stable, keep work in-house and are relatively visible to inspectorates. In this case, they have no incentive to maximise profits by not paying taxes, because they will know that their activities are very visible. However, if there is much sub-contracting, particularly if supply is opaque, then the sub-contractors can do work more cheaply, acting under the official radar, not paying relevant taxes or not providing good conditions for their workers, through using informal economic methods. This is most likely to occur if the official radar, in the sense of enforcement and compliance, is only concerned with relatively large businesses and, because of enforcement costs or because dealing with large businesses maximises the number of workers inspected, is unconcerned with small subcontractors.

(d) Lots of rules, few controls/inspections/enforcement

If there are no regulations, then the distinction between formal and informal work becomes obsolete. But just creating regulations, even criminal legislation, does not necessarily affect the way in which the work is done. In earlier work (Vande Walle and Ponsaers, 2006) we demonstrated that the informal economy in developing countries is indeed being formalised through the globalisation of patent right protection in the pharmaceutical sector (TRIPS). But further international regulations and their implications for the accessibility of the formal medicine market in poor countries have led to an *increase* in non-official sales. At that point we speak no longer of an informal market but of a purely illegal market. In short, the formalised western industry sometimes stimulates the informal market and sometimes annexes it. In many cases the latter is even criminalized by means of international regulations. We have to conclude that creating formalised world trade or intellectual property rules does not affect developing informal world practices in particular cities, although they have an overall effect at the level of inter-country trade.

If there are many regulations, but they are not enforced, then the tendency will be lots of informal work. Opportunities to commit crime exist when suitable targets are present and capable guardians are absent, Nelen (2008) argues, following the crime prevention logic of situational crime prevention, but discussing the sector of real estate. In *Looking for loopholes. Processes of incorporation of illegal immigrants in the Netherlands* Van der Leun (2003) offers a detailed account of how illegal immigrants, who are legally excluded, managed to become incorporated into Dutch society. By combining the perspectives of immigrants on the one hand and of those who had to implement a 'discouragement policy' on the other hand, her study shows how tensions between restrictive rules and day-to-day practices grow. Based on long-term research, attention has been focused on the role of informal employment and criminal involvement. In the Netherlands, Van der Leun observes a shift from semi-formal employment to informal employment, as there have been more crackdowns on whether people have a proper social security number. Illegal workers have moved out of sight, into back premises (e.g. in catering or in private households). They are consequently less visible to inspectors and potentially more able to be exploited.

So, we cannot avoid the general observation that regulation in itself is not the most important determining factor for the presence of a informal economy, *enforcement* is. Absence of enforcement does not result always in bad working conditions for employees or lack of tax payments, etc. We can observe for example widespread activities in the informal economy in Northern Italy, but not by definition in bad working conditions (Palidda, 2003). However, in contradiction to this observation, we see in England, that the informal economy, the sense of paid employment in illegal but not criminal sectors (in garment workshops, restaurants etc.) tends to be synonymous with bad employment conditions. This leads us to the conclusion that what will happen depends largely upon what is seen as 'normal' in the specific sector in terms of conditions, paying taxes, etc. Cultural factors about what workers expect as conditions will affect workers' willingness to work in such environments, as we discussed above, and also employers' provisions.

If there are many regulations and they are only partially enforced, which is the case in the majority of countries, then tensions will be created at enforcement points, for example, at borders or during major transactions. There may also be more informal control – e.g. employers informing on workers who annoy them or who are less useful (Sbraccia, 2008b).

(e) Migration

Market economies work best when there exists a shortage of labour. If there is free movement of labour, more skilled people and those for whom conditions are more favourable will cluster in better paid and, usually, more 'formal' and 'legal' employment. There may be some labour shortages for less skilled work (or work which demands fewer official papers), which may create an overall shortage. If so, both employers and employees have a considerable interest in attracting outsiders. Migration affects the supply of the workforce, not the supply of goods.

There are many instances of managed labour schemes for attracting migrants (student schemes in Australia and New Zealand; licensed gangmasters and farmers in England for agricultural work). In general, however, these will not stop illegal migrants filling these posts more cheaply, unless border controls are very strict (it is interesting that the countries mentioned are islands, making borders more secure). The scheme in Italy (Ferraris, this volume), for example, seems to be less successful, because of slow processing and high demand (by both employers and migrants).

Where borders are more permeable (for example, in mainland Europe) and particularly if legal movement is easy (within the EU), it may become normal for there to be (legal) migration for some age groups etc. It is noticeable that there is now substantial migration of young people in Europe for limited periods. The European tour of the English aristocracy in the nineteenth century, for example, seems now to have become a flood of students on gap years, young educated Europeans deciding to work abroad for a period and people taking career breaks in later life.

Illegal migration, however, creates real problems for both migrants and host countries (exploitation, low tax returns, security concerns). This is particularly so if 'becoming legal' 'requires' the commission of illegal acts, for example, if residence in a country for several years is needed in order to get papers or residence permits, but if there is no legal way to support oneself during this period (Ferraris, 2009). Like all informal economies, migrants obtaining work depend upon social networks, including ethnic networks – it is who you know that counts, not what your formal qualifications are or what your previous workplace has stated you know.

It is unclear to us what the balance of advantage is between, on the one hand, issuing temporary papers to allow illegal migrants to obtain work (as in amnesties, particularly if coupled with strict employment controls, so that people can be traced) and, on the other hand, refusing absolutely to countenance having non-legal people in the country (imprisonment, deportation etc.). In strict economic terms, detaining in custodial establishments many non-legal people, including young fit men (as is the case in England and Wales, or with those reaching Hong Kong or Australia by boat) would seem almost certainly to create a net economic disadvantage (though political and security concerns have to be offset against this).

(f) High demand for low paid workforce, low native supply

The informal economy is encouraged when national or regional formal economies depend for their survival upon low paid workers but where there is an insufficient supply of legally employed native workers to do this. Many Western countries are in this position. However, as Dario Melossi pointed out during the seminars which formed the basis of this book, this situation may have bad long-term effects. Relying on cheap (informal) labour does not encourage modernisation or investment in industry and machinery.

This problem links to the amount the country is prepared to spend on its welfare system (public sector costs) as well as the price of its goods/services (wages, private sector costs). The more illegal the worker, the less the country may have to pay in social benefits (housing, health, education), including the likelihood that informal workers will not bring over their families. Van der Leun (2003) argues that welfare benefits set a floor below which wages have to be paid within the informal economy. If welfare benefits are not paid, however, there are the same problems, potentially, as in creating ghettos, particularly if workers congregate.

In order to deal with these problems of labour supply, some countries have adopted a system of guest workers (for example, Germany and some states in the Middle East). Some have encouraged waves of migration, for example, from former colonies (for example, the UK, the Netherlands). Both solutions may create tensions in terms of whether the temporary workers are granted full citizens' rights and in terms of absorption into the host country (multi-cultural tensions etc.). Some countries and industries have attempted more recently to move the problem offshore, by creating subsidiary companies in lower-waged countries (both in the manufacturing sector and service sector call centres). These can be quite short-lasting solutions, primarily because the offshore country can then develop its own sector with the expertise gained and then compete against the original outsourcing country/company (even maybe taking it over – as has happened in the automobile industry). Occasionally, countries have 'tolerated' substantial elements of the informal economy in order to solve these labour problems, only occasionally checking workers' papers (unless there is an incident) and ignoring non payment of taxes. Police may say 'I don't want to see your face again today – change where you're selling these' (Sbraccia, 2008b).

Do these solutions create problems? The answer, as with so much to do with the informal economy, depends upon whether the 'solution' generates unanticipated problems. If, for example, the presence of a secondary labour force without full citizen's rights (whether a legal or an informal labour force) encourages organised crime elements from the sending countries to infiltrate the host country, then problems may be imported. If the sending countries have different practices in relation to business ethics, again the host business culture may change. This does not always have to be in a negative direction – the sending country may have higher standards or be less prone to organised crime – but there are examples of the encouragement of organised crime in relation to trafficking of women for sexual purposes (through piggybacking illegal transport onto legal links), corruption of regulators and officials, and substandard construction/manufacture/employment practices through subcontracting without adequate safeguards or the use of unlicensed gangmasters. It may be that the potential for negative unexpected consequences is less harmful in the service sector than in manufacturing or construction – because service sector clients can complain more easily than if there are shoddy goods or buildings.

CONCLUSION

National social and economic policies are usually adopted for their own sake, with little thought as to the effect they may have on the labour force, or on the relative sizes of the formal and informal economies in that country. It is often only when workplace regulation or criminal legislation is being considered that the division between criminal and legal, or illegal and legal employment arises in discussion. The crime prevention or crime escalating effect of other social, economic or fiscal policies tends not to be a preoccupation of legislators, though its importance seems to be becoming more visible (Albrecht et al., 2001), because of the increasing salience of crime and law and order to the European public.

We hope, however, that the above discussion shows some examples of how many different national policies may impact on the size and extent of the informal economy in particular countries. This is a relatively new subject for study, perhaps because it intrinsically requires cross-national comparison, a difficult enterprise at any time, but particularly so when speaking of the informal economy, with its varying fiscal, legal and social elements. In setting out the list above, we are not implying that increasing the informal economy is unmitigatingly bad for any country: whether it is desirable or not depends on whether there are alternative avenues for survival of those who are depending upon it. Having no informal economic sector (beyond the supply of criminally proscribed goods or services) implies having a very rigid economy and having little place for new arrivals (without running a continuous deficit in labour in the formal economy).

However, having a substantial informal sector does imply a lack of governmental oversight of work practices in that sector and may include a substantial risk of attracting organised crime. We have also argued that workers in the informal sector will find it difficult to improve conditions by themselves and that informality militates against the creation of organised labour. Changing governmental edicts will affect the size of the informal economy, as Aden (2009) has shown for Germany. It is less clear whether it affects the remaining workers in the informal sector. What we are unable to do, because of the lack of relevant research studies, is to look at the extent of the cultural workplace links between practices in the formal and informal sectors in different countries – and so at whether it is possible to influence conditions in the informal economy through conditions in the formal economy. There is clearly a need for both more governmental consideration of the effects of new social and economic policies, which consider effects on the informal economy as well as the formal economy – and more cross-national study of the implications of governments and international bodies adopting new policies.

REFERENCES

Aden, H. (2009). 'Informal economy, illegal work and public policy'. In J. Shapland & P. Ponsaers (eds.), *The informal economy and connections with organised crime: The impact of national social and economic policies*. The Hague: Boom Juridische Uitgevers.

Albrecht, H.-J., Kilchling, M. & Braun, E. (eds.) (2001). *Criminal preventive risk assessment in the law-making procedure*. Freiburg-I-Br: Max-Planck-Institut für ausländisches und internationales Strafrecht, Paper 5/2001.

Body-Gendrot, S. (2008). 'Urban riots in France: anything new?'. In L. Cachet, S. De Kimpe, P. Ponsaers & A. Ringeling (eds.), *Governance of security in the Netherlands and Belgium*. The Hague: Boom Juridische uitgevers, pp. 261-280.

Bottoms, A.E., Shapland, J., Costello, A., Holmes, D. & Muir, G. (2004). 'Towards desistance: theoretical underpinnings for an empirical study'. *Howard Journal*, 43: 368-89.

Charmes, J. (2000). 'Progress in measurement of the informal sector: Employment and share of GDP'. In *Handbook of national accounting. Household accounting: experiences in the use of concepts and their compilation*. Vol. 1 Household sector accounts. New York: U.N. Statistics Division, pp. 171-188.

Chen, M.A., Jhabvale, R. & Lund F. (2002). *Supporting workers in the informal economy: A policy framework*. Geneva: Employment Sector, International Labour Office, 2002(2): 1-41.

Dobovšek, B. (2008). 'Economic organized crime networks in emerging democracies'. *International Journal of Social Economics*, 35(9): 679-690.

Farrall, S. & Calverley, A. (2005). *Understanding desistance from crime – Emerging theoretical directions in resettlement and rehabilitation*. Milton Keynes: Open University Press.

Ferraris, V. (2009). 'Migrant's offside trap: a strategy for dealing with misleading rules and a hostile playing field'. In J. Shapland & P. Ponsaers (eds.), *The informal economy and connections with organised crime: The impact of national social and economic policies*. The Hague: Boom Juridische uitgevers.

Foucault, M. (1979). *Discipline and punish: The birth of the prison*, trans. A. Sheridan. New York: Vintage.

Godefroy, T., Delaitre, S. & Mollaret, S. (2003). 'L'économie informelle vue du côté français: Une économie "plurielle"?'. In J. Shapland, H.-J. Albrecht, J. Ditton & T. Godefroy (eds.), *The informal economy: Threat and opportunity in the city*. Freiburg-im-Breisgau: Max-Planck-Institut für ausländisches und internationales Strafrecht.

Harriss-White, B. (2008). 'Crime, deviance and the informal economy. Comment on Shapland and Ponsaers'. In A. Groenemeyer & X. Rousseaux (eds.), *Assessing deviance, crime and prevention in Europe (CRIMPREV) – Report of the First General Conference* (Louvain-la-Neuve, 8-10 February 2007), at http://www.crimprev.eu, pp. 103-111.

Henry, S. & Sills, S. (2006). 'Informal economic activity: Early thinking, conceptual shifts, continuing patterns and persisting issues – a Michigan study'. *Crime, Law and Social Change*, 45(4-5): 263-284.

Lippens, R. & Ponsaers, P. (eds.) (2006). 'Re-visiting the Informal Economy: Introductory notes'. *Crime, Law and Social Change*, 45(4-5): 259-381.

Massy, L. (2008). 'The antiquity art market: between legality and illegality', *International Journal of Social Economics*, 35(10): 729-738.

Mars, G. (2006). 'Changes in occupational deviance: Scams, fiddles and sabotage in the twenty-first century', *Crime, Law and Social Change*, 45(4-5): 285-296.

Nelen, H. (2008). 'Real estate and serious forms of crime'. *International Journal of Social Economics*, 35(10): 751-762.

Nelken, D. (2006). 'Immigrant beach selling along the Italian Adriatic coast: De-constructing a social problem'. *Crime, Law and Social Change*, 45(4-5): 297-313.

Palidda, S. (2003). 'Informel, criminel et contrôle sociale dan la ville "post-industrielle": Le cas Italien'. In J. Shapland, H.-J. Albrecht, J. Ditton & T. Godefroy (eds.), *The informal economy: threat and opportunity in the city*. Freiburg-im-Breisgau: Max-Planck-Institut für ausländisches und internationales Strafrecht, pp. 97-132.

Passas, N. (2006). 'Fighting terror with error: The counter-productive regulation of informal value transfers'. *Crime, Law and Social Change*, 45(4-5): 315-336.

Peattie, L. (1987). 'An idea in good currency and how it grew: The informal sector'. *World Development*, 15(7): 851-860.

Ponsaers, P., Shapland, J. & Williams, C. (2008). 'Does the informal economy link to organised crime?' *International Journal of Social Economics*, 35(9): 644-650.

Roché, S. (2006). *Le frisson de lémeute*. Paris: Le Seuil.

Rodgers, P., Williams, C. & Round, J. (2008). 'Workplace crime and the informal economy in Ukraine: employee and employer perspectives'. *International Journal of Social Economics*, 35(9): 666-678.

Ruggiero, V. & South, N. (1994). *Eurodrugs: Drug use, markets and trafficking in Europe*. London: UCL Press.

Saitta, P. (2008). 'Immigrant Roma in Sicily: The role of the informal economy in producing social advancement'. December 31. Available at SSRN: http://ssrn.com/abstract=1322153

Sanders, T. (2008). 'Selling sex in the shadow economy'. *International Journal of Social Economics*, 35(10): 704-716.

Sbraccia, A. (2008a). 'More or less eligibility? Theoretical perspectives on the process of imprisonment of irregular migrants in Italy'. Third Seminar CRIMPREV Workpackage 5 (EU). 17-18 January 2008, Università di Bologna, Palazzo Malvezzi (Facoltá di Giurisprudenza).

Sbraccia, A. (2008b). 'A case study on segregation and the informal economy'. Fourth Seminar CRIMPREV Workpackage 5 (EU). 2-4 April 2008, Faculty of Criminal Justice and Security, University of Maribor, Ljubljana, Slovenia.

Schneider, F. & Enste, D.H. (2002). *The shadow economy: An international survey*. Cambridge: Cambridge University Press.

Schneider, F. (2005). 'Shadow economies around the world: What do we really know?' *European Journal of Political Economy*, 23(1): 598-642.

Seddon, T. (2008). 'Drugs, the informal economy and globalisation'. *International Journal of Social Economics*, 35(10): 717-728.

Shapland, J. (2003). 'Looking at opportunities in the informal economy of cities'. In J. Shapland, H.-J. Albrecht, J. Ditton & T. Godefroy (eds.), *The informal economy: Threat and opportunity in the city*. Freiburg-im-Breisgau: Max-Planck-Institut für ausländisches und internationales Strafrecht.

Shapland, J., Bottoms, A.E., Muir, G. with Atkinson, H., Healy, D. & Holmes, D. (forthcoming). 'Perceptions of the criminal justice system among young adult would-be desisters'. In F. Loesel (ed.), *Transitions to adulthood*. Cullompton: Willan.

Shapland, J. & Ponsaers, P. (2008). 'New challenges of crime and deviant behaviours: Informal economy and organized crime in Europe'. In A. Groenemeyer & X. Rousseaux (eds.), *Assessing deviance, crime and prevention in Europe (CRIMPREV) – Report of the First General Conference* (Louvain-la-Neuve, 8-10 February 2007), at http://www.crimprev.eu, pp. 81-99

Siegel, D. (2008). 'Hawala banking: issues for regulators'. Fifth Seminar CRIMPREV Workpackage 5 (EU). 29-31 October 2008, Rechtsfaculteit, Capaciteitsgroep Criminologie, Erasmus Universiteit Rotterdam, Nederland.

Smettan, J. (2003). 'The shadow economy in Frankfurt-Bornheim: results of an empirical study'. In J. Shapland, H.-J. Albrecht, J. Ditton & T. Godefroy (eds.), *The informal economy: Threat and opportunity in the city*. Freiburg-im-Breisgau: Max-Planck-Institut für ausländisches und internationales Strafrecht.

Sutton, M. (2003). 'Theft, stolen goods and the market reduction approach'. In J. Shapland, H.-J. Albrecht, J. Ditton & T. Godefroy (eds.), *The informal economy: Threat and opportunity in the city*. Freiburg-im-Breisgau: Max-Planck-Institut für ausländisches und internationales Strafrecht, pp. 219-230.

Tarrius, A. (2003). 'Drogues, communautés d'étrangers, chômage des jeunes et renouveau des civilités dans une ville moyenne française'. In J. Shapland, H.-J. Albrecht, J. Ditton & T. Godefroy (eds.), *The informal economy: Threat and opportunity in the city*. Freiburg-im-Breisgau: Max-Planck-Institut für ausländisches und internationales Strafrecht.

Van Calster, P. (2006). 'Re-visiting Mr. Nice. On organized crime as conversational interaction'. *Crime, Law and Social Change*, 45(4-5): 337-359.

Vander Beken, T. & Van Daele, S. (2008). 'Legitimate businesses and crime vulnerabilities'. *International Journal of Social Economics*, 35(10): 739-750.

Van de Bunt, H. (2008). 'A case study on the misuse of hawala banking'. *International Journal of Social Economics*, 35(9): 691-702.

Van der Leun, J.P. (2003). *Looking for loopholes. Processes of incorporation of illegal immigrants in the Netherlands*. Amsterdam: Amsterdam University Press.

Van de Walle, G. & Ponsaers, P. (2006). 'Formal and informal pharmaceutical economies in Third World countries: Synergetic, symbiotic or parasitical?' *Crime, Law and Social Change*, 45(4-5): 373-381.

Van de Walle, G. (2008). 'A matrix approach to informal markets: towards a dynamic conceptualisation'. *International Journal of Social Economics*, 35(9): 651-665.

Verhage, A. & Ponsaers, P. (2009). 'Power-seeking crime? The professional thief versus the professional launderer'. *Crime, Law and Social Change*, 51(3-4): 399-412.

Verhage, A. (2009). 'The anti money laundering complex: power pantomime or potential payoff? Perspectives on practices, partnerships and challenges within the fight against money laundering'. In J. Shapland & P. Ponsaers (eds.), *The informal economy and connections with organised crime: The impact of national social and economic policies*. The Hague: Boom Legal publishers.

Wilson, W.J. (1996). *When work disappears: The world of the new urban poor*. New York: Alfred A. Knopf.

Informal economy, illegal work and public policy

Hartmut Aden[10]

This paper focuses on phenomena that are commonly called *illegal, black, undeclared* or *informal labour*. These terms reflect the labour side of the illegal economy. The boundaries between legal and illegal forms of work are not fixed for all time. They largely depend on political priorities and public policy choices. The paper analyses, using an interdisciplinary perspective from law, politics and administrative science, how political and administrative decision making at the national and European levels influence the labour side of the informal economy and how political and administrative choices influence strategies to combat these forms of behaviour. On the domestic level, the paper starts from the German experience and the major reforms that have led to new strategies and institutions for combating illegal labour in recent years. As a result of these reforms, the *Finanzkontrolle Schwarzarbeit (FKS)*, a unit employing around 6,500 people, was set up in 2004 as part of the customs administration in order to enforce the relevant penal and administrative legislation.

The questions treated in the paper concern the relationship between public policies, illegal labour and the informal economy. The first section asks how public policies define illegal labour. The second section analyses public policies concerning two different phenomena that are usually both labelled as illegal, black, undeclared or informal labour: the definition of boundaries between legal and illegal *labour migration* and between legal help for friends, neighbours or family members as well as legal secondary jobs on the one hand and illegal *moonlighting* on the other (cf. Dallago, 1990: 52-57 for a typology). Do public policies have an impact on illegal and informal labour and to what extent? What are the differences between the impact of public policy on moonlighting and on illegal labour migration? Against this empirical backdrop, the paper draws conclusions concerning the question whether and how public policies are able to reduce illegal work by defining boundaries between the formal and informal sectors.

HOW DOMESTIC AND EUROPEAN PUBLIC POLICIES DEFINE BOUNDARIES BETWEEN LEGAL AND ILLEGAL WORK

There is no universally valid definition of illegal work. Labour statisticians have intensively debated the definition of 'employment in the informal sector' with distinctions to be made between legal and illegal activities, formal and informal

10. The author thanks the organisers and participants of the CRIMPREV seminar at Llubljana in April 2008 as well as the two anonymous referees for their helpful comments to earlier versions of this paper and Joanna Shapland for the stylistic revision of the text.

jobs, formal and informal sector enterprises and work in private households (cf. Hussmanns, 2005:11 *et passim*). In a very broad sense, the informal economy is the reverse side of the official economy (Ponsaers et al., 2008: 645). Illegal work can be described as the opposite of the ideal type of legal employment, characterised by payment and which respects the rules for minimum wages and other labour standards set by legislation or collective labour agreements. A formal contract, social insurance and the fulfilment of other legal requirements such as a safe working place and tax paying also shape legal employment. Illegal work is, on a broad definition, the opposite of all this: working without a formal contract, not respecting obligations to pay social insurance contributions and taxes – and possibly disregarding other legal requirements such as work safety rules.

Beyond the scholarly debate, public policy defines illegal labour by setting rules and requirements for legal labour: who is entitled to work in a jurisdiction, which rules employers and employees have to respect, etc. The lack of a universally recognised definition opens up a margin of discretion for policies to include additional phenomena. In the German case, public policy opted for a broad legal definition of 'black labour' in 2004. [11] It includes not informing the relevant employment officer immediately after having found a new job in order to prevent people from receiving unemployment benefits for longer than they are entitled. It also includes employing workers on a lower salary than the legal minimum wage – a phenomenon becoming more important in Germany with a growing number of economic sectors being included in the obligation to pay the minimum wage. This definition is much broader than the ways in which 'informal labour' are usually used in everyday language as well as in the social sciences.

Informal labour as a domestic policy field: the German example

Informal labour has been a topic for West German public policy since the 1950s. Since the late 1990s, predominantly repressive approaches have been pushed by powerful political and administrative actors, complemented by preventive approaches, especially in the field of mini-jobs and taxation.

Legislative approaches to define and combat informal labour
The political aims and arguments brought forward to justify public policies in the field of informal labour vary with changing political priorities and the perception of problems in a specific historical situation.

The German case demonstrates that the definition of illegal labour and public policy responses vary – depending on the political parties in power and the economic situation in a specific historical period. When the West German parliament, in the 1950s, passed the first legislation intending to combat informal labour, the policy goal was to protect traditional forms of trade. Working as a self-employed plumber, butcher or even painter required a professional qualification[12] and formal registration with the chamber of trades, a semi-public body.[13] A

---

11. § 1(1) Gesetz zur Bekämpfung der Schwarzarbeit und der illegalen Beschäftigung, Bundesgesetzblatt I, 2004, p. 1842.

first *Gesetz zur Bekämpfung der Schwarzarbeit* ('law intending to combat informal [black] labour') came into force in 1957 under a conservative majority and in the period of post-war reconstruction with strong economic growth and relatively low and even decreasing unemployment rates. That law defined it a criminal offence to undertake craft work professionally without the required formal qualification and registration.[14] The conservative government of that time felt the need to protect self-employed craftspeople – traditional conservative voters – against people offering the same services without having the qualification required. Almost 50 years later, in 2004, the newly introduced legal definition of informal labour still included undertaking self-employed professional activities without the qualification and official registration required. However, due to the economic situation in post-war West Germany, the government in the 1950s did not yet feel the need to take measures against undeclared workers offering cheaper labour.

Table 1   Examples of legal approaches to combat informal labour in Germany

Category	Examples
Social security legislation	Obligations for employers and employees to reveal employment, salaries etc.
Legislation for the performance of crafts and trades	Obligation to declare starting to undertake a new craft or trade to the public authorities; requirements concerning the qualifications needed to perform certain crafts
Legislation relating to specific forms of labour	Legislation regulating temporary employment agencies or the employment of workers from abroad
Tax legislation	Obligation to keep bills for a certain time (§14 UStG); sanctions for evading taxes on wages (§370 AO)
Monitoring instruments	Legal base for administrative and criminal investigations; obligation to carry a social security card (for 'risky' crafts)

The West German economy was characterised by stable lifetime employment during the post-war decades. The protection of this employment therefore became another driving factor for the definition of boundaries between legal and illegal work. German legislation formulated strict rules in order to limit the possibilities of hiring personnel indirectly via private agencies. Until the 1960s, temporary employment agencies were strictly prohibited in West Germany. On the one hand, this legal provision was intended to protect workers from being exploited by agencies and short term contracts. On the other hand it was also intended to protect the public labour agency that had a monopoly function as an employment agency at that time. Private agencies were prohibited. In 1967, the Federal Constitutional Court ruled that such a strict prohibition violated freedom of occupational choice.[15]

---

12. *Meister.*
13. *Eintragung in die Handwerksrolle.*
14. Gesetz zur Bekämpfung der Schwarzarbeit, 30.03.1957, Bundesgesetzblatt I, 1957, p. 315.
15. Bundesverfassungsgericht, judgment of January 17, 1967, BVerfGE 21, 261.

Since the 1970s the protection of regular employment became a major concern, especially under governments with social democratic participation (1969 to 1983 and since 1998). The result is a complex body of rules governing legal employment and drawing boundaries between regular employment and informal labour. This legislation includes social insurance obligations, exceptions for secondary jobs ('mini-jobs'), employment rules for immigrants, rules for temporary employment agencies and legal bases for sanctioning breaches of the relevant obligations (for an overview see Riegel, 2003; Kossens, 2004; Buchner, 2004).

Strengthened administrative capacity: the Finanzkontrolle Schwarzarbeit
Besides strengthening repressive legal instruments, the federal government brought together the administrative agencies concerned with combating illegal labour in 2004 under the label *Finanzkontrolle Schwarzarbeit* (FKS) as a part of customs. At the federal level, the relevant tasks had previously been distributed between labour and customs administrations.

In most countries the task of combating illegal labour has been given to labour (work) government departments. Labour inspectorates inspect whether employers adhere to their legal obligations. Germany and Austria have moved away from this traditional institutional setting by giving the task of combating illegal labour to customs. In the German case two factors influenced this institutional choice. First, at that time customs needed new and additional tasks to perform. With the abolition of border controls inside the European Union (EU) and the enlargement of the territory of the EU common customs system as one of the core European policies, member states' customs administrations lost a part of their traditional mission. Customs have therefore developed into general security agencies since the 1990s, fulfilling tasks in fields such as combating illegal drugs trafficking – and in the German case informal labour. In 2004, some of the civil servants who had been deployed on the Czech and Polish borders were redirected towards combating illegal work when these borders became EU internal borders.

The second factor that influenced the new institutional landscape was a major reform of the German federal labour administration that was going on at the same time. Instead of administrating unemployment benefits, this reform intended a shift to a service-oriented agency trying to reduce unemployment by more proactive means and by paying more attention to each individual case. This shift was symbolically underlined by renaming the former *Bundesanstalt für Arbeit* as the *Bundesagentur für Arbeit*. Preparing administrative or criminal investigations against people who had wrongly received social benefits was no longer one of the core objectives of such a service-oriented strategy. Therefore, the political architects of those reforms had no difficulty in redirecting some 2,500 of the agencies' staff to customs in order to combat illegal labour within the new framework.

The high priority that the federal government, dominated by social democrats at that time, gave to combating illegal labour by creating a new institution was also underlined by the fact that around 1,500 additional staff were hired for the new institution – beyond around 2,500 customs officers who were previously working in the field and the around 2,500 staff formerly part of the federal labour administration (Bundesregierung, 2008: 2; Enste and Schneider, 2006: 49; Bundesrechnungshof, 2008: 10-12). Recruiting 1,500 additional civil servants for a new public institution is a remarkable political decision in a period of restrictive budget policy.

The new body was structured into three sub-divisions (Fehn, 2006; Bundesrechnungshof, 2008). About 65 % of the personnel were put in the biggest unit with a mission to conduct criminal and civil investigations ('Prüfungen und Ermittlungen') in cases of illegal work. A second subdivision, with around 15 % of the total personnel, was called a prevention unit ('Prävention'). This unit had the task of undertaking inspections (of construction sites, restaurants and bars, taxi and van drivers etc.) and putting out patrols in order to demonstrate to the wider public that a serious effort was being made to combat illegal labour. This unit's mission thus reflects only a minor part of what criminologists call prevention (Hebberecht, 2002). A third sub-division with the remaining 20% of the personnel administered administrative sanctions and undertook criminal investigations in cases of misuse of social benefits ('Ahndung'). Only four years after the implementation of this new structure, the administrative structures for combating illegal work were again reorganised. The three subdivisions were placed in different departments of customs as a part of a major reform of German customs (for a critique, see Bundesrechnungshof, 2008: 34-37).

Officially the priority given to inspecting employers has been adopted unchanged by the new customs administration. However, in practice, the intensified regime of inspections tend to focus on employees. While the number of employers inspected fell from more than 100,000 to 62,000 from 2004 to 2007 according to the official statistics, the number of employees contacted during inspections rose from 264,000 to 477,000 in the same period (Finanzkontrolle Schwarzarbeit, 2008, for a critique of the official statistics, see Bundesrechnungshof, 2008).

Preventing illegal labour by making it less salient
Some economists researching the informal economy heavily criticise the use of repressive strategies as they have been implemented by the German customs administration. According to these authors, intensified administrative inspections do not significantly raise the probability that instances of informal labour will be discovered and punished, due to the wide extent of that part of the informal economy (e.g. Enste and Schneider 2006: 49-51). Policy makers have taken up this argument. In the German case, in parallel with strengthening the federal administrative structures dedicated to combating illegal labour, additional prevention instruments have been introduced in order to make illegal labour less salient and legal labour less bureaucratic.

One approach is to diminish the extent of bureaucratic hurdles for (legal) employment in private households – a field where informal labour has always been common and widely tolerated. In complex economies with a high level of social security, employers are required to submit to complex administrative obligations: periodic declarations to social security institutions and tax bodies make legal employment not only more expensive but also more bureaucratic than illegal labour. The time needed to employ someone legally to do the housekeeping, gardening or give private lessons to children can therefore easily exceed the time gained by the help. Tolerated forms of illegal work therefore predominate in this field: These activities are a relevant part of the informal economy, the work usually being paid in cash and ignoring employers' obligations. In recent years Germany has followed the example of other countries in reducing the size of the illegal economy in this sector by making it easier and financially more attractive to fulfil legal obligations (Enste, 2002: 194). Employment in private households that does not exceed a salary of 400 Euros per month can now more easily be declared to a specialised agency ('Minijobzentrale') in a simplified procedure called *Haushaltsscheckverfahren*. All taxes and minimum social insurance contributions are covered by a lump sum, and the employer can even partly deduct this sum from his or her income tax. A similar instrument is the French *Chèque emploi-service* introduced in 2005 (Loi no. 2005/841).

These instruments are preventive in a broader sense. Their intention is to prevent people from making use of illegal labour by making it economically less salient. Economists criticising the ineffectiveness of repressive and punitive approaches say that such preventive incentives are a more effective strategy in reducing the extent of the informal economy (Enste and Schneider 2006: 57).

Strong advocacy coalitions in favour of repressive approaches
What are the reasons for this public policy approach being predominant in Germany in recent years strongly favouring more administrative inspection and repressive measures against informal labour? A number of theories on policy analysis developed within political science can help.

The *advocacy coalitions framework* developed by Sabatier and Jenkins-Smith (1999) assumes that 'actors can be aggregated into a number of "advocacy coalitions", each composed of people from various governmental and private organizations that both (1) share a set of normative and causal beliefs and (2) engage in a nontrivial degree of coordinated activity over time' (Sabatier and Jenkins-Smith, 1999: 120ff.). This analytical framework is particularly useful to explain which public policy initiatives are successful. It takes into account the fact that institutional actors, especially representatives from public administrations, generally do not play a neutral role in the process of public policy making. In many cases, they try to influence policy outcomes, driven by their own convictions and institutional interests. They therefore strengthen those advocacy coalitions that want the same result.

In the case of German anti-informal labour policy, a broad advocacy coalition sup-ported the repressive strategies developed in recent years, including more inspec-tion and more onerous sanctions. The social democrats, who were in a govern-mental coalition with the Green party between 1998 and 2005 and with the Christian Democrats since 2005, were the central actors in these coalitions. They wished to protect the types of employment dominant in the West German econ-omy since the invention of the social market economy in the 1950s: stable full-time employment for workers, often over several decades. Policies that protected and favoured this form of employment were strongly supported by trade unions that traditionally recruited most of their members and supporters from people working in stable jobs. Additionally, social security agencies are potential winners from repressive public policy strategies in this field if they succeed in shifting ille-gal employment into legal employment with the effect that social insurance con-tributions paid increase.

However, the strength and power of advocacy coalitions in the field of labour pol-icy largely depends on the participation of employers. Their support is not evident at all. Neo-liberal political ideologies supported by many employers and their associations tend to combat more onerous administrative inspection and sanc-tions as well as any regulation of the labour market, especially that involving a minimum wage and other rules which tend to protect regular employment. Vested interests tend to support this position, especially employers' associations in sectors with a high level of precarious employment. In Germany this is for example the case for the hotel and restaurant sector – one characterised by rela-tively low wages and a high proportion of workers on more flexible part-time employment contracts.

In other sectors, companies and employers' associations are much more pre-pared to combat 'cheap' forms of employment that does not respect the minimum wage and other obligations on employers. In Germany this is especially the case for the construction sector, which is characterised by high 'official' wages based on collective labour agreements between employers' associations and trade unions and partially transformed into legal obligations for a minimum wage. The relatively high 'official' wages in this sector have produced a 'grey' market of sub-contracting, illegal or semi-legal employment that endangers the traditional con-struction market. Hence the construction sector is particularly vulnerable to ille-gal labour. Subcontractors can easily earn extra money, for example by forcing labour migrants to work longer than officially declared hours or by keeping a major part of their salaries back to cover the provision of simple food and hous-ing. Due to the high official wages illegal profits are easier to make in the con-struction sector than in other sectors, such as cleaning companies or restaurants where the official wages are lower. Trade unions estimate the number of workers employed illegally in the German construction sector to be up to 400,000 (see, for example Kirchner, 2006: 176). Therefore 'serious' employers and their associ-ations tend to join advocacy coalitions in favour of stricter inspection and more severe sanctions. The Federal Ministry of Finance responsible for supervising customs in their mission to combat illegal labour therefore created a strategic alliance with these 'serious' employers' associations and the relevant trade unions in the construction industry – a kind of 'good guys' coalition called *Aktionsbündnis* in favour of stricter sanctions for those employers who did not respect the rules. Similar activities have been developed in recent years for the haulage business and for slaughterhouses (Bundesministerium der Finanzen, 2006).

Trade unions regularly publicise the bad working conditions in illegal employment, especially when labour migrants are exploited by subcontractors of companies belonging to the formal economy (e.g. Peter, 2006; Kirchner, 2006). However, their focus is rather to protect their members' regular employments against cheap competition than to help labour migrants (see Kirchner, 2006 on their occasional activities in that field). The fact that left wing advocacy coalitions based on social democrats and trade unions support stricter inspection while conservative and neo-liberal political forces opt rather for non-intervention makes it difficult for those human rights NGOs which assist labour migrants to position themselves in relation to these advocacy coalitions: neither of the two camps focuses on the situation of people who wish to work in rich countries simply to earn their living (Kirchner, 2006).

How European policies contribute to defining boundaries between legal and illegal work

Policy makers in EU member states are not autonomous in defining the boundaries between legal and illegal work. They have to respect the EC internal market rules. As well as these rules the European institutions have developed initiatives to influence domestic strategies in this field, especially in order to transfer parts of the informal to the formal economy. The following sections outline the major patterns within this movement.

Free movement of workers and transitional exceptions in periods of enlargement
The free movement of workers is one of the basic liberties that constitute the European internal market: 'Such freedom of movement shall entail the abolition of any discrimination based on nationality between workers of the Member States as regards employment, remuneration and other conditions of work and employment' (Article 39(2) EC Treaty). This fundamental element of European integration has been shaped by a body of European legislation and by judgments of the European Court of Justice (ECJ) including the limitations justified on grounds of public policy, public security or public health (Articles 39(3) and 40 EC Treaty). A substantial part of the relevant EC legislation and ECJ rulings has strengthened the free movement of workers in the EU and therefore limited the space for domestic policy makers to protect their citizens by using restrictive rules for workers from other EU countries (see for an overview Franzen, 2003). With the dynamics of the EU internal market and the growing mobility of workers inside the EU, restrictive domestic rules have come under pressure. German policy

makers, for example, have therefore reduced the number of professions for which self-employed activities require a special qualification ('Meisterzwang').[16]

However, the free movement of workers within the EU is limited by transitional rules for workers from new member states. Each round of EU enlargement has provoked a debate on the consequences for the labour market in 'older' member states. The accession treaties have therefore made short-term reservations for labour migration from accession countries (cf. Brinkmann, 2006: 373). When Spain, Portugal and Greece joined the European Community in the 1980s, the salaries in these countries were much lower than in the average of the other countries. Germany, France and other 'older' EU member states had already been the destination of labour migration from these countries before their accession to the EC. However, the flow of labour remained rather limited in size after the accession. Developments were not homogeneous. The number of workers from Spain decreased in France and in Germany after accession, whilst the number of labour migrants from Portugal fell in France, but rose in Germany (European Commission, 2001: 41). Even if the EU eastern enlargement in 2004-2006 triggers further migration from Central European countries to Western Europe, that will probably remain a transition issue from a longer term perspective (Zimmermann, 2005; European Commission, 2001).

Transitional exceptions mean that citizens from the countries concerned are allowed to travel to all other EU countries, but generally not to do paid work. If they accept a job there in order to earn their living, they are obliged to do it illegally and thus as a part of the informal economy.

Transitional labour migration inside the EU: the posting rules
If EU citizens are entitled to move freely to other countries as workers, this does not mean that the member states have completely renounced the possibility of defining boundaries between what is allowed and what is forbidden. This is especially the case for temporary labour migration in the form of posting workers to other member states – a field where the rules on the free movement of services potentially conflict with national labour standards (De Vos, 2006; Hatala, 2006).

Even if the EU internal market were to lead to a harmonisation of member states' economies, there are still important differences in the level of wages and other labour standards. The EC posting directive 96/71/EC states the general rule that workers sent to another member state by a company have to be treated and paid according to the rules of the member state where the work is done and they also have to be declared to the social insurance institutions in that country. So far, domestic policy makers have kept the power to require these obligations be respected.

---

16. Drittes Gesetz zur Änderung der Handwerksordnung und anderer handwerksrechtlicher Vorschriften, Bundesgesetzblatt I, 2003, 2934.

However, the posting directive allows exceptions for posting workers for a limited time. In this case, the social insurance rules from the country of origin are applicable. In the service sector this is an advantage for companies from member states with lower wages and lower social security contributions. Consequently, the definition of boundaries between legal and illegal practices has shifted to the question as to whether the country in which the work is done is entitled to check the documents issued by social insurance institutions in the country of origin. The European Court of Justice declared that the principle of mutual recognition was applicable and therefore has obliged the public authorities of the country where the work is done to accept the documents[17] (for an overview of the ECJ judgments on posted workers, see De Vos, 2006). If there is any suspicion that the documents could have been issued falsely, the public authorities will have to check this bilaterally. Here again, the margin for domestic policy makers to define boundaries between legal and illegal practices has been limited by European rules.

Labour migration from outside the EU
If the economy in an EU member state has a need for additional workers, such as seasonal agricultural workers or highly skilled IT specialists, national policy makers are not completely free in their decision making. All workers living legally in the EU are entitled to move freely to the other member states under the European visa regime (Article 62 EC Treaty). The member states therefore have to respect the relevant European rules, which are for the most part characterised by reservations imposed by politicians intending to restrict immigration.[18]

The European Commission, supported by economists (e.g. Zimmermann, 2005), has repeatedly stressed the economic usefulness of legal temporary labour migration from third countries as an instrument to make the economy more flexible (European Commission, 2005; for a critical analysis, see Folmar-Otto, 2007). It has also stressed the importance of opening up labour markets to third-country nationals already living in the EU (European Commission, 2005: 9). Here the European influence on policy making has strengthened the formal sector by opening up opportunities for legal labour immigration and for legal employment of migrants already living in the EU.

COMPARING NATIONAL POLICIES FOR TWO FORMS OF ILLEGAL WORK: ILLEGAL LABOUR MIGRATION AND MOONLIGHTING

The previous section on the influence of national and European public policies on the definition of boundaries between legal and illegal work has shown that a major element of policy making in this field is linked to migration. Immigrants

---

17. Case C-2/05, judgment of 26.1.2006.
18. E.g. by stricter border controls: Cf. Regulation (EC) no. 2007/2004 establishing a European Agency for the Management of Operational Cooperation at the External Borders [...], OJ L 349 of 25.11.2004, 1 (FRONTEX).

are the group most targeted by public policies aiming to combat illegal work or to shift it to the formal sector.

In this section, labour migration will be compared to the second major field in which public policies define boundaries between legal and illegal work: first legally provided help between friends, neighbours or family members as well as legal secondary jobs, and then illegal work by domestic citizens, full time or part time, after having finished their regular job – so called *moonlighting*. These two major types of illegal work will be compared from the perspective of the underlying political choices and respective administrative strategies.

Comparing political choices on legal instruments

The dominant political choices differ considerably between the two major types of illegal work.

Political choices defining legal labour migration
Generally only legally admitted migrants are entitled to regular employment. Possessing a visa to stay legally in a country does not automatically include the right to accept a paid job. The conditions under which asylum seekers and other migrants have the right to accept paid employment depend on political decisions transferred into legal rules (Eichenhofer, 1999). Migrants working illegally are excluded from social security institutions (Vogel, 1999) and risk penal sanctions.

Mainstream politics in the EU member states follow a double strategy to protect their domestic labour markets against unwanted labour immigration and to open them up if there is perceived economic need for additional workers. Consequently there is often a gap in public policies towards the two groups: On the one hand there are migrants working on the margins of modern society with lowly paid jobs as cleaners, dish washers in restaurant kitchens, tough jobs in the construction sector etc. The other group of labour migrants is highly skilled experts, such as engineers and computer specialists actively attracted by government policies to well remunerated positions.

The distinction between legal immigration of highly trained experts and illegal immigration of people working in marginal jobs is a direct consequence of political choices – often driven by political intentions to create favourable conditions for the economy. Policy makers define the categories of workers that are welcome in a specific historical situation – generally depending on the economic and political needs and preferences of the moment. They also define how easy or difficult it is to enter a country – or nowadays the EU – in order to gain paid employment.

Historical studies have shown that immigration has been the subject of social and labour policies at times when additional workers were needed. At times of high unemployment, however, preventing immigration is the predominant pattern, and immigration instead becomes a topic for ministries of the interior and policing (starting from the French example: Noiriel, 1988).

Furthermore, political preferences influence policies concerning immigrants who are already there – legally or illegally. Liberalising immigration and labour law can make it easier for immigrants to earn their living. Generally it is rather difficult for illegal immigrants to organise themselves in order to defend their interests – due to their illegal status. Only if there is an economic need for supplementary labour or if strong other groups act in favour of illegal immigrants do they have a chance to improve their status – as was the case for the French *sans-papiers*, who were supported by a substantial body of people a while ago.

Preferential rules towards domestic workers, which exist in many countries, press less qualified immigrants to do work that nationals from the middle classes do not want to do – for example, cleaning the streets or collecting rubbish. If someone offers them another job, it will often be on an illegal basis. In contrast, public policies tend to soften preference rules in order to attract highly skilled experts where they are needed in the labour market. Industrialised countries find themselves in a competition to attract the most qualified engineers or scientists (European Commission, 2005: 7).

The general purposes of immigration policy and economic arguments are dominant in political decision making on labour migration. Political decision makers have some margin for acting when they define which migrants are entitled to work legally. But in making their political choices, they often depend on economic pressure groups, for example, employers' associations lobbying in favour of making access to the labour market easier for qualified labour migrants – or in favour of protecting the domestic market against 'cheap' competition from abroad. The individual migrant and his human rights only play a secondary role for mainstream politics in this field – which is a perspective that human rights specialists and NGOs take in the political debate (Follmar-Otto, 2007).

Political choices for defining boundaries between illegal moonlighting and legal work
Moonlighting involves having multiple jobs with partly legal and partly illegal employment, together with informal self-employed activities in one's free time (Leonard, 1998: 60-65; Dallago, 1990: 61). People who feel a need for more income may be prepared to renounce a part of their free time in order to make some extra money in the informal sector (Enste, 2002: 121). In another variation of moonlighting self-employed people circumvent legal obligations in relation to a part of their activities, for example by separating bills into a (lower) official part and additional cash payments in order to save on taxes and social security contributions.

Being prepared to help family members and friends in one's free time is something that contributes to social cohesion in modern fragmented societies. Public policies therefore would cause more damage than benefit by limiting this form of work by legal rules and bureaucratic obligations. In fact, many governments have started programmes to promote voluntary engagement in civil society. Therefore defining boundaries between legal and illegal work is particularly difficult in this field.

The easiest way that most legal systems have chosen to define what is allowed is to leave unpaid work and help unregulated and to establish rules for paid employment: obligations to register as a self-employed craftsperson or to declare employees to tax and social security authorities (see Leonard, 1998 for the distinction between work and employment). However, this solution for defining the boundaries between the legal and illegal sectors leaves questions open: does it make sense if public policy forces people who earn relatively little money to comply with bureaucratic requirements? What about receiving non-monetary advantages for work? Instead of a salary people might receive free meals, gifts or other payment in kind for their help. Does this oblige them to fulfil the same requirements as people who work for money?

Public policy has developed repressive and preventive strategies to combat moonlighting and fraud related to illegal work. Repressive strategies include sanctions for not respecting legal obligations to declare employees or to register as self-employed. In the German case, a mix of administrative and penal sanctions has been included in the relevant legislation (Fehn, 2006).

In recent years preventive public policy strategies have become more important in this field. In Germany and France for example, they include efforts to reduce the bureaucratic burdens in relation to minor forms of employment in private households such as cleaning or private lessons (see above), complemented by tax deductions for employing officially registered tradespeople in the private sector, e.g. for renovating or gardening. These strategies transfer a part of the grey zone that exists between legal and illegal activities to the formal economy – especially in the private sector.

Strategies for administrative implementation compared

Political choices only have practical impact if they are implemented. Without any kind of administrative implementation, many public policy choices would probably not have any consequences. Legal obligations that make labour more expensive or exclude people from legal work are likely not to be respected if the risk of detection is low. Policy makers that have more than symbolic intentions for their policies therefore have to work out how to implement and enforce the substantive legal rules. As policy makers can choose more or less repressive implementation measures, implementation strategies are another point of intervention for political decision making.

The existence of administrative inspection strategies does not automatically lead to perfect implementation. They may make people more aware of the existing rules and more motivated to respect them. But administrative inspections can never reduce to zero the number of cases of flouting the rules.

Administrative implementation of strategies against illegal labour migration
Administrative inspection strategies as they have been developed in Germany in recent years have involved increasing the number of 'street level bureaucrats' (as defined by Meyers and Vorsanger, 2007). This has proved to be a major factor influencing whether public policies lead to policy outcomes. Inspections are the classical form of administrative supervision – visiting construction sites, restaurants or other businesses known to have labour migrants among their staff, on the premise that some of these workers might be illegal. If the 'success' of inspections is measured by the number of infringements detected, inspecting employers who might have illegally employed labour migrants is particularly salient. Restaurants, shops and other businesses run by immigrants therefore are preferred targets for inspectors. This effect is amplified by the high visibility that characterises many of the immigrants' professional activities – as much for public administrations preparing inspections as for whistle-blowers. Among the cases on which action has been taken after inspections and investigations by the German *Finanzkontrolle Schwarzarbeit*, there are many violations of the legislation on the employment of foreigners (Bundesrechnungshof, 2008, 32).

In the European context, administrative inspection strategies can easily become the subject of political conflicts. Intensified inspections may be perceived as a strategy to keep workers from other European countries away from the domestic labour market (Hatala, 2006).

Administrative implementation of strategies against moonlighting
In some respects, administrative strategies against moonlighting are similar to those against illegal immigration. Control bodies have to demonstrate that they are successful and therefore tend to concentrate their activities where they think they will find many illegal workers. Inspection strategies are therefore developed based mainly on previous experience and hints from neighbours or other people on the basis of more or less concrete suspicions.

However, the visibility of illegal work makes a major difference to administrative control strategies. Illegal immigration generally is much more visible than most forms of moonlighting. While moonlighting in the construction sector is relatively easy to detect by inspecting construction sites, most types of moonlighting are rather difficult to detect and to prove. If a self-employed plumber or joiner works without sending an officially declared bill or only partly bills his work, the fiscal fraud is difficult to detect. Combating moonlighting in private households is even more difficult. A cleaner, plumber or joiner working in a private household is almost invisible to the public administrations. Only a tip from an insider enables inspectors to detect illegal activities in this field. As illegal employment in private households is a widespread phenomenon, there is also little political will to combat these forms of illegal work by inspection strategies or to transfer them to the formal sector (for the German case see Berwanger, 2004). In sum, compared to illegal labour by immigrants, characterised by a concentration in certain sectors and a high degree of visibility of illegal activities, moonlighting is rather difficult to combat by administrative inspection strategies.

CONCLUSION: ILLEGAL WORK, PUBLIC POLICY CHOICES AND THE INFORMAL ECONOMY

This paper has shown that the boundaries between legal and illegal work are floating, but that public policies have some possibility of influencing them by defining boundaries between what is allowed and what is forbidden. Thus far, the paper confirms the results of previous studies in this field, such as those from other countries such as Castells and Portes (1989) and Leonard (1998).

The choice of public policy strategies depends on the strength of advocacy coalitions for more restrictive or more liberal strategies in a specific historical situation. The perceived need for labour, intentions to reduce the informal economy or putting considerable importance on human rights can lead policy makers to transfer certain activities to the legal sector, supported by employers' associations and trade unions. High unemployment rates or populist anti-immigration pressure tend to have the opposite effect: As the German example shows, policy makers then tend to opt for a broader definition of illegal labour. In Europe the debates on illegal work as a part of the informal economy are largely dominated by economic strategies aiming at more flexibility for the labour market. Workers' social and human rights therefore only play a secondary role in these debates (for a critique, see Follmar-Otto, 2007; GCIM, 2005).

In the European multi-level polity, the rules that decide whether labour is legal or illegal are often complex and therefore difficult to understand for the workers concerned and also difficult for public administrations to apply. As in other sectors of the informal economy (Vande Walle, 2008: 654), the dualist distinction between legal and illegal activities is fading. Grey zones are emerging where rules are unclear or contested. The classification of activities as legal or illegal often depends on the interpretation of legal rules that has to take into account the multi-level character of many rules in the EU. The substantial number of judgments by the European Court of Justice and national courts on questions related to boundaries between legal and illegal work is a direct consequence of these grey zones.

A symbiotic and synergetic relationship between legal and illegal work tends to dominate (in the sense of the analytical framework developed by Vande Walle, 2008: 658). The example of defining boundaries between legal and illegal work demonstrates that public policy can most efficiently reduce illegal labour by removing phenomena from the field of illegality. If employment can be gained without any formal requirements, it cannot be illegal work. Public policy can also reduce the market for illegal work by making legal work more attractive and salient for workers and employers.

Since the 1980s, academic political economy debates have focussed on the question whether the state is able to regulate markets successfully. While the idea that markets are producing better results than public policy was dominant for a number of years, the idea of the state as an important regulator has been brought back in, especially since the major crisis in the international financial markets in 2008. The public policies which create the boundaries between legal and illegal work demonstrate that political decision makers can influence markets in multiple ways. If they decide to legalise certain forms of work or to make legal work more attractive, they reduce the market for illegal work. If they opt for restrictive policy solutions, for example by excluding asylum seekers or workers from new EU member states from legal work, they indirectly set incentives for the illegal labour market. In making these kinds of decisions, they follow economic interests, which are themselves determined by the needs of the labour market.

Measuring the effects of preventive or repressive policy solutions poses methodological problems. On the basis of the available studies, it is not possible to say if the new repressive strategies, as they have been adopted by German policy makers in recent years, have significantly reduced illegal work (Boockmann and Rincke, 2005; Schneider and Enste, 2002: 43-53). While the relevant authorities say they are convinced that their strategies are successful, the relatively few empirical studies available in this field do not demonstrate any clear reduction in illegal activities (Feld and Larsen, 2005; Enste and Schneider, 2006; Bundesrechnungshof, 2008). From a criminological point of view, measuring illegal work poses similar methodological problems to measuring the dark figure of crime. In order to measure the impact of public policy measures it would be essential to know more about the extent of (unreported) cases of different types of illegal work. However, only few criminologists have discovered this as a field of empirical research up to now (Albrecht, 2006). In the case of labour migration, the extent of illegal immigration is another dark figure phenomenon that is methodologically difficult to estimate (Vogel, 1999). Future empirical research should have a closer look at labour migration and moonlighting and analyse specific parts of these fields in order to identify ways in which public policies can contribute to transferring relevant forms of labour from the informal to the formal sector. In addition, the fact that domestic public policies are restricted in their decision making by a growing body of European rules on labour conditions and labour migration makes the relationship between the informal economy, illegal work and public policy an interesting subject for further comparative research.

REFERENCES

Albrecht, H.-J. (2006). *Illegalität, Kriminalität und Sicherheit*. In J. Alt & M. Bommes, M. (eds.), *Illegalität. Grenzen und Möglichkeiten der Migrationspolitik*. Wiesbaden: Verlag für Sozialwissenschaften, pp. 60-80.

Berwanger, J. (2004). 'Private Putzhilfen und Schwarzarbeit. *Betriebs-Berater*, 59(2): 10-16.

Boockmann, B. & Rincke, J. (2005). *Wirksamkeit der Bekämpfung der Schwarzarbeit durch die Finanzkontrolle Schwarzarbeit: Empirische Untersuchung der Entwicklung der Schwarzarbeit und des hierauf bezogenen Bewusstseins- und Wertewandels Machbarkeitsstudie*. Mannheim: Zentrum für Europäische Wirtschaftsforschung, Forschungsauftrag 5/05.

Brinkmann, G. (2006). 'Die Übergangsregelungen zur Arbeitnehmerfreizügigkeit unter besonderer Berücksichtigung der Entscheidung der deutschen Bundesregierung'. *ERA-Forum*, 7(3): 370-380.

Buchner, H. (2004). 'Neuerlicher Anlauf zur Bewältigung der "Schwarzarbeit"'. *Gewerbe-Archiv*, 50(10): 393-403.

Bundesministerium der Finanzen (2006). *Aktionsbündnisse gegen Schwarzarbeit und illegale Beschäftigung*. BMF-Monatsbericht (June), 65-71.

Bundesrechnungshof (2008). *Bericht nach § 99 der Bundeshaushaltsordnung über die Organisation und Arbeitsweise der Finanzkontrolle Schwarzarbeit*. Bonn/Berlin, Bundestags-Drucksache 16/7727, at http//www.bunderechnungshof.de/veroeffentlichungen/schwarzarbeit.pdf.

Bundesregierung (2008). *Antwort [...] auf die Kleine Anfrage [...] der Fraktion DIE LINKE [...]*. Bundestags-Drucksache 16/8156.

Castells, M. & Portes, A. (1989). 'World underneath: The origins, dynamics, and effects of the informal economy'. In A. Portes, M. Castels & L. Benton (eds.), *The informal economy. Studies in advanced and less developed countries*. Baltimore and London: John Hopkins University Press.

Dallago, B. (1990). *The irregular economy. The 'underground' economy and the 'black' labour market*. Aldershot: Dartmouth.

De Vos, M. (2006). 'Free movement of workers, free movement of services and the Posted Workers Directive: A Bermuda triangle for national labour standards?' *ERA-Forum*, 7(3): 356-370.

Eichenhofer, E. (1999). 'Migration und Recht'. In *Migration und Illegalität*. Osnabrück: Universitätsverlag Rasch, pp. 29-40.

Enste, D. (2002). *Schattenwirtschaft und institutioneller Wandel*. Tübingen: Mohr Siebeck.

Enste, D. & Schneider, F. (2006). 'Schattenwirtschaft und irreguläre Beschäftigung: Irrtümer, Zusammenhänge und Lösungen'. In J. Alt & M. Bommes (eds.), *Illegalität. Grenzen und Möglichkeiten der Migrationspolitik*. Wiesbaden: Verlag für Sozialwissenschaften, pp. 35-59.

European Commission, Directorate for Economic and Financial Affairs (2001). *The economic impact of enlargement*. Enlargement Papers, no 4. Brussels: European Commission.

European Commission (2005). *Policy plan on legal migration* (COM(2005)669 final). Brussels: European Commission.

Fehn, B. (2006). *Finanzkontrolle Schwarzarbeit. Prüfen und Ermitteln nach dem Schwarzarbeitsbekämpfungsgesetz*. Köln: Bundesanzeiger Verlag.

Feld, L. & Larsen, C. (2005). *Black activities in Germany in 2001 and in 2004. A comparison based on survey data*. Copenhagen: News from the Rockwool Foundation Research Unit.

Finanzkontrolle Schwarzarbeit (2008). *Bekämpfung der Schwarzarbeit und der illegalen Beschäftigung*, at www.zoll.de, April 4, 2008.

Follmar-Otto, P. (2007). *Temporäre Arbeitsmigration in die Europäische Union. Menschrechtliche Anforderungen*. Policy Paper no. 7. Berlin: Deutsches Institut für Menschenrechte.

Franzen, M. (2003). 'Kommentierung zu Art. 39 EGV'. In R. Streinz (ed.), *EUV/EGV*. München: C.H. Beck, pp.564-623.

GCIM (Global Commission on International Migration) (2005). *Migration in an interconnected world: New directions for action*. Geneva: GCIM.

Harding, P. & Jenkins, R. (1989). *The myth of the hidden economy. Towards a new understanding of informal economic activity*. Milton Keynes: Open University Press.

Hatala, R. (2006). 'Beschränkungen der Arbeitnehmerfreizügigkeit. Umsetzung der Beitrittsakte 2003 und deutsche Arbeitsmarktsituation'. *Forum Recht*, 24(2): 40-43.

Hebberecht, P. (2002). 'On prevention and security policy in Europe'. In P. Hebberecht & D. Duprez (eds.), *The prevention and security policies in Europe*. Brussels: VUB Brussels University Press, pp. 7-13.

Hussmanns, R. (2005). *Measuring the informal economy: From employment in the informal sector to informal employment*. Working paper no. 53. Geneva: International Labour Office, Policy Integration Department; Bureau of Statistics.

Kirchner, M. (2006). 'Wem nützen bzw. schaden "illegale" Migranten?' In J. Alt. & M. Bommes (eds.), *Illegalität. Grenzen und Möglichkeiten der Migrationspolitik*. Wiesbaden: Verlag für Sozialwissenschaften, pp. 170-179.

Kossens, M. (2004). 'Das Gesetz zur Intensivierung der Bekämpfung der Schwarzarbeit und damit zusammenhängender Steuerhinterziehung'. *Betriebs-Berater*, 59(2): 2-9.

Leonard, M. (1998). *Invisible work, invisible workers. The informal economy in Europe and the US*. Basingstoke: Macmillan.

Meyers, M. & Vorsanger, S. (2007). 'Street-level bureaucrats and the implementation of public policy'. In B. Peters & J. Pierre (eds.), *Handbook of public administrations*. London: Sage, pp. 153-163.

Noiriel, G. (1988). *Le creuset français. Histoire de limmigration. XIXe-XXe siècle*. Paris: Éditions du Seuil.

Peter, A. (2006). *Die Fleischmafia. Kriminelle Geschäfte mit Fleisch und Menschen*. Berlin: Ullstein.

Ponsaers, P., Shapland, J. & Williams, C. (2008). 'Does the informal economy link to organized crime?' *International Journal of Social Economy*, 35(9): 644-650.

Riegel, M. (2003). *Schwarzarbeit aus öffentlich-rechtlicher Sicht*. Hamburg: Dr. Kova.

Sabatier, P. & Jenkins-Smith, H. (1999). 'The advocacy coalition framework'. In P. Sabatier (ed.), *Theories of the policy process*. Boulder, Colorado: Westview Press, pp. 117-166.

Schneider, F. & Enste, D. (2002). *The shadow economy. An international survey*. Cambridge: Cambridge University Press.

Vande Walle, G. (2008). 'A matrix approach to informal markets: towards a dynamic conceptualisation'. *International Journal of Social Economics*, 35(9): 651-665.

Vogel, D. (1999). 'Illegale Zuwanderung nach Deutschland und soziales Sicherungssystem'. In E. Eichenhofer (ed.), *Migration und Illegalität*. Osnabrück: Universitätsverlag Rasch, pp. 73-90.

Zimmermann, K. (2005). 'European Labour Mobility: Challenges and Potentials'. *The Economist*, 153(4): 425-450.

Migrant's offside trap: a strategy for dealing with misleading rules and a hostile playing field

Valeria Ferraris[19]

INTRODUCTION

In Italy today deviance and immigration are two closely linked issues in public debate and on the political agenda. It is not by chance that they are the object of many academic studies.[20] I will here seek to examine the issue of deviance in connection with achieving legal status to reside in Italy. I will first briefly present the methodology used and clarify some terminology and then explain the theoretical basis of the analysis.

At the core of the research is the Italian immigration rules and their implementation concerning admission and stay of foreigners, focusing on how they produce 'institutionalized irregularity' (Santos 1993, cited by Calavita 2003: 405), i.e. an illegality caused or at least facilitated by the law. I shall then outline the relationship between immigration admission rules and the position of foreigners in the labour market. Once this scenario is clarified, I will illustrate some adaptation behaviour adopted by migrants to deal with the Italian legal and economic framework. I will show how they use illegality to become legal, and how migrants implement strategies to overcome their precarious condition. The success of the strategies adopted largely depends on the ability of migrants to understand the essential 'normative features' of the host country and to exploit available opportunities. Looking for a way to legality, migrants will reveal the essence of the Italian way of life.

TERMINOLOGY AND METHODS

Immigration is a complex issue, as is its vocabulary. In the article I have chosen to use 'foreigners' and 'migrants' interchangeably, because the first one is the word used by legislators and the second I believe is better able to define the situation of people who leave their own country and arrive in a new one. Similarly, the terms 'amnesty' and 'legalisation/regularisation programme' are used as syn-

---

19. This paper is derived from a paper in *Studi sulla Questione Criminale*, 2009, 3, March 2009.
20. See Ambrosini (2005); Ambrosini and Salati (2004); Barbagli (2008); Barbagli et al., (2004); Calavita (2005); Melossi (2003). Immigration reports are published yearly by Fondazione ISMU (from 1995 to 2008). See also the journals *Studi Emigrazione*, especially no. 145/2002, *Dei Delitti e delle Pene*, especially no. 3/1999, *Studi sulla Questione Criminale* no. 1/2007.

onyms. Italian legislation distinguishes a 'regularisation/legalisation programme' from an amnesty. In the first, proof of an employer-employee relationship is required, whilst in the second access to legal status is guaranteed to everyone who can prove they are living and staying in Italy when the amnesty comes into force – however, it is not the purpose of this chapter to track differences in the features of the different legalisation mechanisms.

Finally, I have chosen to use the word 'underground economy' for the informal economy because it is broad and understandable. I have avoided using terms such as informal, illegal or black when referring to either markets or the economy. Each word has a specific meaning, and sometimes economists and statisticians do not agree on their meaning or their use. For the purpose of this thesis, I believe the underground economy is the most appropriate.

The present analysis is the result of research and fieldwork carried out in Italy between January 2006 and April 2007 using different methodologies. Considering the importance of the legislative background, the research starts with an in-depth examination of immigration law and its implementation, using textual analysis, the study of articles in the relevant journals and several informal interviews with practitioners working in the offices involved in admission procedures in Italy. For particular circumstances, such as the enactment of the last flow decree and the changes in procedure for renewal, I carried out observations at the post office and at the so-called *Sportello Unico* (i.e. the office in charge of the procedures for the admission of foreigners from abroad). Moreover, I interviewed 15 experts (lawyers, public prosecutors, law enforcement officers, academics) using open-ended questions covering four main areas: the development of immigration laws and policies, difficulties of implementation, the economic role of migrants and their involvement in the crimes of fraud and forgery.

Subsequently, I collected 25 life histories of foreigners, focusing on their experiences in entering Italy and on the procedures that they followed to gain legal status. Most of the interviews were carried out in Piedmont and in Lombardy but some were also held in Lazio and Puglia. Due to the lack of feasibility of having a sampling frame (because of the difficulty of distinguishing the target population – people who uses illegality to become or remain legal – 'general' legal migrants), the interviewees were chosen through a snowballing sampling process. In order to select the interviewees I attempted to pay attention to the many possible important variables involved, in particular, nationality, place in the labour market and period of migration. Moreover, I tried to reach people through different channels (charity organisations, lawyers, trade unions, acquaintances, etc.), trying to consider as many different ties and networks as possible. Wherever possible, people were chosen because they were capable not only of describing their experiences but also of giving insights on the issue.

THE THEORETICAL FRAMEWORK

Due to the intrinsic interdisciplinary nature of immigration research, the theoretical scenario guiding this work is rather complex. The first part of the work is mainly normative and dedicated to present immigration law and policies and demonstrating that they tend to obstruct legal entry into Italy and place foreigners in a particularly disadvantaged position in relation to the labour market.

Law is seen as a dialectic process (Chambliss and Seidan, 1982), as the result of a process stemming from the political balance between parties (sometimes including political exchange), intervention of the State bureaucracy, the consent of public opinion, 'symbolism' and finally (though increasingly rare) adequacy for the purpose.

Immigration law, especially in Italy, is an amazing example of the result of these processes. Factors shaping immigration law in present societies are global: the social dynamics of the migratory process, globalisation (north-south divide, availability of cultural capital and techniques, deregulation), and national and international political systems (Castles, 2004). In facing this scenario immigration law is, as a consequence, stuck between conflicting forces which shape it.

Highlighting the fact that legislation is a result of a struggle amongst complex interest groups, yet at the same time tries to be functional in relation to precise socio-economic and political interests, is not a contradiction. On the contrary, it makes clear to what degree interests in a complex society are various, contradictory and often hidden. As a consequence and not by chance, rules are thus often conflicting, confused and changeable. They are often the result of hidden agendas: officially, certain objectives are followed but practice may aim at totally different results. There are many doubts as to whether the results are unwanted but they are a consequence of a combination of factors which characterize Italy – hot political debate, the strong symbolic significance of the issue, the widespread underground economy, the crisis of welfare and, lastly, the inefficient and discretionary bureaucratic and administrative apparatus. As a matter of fact, the policies that 'claim to exclude undocumented workers often conceal practices that allow them to enter in covert ways, so they can be more readily exploited' (Castles, 2004, p. 871).

The core of the paper concerns the adaptation of a foreigner to the legal and economic framework which tends to marginalise him/her. Hence analysis will focus on the behaviour of the foreigner who wants to achieve legal status and, due to the impossibility of achieving this legally, finds other means to reach the goal. These behaviours can be related to the category of the innovator, elaborated by R.K. Merton (Merton, 1968). The Mertonian scheme regarding conflict between goals and means can be applied as an analogy, with reaching legal status in Italy as the goal and innovation in the mode of adaptation. The achievement of legal status is an attractive goal because not only does it allow access to most of the benefits guaranteed to citizens and permits general improvement in one's own conditions, but also keeps migrants safe from expulsion and from the ordinary controls made by formal social control agents.

Migrants need to be innovators because they cannot conform. The following thorough examination of the immigration rules and their implementation will clarify why law 'forces' them to use deviant means instead of normal ones to achieve their goal. Merton's statement on the genesis of the deviant behaviour is incomplete without an explanation about the process which drives foreigners to learn the necessary criminal behaviour.

I believe that an explanation can be found by using and adapting Sutherland's approach of differential social organisation (Sutherland and Cressey 1978). Sutherland's theory postulates that criminal behaviour is learned by relationships with people close to one. A person learns techniques (how the actions can be committed) and 'the specific direction of motives, drives, rationalisations and attitudes' (why the actions are committed). Criminal behaviour occurs 'because of an excess of definitions favorable to violation of law'.

Sutherland's approach seems to me fruitful in the sense that it provides – as it will be shown – an adequate explanation of the deceptions and forgeries committed by foreigners. Migrants are encouraged to commit deception and forgery by a widespread definition favourable to the violation of the rules governing entrance to and staying in Italy. These violations are not perceived as crimes. Migrants learn techniques and justifications, because of the help of people, natives and foreigners, connected to them by networks.

The hypothesis is that a foreigner, who has been socialised into specific deviant patterns of behaviour typical of Italian society, succeeds. S/he overcomes obstacles by avoiding them and cheating. Committing fraud or forgery concerning one's residence status is the 'obligatory' short cut to legality. Discovering and using shortcuts is not sanctioned or socially censured. It is a consolidated social custom. Moreover, this strategy is possible due to the help given by natives and other migrants. The lesson learnt is that in Italy solutions to problems and difficulties can be found more easily by working indirectly and taking short cuts.

THE PILLARS OF THE IMMIGRATION LAW: AMNESTY AND THE FLUID BOUNDARIES BETWEEN UNDOCUMENTED AND DOCUMENTED MIGRANTS.

In recent years, there have been five[21] key mechanisms for entry onto Italian territory: three based on quotas[22] (employee entrance systems or so called *chiamata nominativa*, seasonal jobs, so-called sponsor system[23]), one outside the quota

---

21. To complete the list there is also entry for the self-employed (the so-called *chiamata numerica*, which is never used), and the so called 'training for migration' certificates' (in Italian *titoli preferenziali*) which, as will be explained below, have replaced the so-called sponsor system.

system, in particular cases related to highly skilled activities or because they have unusual mobility or time constraints and last, but by no means least, legalisation programmes for people already in Italy.

Admission procedures for employees take place in five key phases: the employer's request to hire a foreign worker living abroad, subsequent authorisation from the Italian administrative authorities,[24] the issue of a working visa from the Italian consular authority in the foreigner's native country and finally the stipulations of the residence contract which entitle the foreigner to legally stay in Italy followed by the issue of a residence permit for work reasons.

A similar procedure is in place for seasonal jobs. But here employers' associations may apply for these for their members and the issuing procedure is simpler and faster (mainly due to the fact that these requests have to be examined prior to those of ordinary employees, considering the immediate need for seasonal workers).

The third admission procedure is called 'entrance in particular cases'. It is designed for specific categories of workers and employees and it takes place out of quota,[25] if there is a need for foreigners included in one of the categories described in article 27, legislative decree no. 286/1998. These are highly skilled professionals or people working in niche sectors. Through legislation enacted on 30 July 2002, no. 189, the category of professional nurses has been included (article 27, c.1, lett. r-*bis*).[26]

---

22. A quota is the maximum number of people who can enter in a country within a defined period. The enactment of a flow decree is essential for employers wishing to hire foreigners. An employer cannot apply to hire a foreigner when s/he wants but has to wait until the government enacts the flow decree.

23. The sponsor system allowed a person or a private or public entity to sponsor migrants to come to Italy as long as they could guarantee housing, health assistance and a source of livelihood for one year. Foreigners can enter and look for a job. It has now been replaced by so called 'training for migration certificates' (art. 23 d.lgs. no. 286/1998). These give priority to foreigners who follow specialised vocational training courses in their native countries, which are aimed at placing them on the job market in Italy, or at them getting a job in their native countries after a training period in Italy.

24. The Italian authorities only give authorization, within the limit of the available quota, under specific conditions. First there must be insufficient personnel available (from Italy or the rest of the EU). Then the authorities have to check the effective economic capability of the employer to hire workers. Lastly employer and worker must not have a police record or a previous prohibition to enter in the Schengen area, etc... (i.e. so called *motivi ostativi all'ingresso*).

25. Foreigners entering for training in Italy are included in this admission procedure (*ex* article 27 c.1, lett. f) d.lgs. no. 286/1998) together with sportsmen who benefit from a special quota defined in a specific flow decree.

26. This new procedure is interesting because for a category of workers that Italy needs, the legislators have decided to change admission procedures. It seems to suggest that when it is essential that things work relying on the ordinary admission channel using *chiamata nominativa* is not a good way.

Apart from using these procedures involving entry from abroad, a legal permit to stay in Italy can be acquired through legalisation. These regularisation programmes have been enacted to amend the position of people employed illegally who cannot rectify their working position and make contributions to social security systems due to their status as undocumented migrants.[27]

Most European countries have instituted legalisation programmes (Pastore, 2004: 25-35) but Italy is remarkable due to the distinctive features of 'its amnesties': these are massive and recurrent,[28] with a large number of accepted applications and a high degree of administrative discretion in the implementation procedures. Looking at the data for the legalisation programmes in the 1990's, 42% (52% if we look only at the countries with high migratory pressure) of foreigners legally in Italy at the end of 1999 benefited from an amnesty (Carfagna, 2002: 85). Including estimates based on the most recent regularisation programme (Cesareo, 2004: 16-19; Blangiardo, 2004: 45-46), this amounts to two thirds of all the people legally present in Italy.

The countries of origin of the legalised immigrants are also in line with migratory flows. Empirical research demonstrates that most of the legalised immigrants have managed, at least in the short term, to retain their residence permit: data regarding amnesties in the 1990s show that a high proportion of people keep their legal status after the regularisation programme (Carfagna, 2002: 78-87; Blangiardo, 2004). The data available for the 2002 legalisation come to similar conclusions (Cesareo 2006). This means that legalisation is the gateway to becoming legal in Italy. It has been used as a 'safety valve' in immigration legal policy making,[29] which has been characterised – since the so called Martelli law (law no.39/1990) and up to the Bossi-Fini law (law no. 189/2002) – by a progressive tightening of entry rules and restrictions on the conditions for undocumented migrants. It has indeed been stated that the amnesty is the price for closing the borders to immigration for work reasons (Ambrosini, 2004: 11).

Hence, legalisation programmes have become an *'equivalente funzionale di una politica attiva degli ingressi'* (i.e. equivalent to an active entry policy) (Barbagli et al., 2004: 15), a mechanism to bring the legal position of migrants closer to their working and social conditions when the distance between them becomes critical.

---

27. According to Italian immigration law, the words 'undocumented migrants' identify two different categories of migrants. One category, named 'irregular migrant', refers to those migrants who enter legally and then overstay, while another named 'illegal migrants' refers to those who enter illegally. I normally use the term 'undocumented migrants' if I do not need to be specific, given that there is no difference in the situation they face, according to those interviewed for this research. The terms 'irregular' and 'illegal' will be used when there is a need to differentiate this difference in Italian law.

28. The first programmes were enacted at the beginning of the 1980s. They have been followed by more significant and bigger amnesties in 1986, 1990, 1995, 1998 and 2002.

29. For more information about the history and changes in immigration policies see Einaudi (2007) and the journal *Diritto, Immigrazione e Cittadinanza*, published since 1998 and specifically dedicated to immigration legal matters.

In other words, comparison between legalised migrants and those who have entered using the 'normal' admission channels reveals one important factor about Italian immigration policy: legally resident foreigners are mostly former illegal or irregular migrants (see Table 1). There is no clear boundary between documented and undocumented foreigners; they are not distinct populations but, as has been stated, these legal statuses are but moments in the life of migrants (Calavita, 2005: 37-47). Legal positions change over time. People remain the same.

Alongside the positive role of legalisation as a surrogate for an absent active entry policy, each legalisation programme brings about new exclusion effects. In fact for each amnesty there are foreigners excluded because they are not equipped with the correct documents, or who fall into one of the exclusion rules provided by the law (e.g. those who were convicted of a crime) (Pastore, 1995). The closely related so called 'pump effect' is also worth considering; indeed the estimates of the numbers of undocumented migrants present in the country show that any legalisation programme attracts new clandestine immigrants (Blangiardo and Tanturri, 2006), a great number of whom are not able to take advantage of the new legalisation.

Therefore, legalisation programmes make the old migrants legal but in the meantime create new undocumented immigrants. This is especially true in a country like Italy where amnesties have the points mentioned above: a wide application, frequent recurrence, huge administrative discretion. It is interesting to note that as well as calling into doubt the validity of certain legalisation programmes the very nature of an amnesty can be questioned. It is a mechanism which, as already emphasised, calls into question the validity of any precedent rules.

All of the above emphasises how rules in Italy are variable, can be changed, even denied by the legislators themselves. Every legalisation programme has been emphatically proclaimed to be 'the last in the history of the Italian Republic'. But each of them has been followed by another one, real or disguised as a flow decree. The message this sends to foreigners is clear: in Italy 'everything can happen', nothing is true or false. The idea that 'it is always worth giving it a try' is amplified and is part of the normative socialisation of foreigners (Ruggiero, 2008).

Table 1   Comparison between the numbers of people entering through a flow decree and the legalisation programme

	1996	1997	1998	1999	2000	2001	2002	2003	2004	2005	2006 (Belusconi-Maroni)	2006 bis (Prodi-Ferrero)	Total	% of all migrants entering Italy
Foreigners legalised by amnesty*	246,000		217,000				650,000						1,113,000	45.9
Foreigners entering through flow decree	23,000	20,000	58,000	58,000	63,000	83,000	79,500	79,500	79,500	79,500	170,000	520,000	1,313,000	54.1
'Privileged quota'	0	0	6,000	6,000	18,000	15,000	14,000	3,800	20,400	20,800	37,500		141,500	5.8
% privileged quota on flow decree			10.3	10.3	28.6	18.1	17.6	4.8	25.7	26.2	22.1			
Seasonal workers						33,000	56,000	68,500	50,000	49,500	50,000		307,000	12.7
% seasonal workers on flow decree						39.8	70.4	86.2	62.9	62.3	29.4			
Non seasonal workers						50,000		11,000			120,000	520,000	701,000	28.9

* The data refer to accepted applications (in 1996 95%, of the application made, in 1998 86.8%, in 2002 92.3%).
Source: data processing of flow decree and Ministero dell'Interno (2007).

If the perception of widespread illegality in Italy has been strengthened by the use of the amnesties, we need to add that it is a common opinion that the legalisation programme is a moment of frantic business. The sale of work contracts and other documents is affirmed by nearly all the people interviewed and it is a constant for all the regularisation programmes (Ciafaloni, 2004).The fact that money changes hands is also confirmed by ethnographic research carried out during the 2002 legalisation programme (Semi, 2004) and by empirical research into renewal of the residence permits given during the 2002 amnesty[30] (Cesareo, 2006; Codini, 2006).

AT THE CORE OF THE ENTRY PROCEDURE: LOGICAL ABSURDITY AND BUREAUCRATIC IMPRACTICABILITY

As clarified in the previous section, the two pillars of migrants' status are entry through the back door (Sciortino, 2005: 291), i.e. amnesty, and the impossibility of separating documented and undocumented migrants into two distinct populations. To continue, let us now delve into the operation of entry procedures from abroad.

In the main entry mechanism (so called *chiamata nominativa*), an individual is specifically named in relation to a particular job; however, the peculiar thing is that the employer does not know the employee from a professional point of view. S/he should be abroad and enter Italy following a call from an employer. In order to hire this *unknown* worker, the employer must follow onerous proceedings recently labelled as 'fragmented, without any clear identification of the people responsible to the users (employer and migrants) and in general of the tasks and responsibilities of the whole procedure'[31] (Corte dei Conti, 2008). Moreover, the average length of the procedure is between 350 and 400 days (with this result only reached after good co-ordination between different administrative agencies). This situation has been defined by the State's Auditors Department as 'pathological'. The procedure has proved to be not only complex and muddled, due to the endless checks needed to issue the administrative authorisation and the continu-

---

30. The data from the research show that at the first renewal 40% of legalized people declared they had renewed their residence permit with another employer and 3% with a fictitious employer. This result is interesting because after one year 3% of foreigners still declared renewal using a false employer and, as commented by the researcher, this percentage is certainly below the real figure. Moreover, it is also not difficult to imagine that within the 40% of renewals with another employer there are people who concluded the amnesty with a fictitious employer or under very bad conditions (e.g. the migrant is forced to pay social security contributions or has had a reduction in salary due to the costs of regularization for the employer) and to improve his/her condition have, during the following year, tried to find a real or a better employer.

31. In Italian the original text is as follows: 'frammentato e tale da non permettere di individuare i titolari, sia di forme concrete di responsabilità nei confronti dell'utenza (costituita dai datori di lavoro e dagli immigrati), sia dei compiti (e delle conseguenti responsabilità) di coordinamento delle operazioni complessive'.

ous exchange of documents between administrative entities, but also totally dys-functional.

In 2006 queues in front of post offices even started some days before the enact-ment of the admission quota decree: the availability of the forms and rumours about the date of enactment of the decree caused long hours of waiting outside post offices in order not to miss the chance. Applications were to be processed on a first-come/first-serve basis until the quota was filled. The number of applica-tions submitted after the first entry-quota decree was 540,058. As the number of applications was much higher than determined by the entry-quota decree (170,000), the new government issued an additional quota of 350,000 entries in October 2006 (when the application processing procedures were far from being complete). This was meant to cover the regularly submitted applications up to 21 July 2006, in accordance with the first entry-quota decree of the year. The Gov-ernment therefore realised not only that, after the first entry-quota decree, a great number of applications had been submitted, but also that the processing proce-dure was faulty[32] and slow, making it difficult to reject applications because they did not respect deadlines.

Similarly, the decision to use an electronic readable form system for the renewal procedure has created situations which border on a paradox: foreigners request the renewal of their residence permit, then they wait for it for 9-12 months, often for a period longer than the remaining validity of the residence permit. Conse-quently the rights of the foreigners are severely damaged. Indeed, even if the receipt stating the submission of the renewal application (in compliance with the law) allows foreigners all the rights that derive from possessing a valid residence permit (as also stated by the Ministry of the Interior in a memorandum issued on 5 August 2006 and in the following circular in December 2006), cases of failed hiring have been registered, together with loss of work, failed assistance from the health system and failed issuing of driving licences, all because of a lack of will-ingness to recognise the receipt as valid. This malfunction due to bad implemen-tation of the law increases the risk of not meeting the requirements for renewal (i.e. house and work) and moreover, paradoxically, allows those who do not have the right to obtain a renewal of their residence permit to take advantage of the faults in the system, as the validity of their residence permit is extended until the renewal applications are rejected.

After the experience of the 2006 flow decree, the Government established a new procedure, starting from the 2007 flow decree. This allows people to send appli-

---

32. On the first day on which applications could be submitted, in many Italian post offices the comput-erised system that ensured the correct marking of the date and time, broke down. For some points the system broke down for several minutes and started to work again after the intervention of qual-ified technicians. In some cases, post office employees handwrote the time on the applications using their own watches; in other cases operations were held up for a few minutes while waiting for the system to work again. Following the system breakdown, many people presented claims to the Italian Postal Authority that indeed admitted its mistakes.

cations over the internet. Even though some problems were encountered when trying to apply for new requests (internet website overloaded, with subsequent delay in receiving requests, lack of confirmation to the sender about the registration, and so on), during the examination phase this system seemed to guarantee a faster processing of requests. No improvements were achieved for the renewal requests applied for using the mail system, which recorded a waiting time of 9 months in January 2008.

We therefore need to reconsider not only the concept of admission quotas (that can, at least, be criticised as being too low because of lack of capability at a ministerial level to forecast the need for workers) but also the operation of the entry mechanism that is based on the idea that one has to find a job from abroad and then migrate into Italy.

On the basis of observations made during the 2006 flow decree application procedure, I have noticed that those standing in the queue in front of the post office to apply for legal entry in Italy were indeed foreigners already living and working in Italy. In a piece of unintentional irony, some post offices pasted notices on their front door for amnesty application forms, confusing amnesty and flow decree. As recently noted: 'i decreti di programmazione flussi sono divenuti una sorta di equivalente funzionale delle operazioni di regolarizzazione di massa' (i.e. now, flow decrees have become a functional equivalent to the mass amnesties) (Zanfrini, 2007a: 103). This idea of immigration as 'acquisizione di braccia per lavori prestabiliti' (i.e. a way to acquire a workforce for pre-established work places) (Pepino, 1999: 19) is completely out of date and inadequate for the real functioning of the labour market, based upon existing relations between employers and workers and assessment of workers' skills and competences. This is particularly true in some of the major areas of employment for immigrants, such as domestic work and care of the elderly that require the establishment of a relationship of mutual trust between the employer and the worker, and immediate availability that is hard to obtain given the endless length of time it takes to process applications through the admission-quota decree.

This time-consuming procedure makes it impossible to use the admission-quota mechanism for any job that is linked to time or production requirements based on immediate needs and which is not able to withstand indefinite bureaucratic time scales. Hence, the flow decree has been used to hire a foreigner already employed, but illegally. Only this way an employer can wait for an indefinite time to formally hire the migrant, who will be willing to keep working in the informal economy.[33]

It is not by chance that the State Auditors Department has underlined the fact that: 'The inconvenience created by the time needed to examine applications does not rule out the possibility that the complex procedure, highly demanding for the

---

33. See Ministero dell'Interno (2007: 81-92); Einaudi (2007: 265-381).

users, will increase, instead of containing the number of undocumented migrants.'[34] Remarking on the large number of uncollected visas in Italian embassies abroad, the State Auditors Department adds: 'The big difference in number between the granted visas and the requested ones forces us to think about, beyond any remarks on the efficient management of the procedure, the real correspondence of the procedure to hire foreign workers to reality in the country. Considering the high number of undocumented migrants already in Italy, the procedure has involved many who do not go back to their country of origin to collect the visa. Consequently, the lack of results for the procedure together with the useless expenditure of resources, leads us to think about the advantages and disadvantages of this procedure and seems to prove that the proposal to modify the rules is right.'[35] (Corte dei Conti, 2008).

What can we say? The emperor is naked and the fact is being pointed out, not by the jester, but by the Court Great Chamberlain.

THE DISADVANTAGED LABOUR POSITION OF FOREIGNERS AS A RESULT OF CUMBERSOME LEGAL PROCEDURES FACING AN 'IMPATIENT' ECONOMY

To sum up, it is undisputed that legalisation programmes have become the main immigration management tool for entry and staying in Italy and that the flow decree has turned into a ratification of the status of migrants already in Italy, i.e. an amnesty. Therefore legal migrants are often former undocumented migrants who benefit from legalisation or who use a flow decree amnesty in order to obtain the necessary papers. Another undisputed fact is that in general, legislative policies on immigration are in great disarray, or rather their practical application is not in accordance with what is written.

Looking at all developed countries, it has been argued that immigration policies are increasingly similar amongst developed countries (the so called convergence hypothesis), and tend to leave important gaps in their outcomes (the so called gap hypothesis) (Cornelius and Tsuda, 2004). These gaps are caused by the unintended consequences of policies or by their inadequate implementation or

---

34. In Italian the original text is as follows: 'Il disagio prodotto dalla durata dell'esame delle istanze concorre a non escludere che la complessità del procedimento, rivelatosi alquanto faticoso per l'utenza, possa accrescere, anziché reprimere, il fenomeno della clandestinità.'

35. In Italian the original text is as follows: 'il forte divario che si rileva tra visti rilasciati e permessi richiesti, induce a riflettere, al di là di ogni valutazione sull'efficiente gestione del procedimento, sull'effettività della rispondenza dell'impianto normativo della legge 189/2002, per quel che attiene alle modalità di acquisizione di lavoro straniero regolare, alla realtà del Paese. La considerevole presenza irregolare sul territorio, infatti, ha certamente comportato l'espletamento del procedimento anche in favore di soggetti già soggiornanti nella clandestinità, con la conseguenza che questi non si sono recati nel Paese di provenienza per il ritiro del visto. La vanificazione del risultato del procedimento, unitamente all'inutile dispendio di risorse per perseguirlo, induce a riflettere sull'opportunità di perseverare nella direzione propria della normativa in argomento e sembra dare ragione delle iniziative di rivisitazione delle disposizioni ancora vigenti in materia.'

enforcement. Italy is a case in point. Due to the features of the Italian socio-political system and its way of creating legislation, the Italian legislation in most socially and politically sensitive fields (e.g. penitentiary sector; mental illness; drug use; prostitution) is full of examples of laws which bring with them unintended consequences and inadequate implementation. Upon examination of Italian immigration law there are three main reasons for these gaps.

First of all, the obstacle race in relation to entry and becoming and remaining a legal resident, is rewarded by one of the 'largest underground economies in the developed countries' (Calavita, 2004: 353), which gives thousands of opportunities to find jobs, albeit on the black market. The underground economy, present before the arrival of foreign workers, is therefore both strongly attractive to unauthorised immigrants and obstructive to the stabilisation of immigrants who have been legalised through amnesties, due to the difficulties in maintaining a job under legal conditions (Reyneri, 2004a; 2004b).

Secondly, immigration law is the product of the difficult balance which exists between the interests of different lobbies, political parties and public opinion. Its aim was to serve the purposes of the different individuals who make up the complex Italian socio-political framework. By trying to satisfy everybody, it does not give pragmatic and fitting answers to the real problems.

Lastly, the endless legal and procedural changes would require an efficient bureaucracy to be well implemented. This is nearly impossible in a country where 'bureaucratism', deficits in implementation and territorial differences are chronic vices in administrative agencies and where in most cases, we are left with the impression that there is a lack of political will to enforce laws and regulations (Triandafyllidou, 2003).

The system does not work. It cannot be said that the executive and parliament wishes to directly obstruct foreigners in gaining legal status, but it is evident that the difficult situation is due to some hidden (both intended and unintended) objectives of the law. Moreover it cannot be ignored that these dysfunctional policies can in fact force foreigners into an economic position in the underground economy (Reyneri, 2001; 2004a; 2004b). The labour market needs migrants and in any developed country, foreign workers 'enjoy a special position' in the so called secondary sector of the labour market (Piore, 1979), taking dirty, dangerous and demanding jobs (Abella et al., 1995: 9) which the post-Fordist economy needs in order to survive and which are refused by native workers (Castels, 2002; Sassen, 2006: 151-175). Italy is a country where this is especially true. The Italian economy has always been characterised by certain traditional elements (small businesses, artisans, specialised agriculture, small shops, i.e. so called pre-Fordist jobs), even during the phase of intense industrial development, which lasted until the middle of the 1970s. Moreover, the underground economy is well developed, as is the presence of a certain amount of unemployment and at the same time an unsatisfied demand for labour. Today, the Italian post-Fordist economy model is strongly characterised by a mix of pre- and post-Fordist elements, embedded in the global economy but with a huge underground sector (tolerated or at least not adequately opposed by the state) and a new revival of pre-Fordist labour relations (Calavita, 2005:72-74), i.e. employer-employee relationships where traits such as reliability, respect for the employee and obedience are significant, often more important than competencies.

In this framework, foreign workers find jobs in small and medium-sized firms, which require low qualifications, in labour-intensive agricultural sectors and in the low level urban tertiary economy. The Italian economic system has a significant degree of light industry, which is very much in competition with newly developed countries and often includes difficult and unhealthy working conditions. It is now common knowledge that immigrants are concentrated in work where the conditions are harder, requiring greater physical effort, strength and willingness to work overtime and multiple shifts, with greater danger and greater risk of accidents. Immigrants in industries often have a regular job and companies save money by paying immigrants the contractual minimum and paying overtime in cash.

In addition, construction is an emerging sector for immigrant labour. The increasing competition and the subsequent need to reduce prices in order to work, have created fertile ground for the spread of an immigrant workforce. Moreover, a grey market of subcontracting co-operatives, a new development of the traditional 'hands' market, often due to recruitment carried out by a migrant middleman, do the rest.

The situation in the labour intensive agricultural sector is the worst of all. Migrants are a structural component of Italian Mediterranean agriculture and they guarantee the survival of the most obsolete parts of the sector. Many are hired by the day, under the old-fashioned 'day labour market' system; people are hired by middlemen, mostly migrants, who take them to their workplace and in turn hire them out to the owners. They are paid piece rates (per box of vegetables or fruit picked). Foreigners also work in greenhouses and on livestock farms.

Many migrants have abandoned agriculture in favour of the low urban tertiary sector, which cannot be transferred to lower labour cost countries. It is a sector that demands workers for low maintenance jobs (i.e. garage repair workers, cleaning industries, doorkeepers), low jobs in the catering sector (i.e. dishwashers, waiters, cooks) and other badly paid jobs – which are still highly necessary to the daily life of a city (e.g. porters, caretakers, messengers, market workers, butchers' and bakers' assistants, service station attendants).

To these economic activities, the tourism sector and jobs with families must be included. The first of these employs mostly women who work in catering and in the hotel trade. Jobs inside the family, such as carers for the elderly, child care assistants and maids, are the first option for foreign women, especially in a big city. It is a growing sector due to the lack of support by the welfare system (Esping-Andersen, 1995) and the new economic role of women coupled with a lack of redistribution of domestic tasks inside the family. This need for more personnel is mainly a need for weak, precarious, temporary labour with few or no rights. This kind of job is the only attraction of an economy, which requires a poorly qualified workforce, where the welfare state is in crisis and where underground economic activities and casual jobs are widespread, bordering on the endemic.

There are three main characteristics of the Italian labour market that make this placement of foreigners in the labour market possible and in a certain sense, forced. The first is the process of labour market segmentation as result of a combination of factors that characterise the Italian economic and social system. I refer mainly to the relative lack of innovation in some production sectors, the continuance of dirty and low qualified jobs inside highly developed economic sectors, the increasing educational level of young Italians, and the crisis in the welfare state (Castels and Miller, 2003). Segmentation produces niche sectors from which it is nearly impossible to move; natives and foreigners are employed in different environments.

The second is widespread illegality. Labour market segmentation and widespread illegality are two sides of the same coin. The underground economy has a strong presence in the economic system. It was present before the arrival of foreign workers and is both strongly attractive to unauthorised immigrants and obstructive to the stabilisation of immigrants who have been legalised through amnesties (Reyneri, 2004a; 2004b).

Finally, as in all post-modern economies, supply and demand for manpower are mostly met via personal acquaintance, by introductions made by a reliable source (so called weak ties, see Granovetter, 1973; 1983).

These features of the Italian labour market, combined with the current immigration regulations, create a perverse situation. The economic system requires workers, but the law does not give many opportunities to enter Italy legally. At the same time, the Italian economic system, with its high level of reliance on the underground economy, attracts undocumented immigrants who know they can work in some way, while waiting for an improvement in their status (passing from illegal to legal) (Reyneri, 2001). Therefore, foreign undocumented workers are the main actors in the sectors where black market jobs dominate and 'immigrants, while they certainly do not bring the underground economy into existence, contribute to its reproduction because they are particularly disposed towards accepting, whether *through constraint or otherwise, unrecorded remuneration*' (Reyneri, 2004a).

ADAPTING TO THE LEGAL AND ECONOMIC FRAMEWORK, STEERING A NECESSARY COURSE BETWEEN COLLUSION AND OPPORTUNITY

Given the economic and legal framework examined above, what are migrants' reactions? If they define the achievement of legal status as their aim, migrants, acting as Mertonian innovators, use whatever available means there are in order not to be defeated by a situation, which tends to marginalise them and leave them as illegal. The research carried out has shown how foreigners chase legality. They want to be legal but they cannot achieve their aim by legal means. These people are united in their search for resources and the use of social ties to obtain them.

Not all migrants have the same experience: some find positions in some sectors and not in others, some of them develop success or at least survival strategies, and others do not. Individual resources (such as cultural background and ability to adapt to certain environments and contexts) combine with resources drawn from their social context. Personal histories are different but the social capital activated is considerable in terms of quantity and quality. What are these resources and how can migrants reach out to them? From the collected life histories, four typologies of resources can be identified, all giving the possibility of changing a foreigner's life.

FRIENDS

Living abroad also means starting friendly relations with local people and compatriots. It is common knowledge that friendship networks are one of the main ways of socialisation. Having an illegal status is so widespread and such a common life experience (Calavita, 1998; 2005; Schuster, 2005) that an undocumented migrant does not live 'out of the world'. People meet each other in public places, in the street, through common friends (both foreign and native). All these relationships play a role in the solution of 'status problems' and help migrants to discover their own resources. An example can be found in this story about a Moroccan peddler employed as a maid by an Italian family:

> *'I saw A. every day in the city centre. He stopped me and we spoke a little bit (...) I always thought he was 'a peddler of great talent': he knew how to stop people, how to speak with them; he knew also when it was better only to speak and not try to sell things. After some time we had a sort of friendship (...) One day he explained to me his illegal status and his need for a residence permit. I told him that if it was possible I would like to help him. I followed the procedure to legalise him as a maid. I just thought it was a good idea. He is a nice guy. Why not help him?' (Teacher, Piedmont)*

Another person from the Cameroon graduated in medicine and, stuck between the right to renew his study permit until the qualifying examination and the request by the Medical Association for a work permit in order to be enrolled in the Association immediately after the exam, is being hired as a maid by a friend of his girlfriend:

> 'Questura renews the study permit so one can to take the qualifying exam but the Medical Association requires a work permit to enrol someone in the Association (…) It's a little bit strange, isn't it? As a maid I could but as a student of medicine I couldn't enrol.' (Doctor, Cameroonian)

Moreover people can get married, one revealing:

> 'We got married, we had a baby. Then, he disappeared (…) Now, every day I think he married me only to take advantage: to get his residence permit and getting away from the mess.' (University student, Campania)

Or without deception or bad faith:

> 'My brother married an Italian girl. Their marriage is not a real one. They have known each other since 2000. When my brother got in trouble with the residence permit, she helped him. And in this way she is helping also me.' (Worker in the underground economy, Moroccan)

Finally, friends can act as a launch pad for upward social climbing. This can happen when work or personal networks initiate acquaintances with influential people:

> 'Being always sure to have the right lifejacket in any situation is strictly linked to my origin. I think that Italy is a Mediterranean country where personal ties are worth more than rules. I don't think I have broken rules. I try to explain it. I have always thought that Italy as an immigration country can accept everything except illegal activities, crimes. It was my hypothesis at the beginning and I follow the rule. (…) I have always been inattentive to bureaucratic papers and the deadlines. Every time a delay of months in asking for the renewal of the residence permit. But every time I put things in order by asking someone to make the right telephone call. I think that your country works in this way (…) I haven't met some milieu for this reason, but meeting a certain kind of people helps me have an advantage. I'm not the only one. The "exceptions" are many. There is a compatriot of mine who applied for citizenship and obtained it in two months. I know with whom he spoke and which political "procedure" he followed.' (Employer, Lebanese)

Friends are at least a safe shelter, but they can be an opportunity, a card played that will improve their own life. And in general they do not ask for anything in return.

SOLIDARITY NETWORKS

Italy is a country with a high number of non-profit organisations, both religious and lay.[36] In immigration matters solidarity networks support and sometimes replace the state in the reception of foreigners, in management of residence permits and in the search for work. In this way a foreigner can find information that will take advantage of any opportunity given by the law:

> 'After 5 years, I could not renew the residence permit. Going back to Argentina? Not easy with my wife who works here and children at school. Luckily my wife at church got to know I could change the residence permit because we are married and she works. So we did it.' (Engineer, Argentine)

These networks often act as a mediator between demand and supply for manpower, influencing employers in order to overcome discriminatory attitudes that sometimes affect the reputation of foreign workers. Foreigners can therefore approach work contacts that they could not have otherwise.

> 'I found the job in their family through the nuns. They needed help and Sister X introduced me to them, suggesting that I could be the right person for that job.' (Carer, Ukrainian)

The presence of networks is not always totally positive. Sometimes it forces foreigners into a labour niche rendering their situation powerless. However it will save them from the risk of drowning. They fill the holes in the public resources for assistance to foreigners which are lacking and they take advantage of their privileged position. The state cannot do without them and they know perfectly well they can trick the state within certain limits. Solidarity networks often move along a borderline between legal and illegal, in a grey zone where illegality seems to be harmless and socially accepted.

> 'Is it illegal to help a man working illegally to gain a residence permit through a fictitious employer? I try to solve concrete problems (...) Should I stare at the ceiling or denounce the employer with the only result that the foreigner risks expulsion? Any chance to fix things is an opportunity and it is better to grab it.' (Priest, Piedmont)

> 'What should be taken into greater consideration is that a system built on a certain degree of exploitation of the people cannot expect that foreigners follow rules. How can you consider not rightful any means to help foreigners to be emancipated?' (Immigration policy expert, Piedmont)

ETHNIC NETWORKS AND FAMILY CLAN

Ethnic and family networks vary according to many dimensions: size, cohesion, concentration (spatial and employment) and composition.[37] They are not all equally efficient. Integrated networks, not too large and formed by people with

---

36. For a description of all the different typologies of solidarity networks, see Ambrosini (2005).
37. For more about the features and capability of ethnic networks in Italy, see Ambrosini (2005); Zanfrini (2007b).

good management abilities and levels of education, offer a real possibility of integration and upward social climbing:

> 'My friend's family is now in the south of China. They do business with Chinese. They tell me to go. I can even find friends there.' (Boy, Egyptian)

Other networks, like the solidarity one, can bring downward integration (it is what normally happens to a group with strong cohesion and concentration in employment):

> 'I found a job very quickly. My compatriots helped me and I started working in a house of a well-off family. Most of my compatriots worked in the domestic sector. Now I manage a Japanese restaurant with my uncle. It wasn't easy. Coincidence: an uncle arrived in Italy and the husband of the family where I used to work who helped me.' (Restaurant owner, Philippines)

In any case, they can advise, protect and help locate the necessary documents to be legalised.

CRIMINAL NETWORKS

Criminal networks are apparently an efficient way to achieve legal status, but also very risky and costly. Normally the costs and risks become clear at a later date. They sell false employment contracts, marriage certificates and other papers useful for legalisation. If the networks have sufficient finance and connections they can directly provide false visas and residence permits, they often succeed. The foreigner has his/her residence permit but, in almost all the cases, has to pay back a debt:

> 'I found an employer who hired me. I gave him 1,500 euro. Each month I pay social security contributions on my own. Now I have found a job in an ice cream powder factory. They hire me. Legally. Nothing to pay. I resigned the previous job, the one which gave me the residence permit. Everything should work.' (Worker, Moroccan).

> 'It works in this way. A woman working in the night club persuades a customer to hire her as maid or caregiver. So, she gains the residence permit and if she is quite smart she can reach a condition of autonomy. Other situations are much more serious. The owner of the night club can find fictitious employers. Normally, these men hire the girls as maids. So the owner increases his power; the girls are linked to him also for the residence permit.' (Law enforcement officer, Lombardy)

In other cases expulsion or prison are the only result:

> 'He guaranteed to me that it was a true residence permit; there were some Italian policemen in Milan who gave residence permits after payment. They could do that when the

colleagues have holiday. They were alone in the office and they could insert in the information system what they want. Well I said OK (...) If you looked at the paper it seemed a real one (...) Using that permit I enrolled on the training to became a social sanitary worker. I started to work (...) But the day of the exam two policemen came to catch me at home.' (Nurse, Tunisian)

'Così FAN TUTTI': IMMIGRANTS MIRROR ILLEGAL ITALIAN SOCIETY.

All the stories set out above are histories of everyday illegality. Foreigners' lives are distanced from reality. Most of them have experienced a period as an undocumented migrant or at least a period in which their formal condition did not correspond with their papers. The passage through illegality to gain legal status is a constant in a foreigners' life. Most fraud and forgery seems harmless. At first sight, nobody gets hurt. Legality is not however seen as a launching pad for the affirmation of one's rights. 'The residence permit is used to go to the Questura' is a good summary of the position, made by an interviewed law enforcement officer. The justification presented for their own behaviour is strong, even when they are criminals. Becoming a legal migrant through a flow decree even if s/he already lives in Italy is normal. If the job behind the admission or the amnesty application is true or false it is of minor importance. The goal is 'to fix the paper'. After all, as an undocumented Moroccan worker told me: 'Also the Ministry said that we were here because there is no other way to enter Italy. We could not do otherwise'. Italy is seen as a place where a foreigner takes a gamble on him/herself and tries to make the most of any opportunity.

Can foreigners' behaviour say something about the Italian way of life? What kind of country is Italy? If it is true that immigration gives us the possibility to 'make obvious what is latent in the constitution and functioning of all social order, to unmask what is masked, to reveal what it is preferably ignored and left in a state of ignorance and societal naiveté. So, immigration enlarges, as would a fun house mirror, what is normally hidden in the social consciousness and left, as a secret, in the shadow of the unthinkable. Immigration represents the limits of the nation state; that limit demonstrates the essence of the nation state, which permits the comprehension of the fundamental truth of the nation state.'[38] (Sayad, 1996: 13), which image is reflected in this mirror? The image is that of a formally strict society where everything is 'arrangeable', if you know the right people: a society where the 'smartest' wins over the 'honest'. A society where illegality is wide-

---

38. In French the original text is as follows: 'L'immigration rendre patent ce qui est latent dans la constitution et le fonctionnement de tout ordre social, pour en démasquer ce qui est masqué, pour en révéler ce qu'on a intérêt à ignorer et à laisser à l'état d'ignorance ou d'innocence sociale, pour porter au grand jour et grossir – d'où l'effet du miroir grossissant – ce qui est habituellement enfoui dans l'inconscient social et voué de cette façon à rester dans l'ombre, à l'état de secret (l'ombre et le secret de l'impensé social), l'immigration constitue comme la limite de ce qu'est l'Etat national, comme un limite qui donne à voir ce qu'il est intrinsèquement, qui donne à comprendre ce qui est sa vérité fondamentale.'

spread because *così fan tutti* and where a sort of national excuse is ready for illegal behaviour, on condition that it is kept silent, in the shadow and formally respectful of the law.

If a foreigner can be considered integrated when s/he is able to understand in which country s/he lives, what its rules are, written and unwritten, the deduction (after listening to and reading migrants' histories) is that integration in Italy passes through illegality, informality and an 'equilibrium of transgression' (Melossi, 2003: 382). Most of the solutions can be found using the window and not the front door. Behaving like Italians means being able to take short cuts. Incidentally, is it not true that there is a 'great subtlety in the way we, Italians, distinguish in our acts what is allowed and what is not, what is right and wrong? It is a subtlety elaborated in centuries of practice of legal and moral Pharisaism, the more evident sign of the lack of a true law[39] (Melossi, 1999: 8).

For any rule, there exists an exception. Or, in some cases, a dispensation can be proposed. Legality is synonymous with being below deck. It is not a value. It is a result to reach, using any means. And the means used reveal another feature of Italian society: 'clan' solidarity. Foreigners become legal through the help of natives (friends or solidarity networks) or compatriots. The help given is essential and it summons up the idea that if s/he is recognised as a 'member', s/he has a chance to find a way to solve problems. When a foreigner stops being a foreigner but becomes the one who takes care of our grandparents, or with whom we work, something happens. Consequently, a foreigner is not even an illegal migrant, let alone a criminal. S/he is only a foreigner who deserves a second chance. And to give it to him/her is right, even incumbent on one. Italians help migrants because they perceive in *that specific cases* the injustice of the rules and they are used to solve problems *prater legem* if not *contra legem*.

Similarly foreigners help their compatriots with no qualms about violating rules. They justify their acts with the need to help their group in a hostile and also hypocritical context. Consequently, there is hardly ever a real claim for the respect of rights. The solution searched for is the most fruitful. No surprise then if foreigners consider violating the law as an easy path. The favourable definitions of these criminal behaviours, the techniques, the specific directions as to motives, rationalisations and attitudes are all learnt by interaction with Italians or people familiar with the Italian context. During their stay in Italy foreigners experience this kind of normative socialisation. It is not a deviant socialisation, it is absolutely consistent with the prevailing mode of proclaimed but not exercised legality.

It is a formal illegality, which does not imply the absence of a superior substantial legality.

---

39. In Italian the original text is as follows: 'Grande finezza con cui noi italiani distinguiamo nelle nostre pratiche il lecito dall'illecito, il giusto dall'ingiusto, finezza elaborata in secoli di abitudine al fariseismo giuridico e morale, il segno forse più evidente della mancanza di vero diritto.'

REFERENCES

Abella, M., Park, Y.B. & Bohning, R. (1995). 'Adjustments to labour shortages and foreign workers in the Republic of Korea'. *International migration papers*, 1. Geneva: ILO, at http://www.ilo.org/public/english/protection/migrant/download/imp/imp01.pdf, accessed December 9, 2008.

Ambrosini, M. (2004). 'Introduzione. Uscire dall'ombra: un processo da proseguire'. In M. Ambrosini & M. Salati (eds.), *Uscendo dall'ombra. Il processo di regolarizzazione degli immigrati e i suoi limiti*. Milano: Franco Angeli, pp. 11- 29.

Ambrosini, M. (2005). *Sociologia delle migrazioni*. Bologna: Il Mulino.

Ambrosini, M. & Salati, M. (eds.) (2004). *Uscendo dall'ombra. Il processo di regolarizzazione degli immigrati e i suoi limiti*. Milano: Franco Angeli.

Barbagli, M. (2008). *Immigrazione e sicurezza in Italia*. Bologna: Il Mulino.

Barbagli, M., Colombo, A. & Sciortino, G. (2004). 'Introduzione'. In *I sommersi e I sanati. Le regolarizzazioni degli immigrati in Italia*. Bologna: Il Mulino, pp. 7-18.

Blangiardo, G.C. (2004). 'La presenza straniera in Italia. Primo bilancio dopo la regolarizzazione del 2002'. In Fondazione ISMU, *Nono rapporto sulle migrazioni 2003*. Milano: Franco Angeli, pp. 41-53.

Blangiardo, G.C. & Tanturri, M.L. (2006). 'La presenza straniera in Italia'. In G.C. Blangiardo & P. Farina (eds.), *Il mezzogiorno dopo la grande regolarizzazione. Immagini e problematiche dell'immigrazione. Volume III*. Milano: Franco Angeli, pp. 25-51.

Calavita, K. (1998) 'Immigration, law and marginalization in a global economy: notes from Spain'. *Law and Society Review*, 32(3): 529-566.

Calavita, K. (2003). 'A "reserve army of delinquents"'. *Punishment and Society*, 5(4): 399-413.

Calavita, K. (2004). 'Italy: economic realities, political fictions and policy failures'. In W.A. Cornelius, J.F. Hollifield, P.L. Martin & T. Tsuda (eds.), *Controlling immigration. A global perspective*. Stanford: Stanford University Press, pp. 345-380.

Calavita, K. (2005). *Immigrants at the margins. Law, race and exclusion in Southern Europe*. New York: Cambridge University Press.

Carfagna, M. (2002). 'I sommersi e i sanati. Le regolarizzazioni degli immigrati in Italia'. In A. Colombo & G. Sciortino (eds.), *Stranieri in Italia. Assimilati ed esclusi*. Bologna: Il Mulino, pp. 53-87.

Castels, S. (2002). 'Migration and community formation under conditions of globalization'. *International Migration Review*, 36(4): 1143-1168.

Castels, S. & Miller, M.J. (2003). *The age of migration. International population movements in the modern world*. New York: Guilford.

Castels, S. (2004). 'The factors that make and unmake migration policies'. *International Migration Review*, 38(3): 852-884.

Cesareo, V. (2004). 'Migrazioni 2003: un quadro di insieme e un'agenda per il futuro'. In Fondazione ISMU, *Nono rapporto sulle migrazioni 2003*. Milano: Franco Angeli, pp. 7-38.

Cesareo, V. (2006). 'La ricerca: obiettivi e risultati'. In V. Cesareo & E. Codini (eds.), *Il mezzogiorno dopo la grande regolarizzazione. L'esperienza italiana nel contesto internazionale. Volume I*. Milano: Franco Angeli, pp.1-78.

Chambliss, W.J. & Seidman R.T. (1982). *Law, order and power*. Reading: Addison-Wesley

Ciafaloni, F. (2004). 'I meccanismi dell'emersione'. In M. Barbagli, A. Colombo & G. Sciortino (eds.), *I sommersi e I sanati. Le regolarizzazioni degli immigrati in Italia*. Bologna: Il Mulino, pp. 187-200.

Codini, E. (2006). 'Un confronto con le esperienze straniere'. In V. Cesareo & E. Codini (eds.), *Il mezzogiorno dopo la grande regolarizzazione. L'esperienza italiana nel contesto internazionale. Volume I*. Milano: Franco Angeli, pp. 79-109.

Cornelius, W.A. & Tsuda, T. (2004). *Controlling immigration: the limits of government intervention*. In W.A. Cornelius, J.F. Hollifield, P.L. Martin & T. Tsuda (eds.), *Controlling immigration. A global perspective*. Stanford: Stanford University Press, pp. 3-48.

Corte dei Conti (2008), *Programma controllo 2006 Lattività di gestione integrata dei flussi di immigrazione*, at http://www.corteconti.it/Ultimi-doc/Attivit--23/index.asp, accessed December 8, 2008.

Einaudi, L. (2007). *Le politiche dell'immigrazione in Italia dall'Unità a oggi*. Roma/Bari: Laterza.

Esping-Andersen, G. (1995). 'Il Welfare State senza il lavoro. L'ascesa del familismo nelle politiche sociali dell'Europa continentale'. *Stato e mercato*, 45: 347-380.

Granovetter, M.S. (1973). 'The strength of weak ties'. *American Journal of Sociology*, 78(6): 1360-1380.

Granovetter, M.S. (1983). 'The strength of weak ties: a network theory revisited'. *Sociological Theory*, 1(1): 201-233.

Melossi, D. (1999). 'Immigrazione e insicurezza: un'introduzione'. *Dei delitti e delle pene*, 6(3): 7-17.

Melossi, D. (2003). 'In a peaceful life. Migration and the crime of modernity in Europe/Italy'. *Punishment and Society*, 5(4): 371-397.

Merton, R.K. (1968). *Social theory and social structure*. New York: Free Press.

Ministero dell'Interno (2007). *Primo rapporto sugli immigrati in Italia*, at http://www.interno.it/mininterno/export/sites/default/it/assets/files/15/0673_Rapporto_immigrazione_BARBAGLI.pdf, accessed December 19. 2008.

Pastore, M. (1995). *Produzione normativa e costruzione sociale della devianza e criminalità tra gli immigrati*. Milano: Fondazione Cariplo I.S.M.U.

Pastore, F. (2004). 'Che fare di chi non dovrebbe essere qui? La gestione della presenza straniera irregolare in Europa, tra strategie nazionali e misure comuni'. In M. Barbagli, A. Colombo & G. Sciortino (eds.), *I sommersi e I sanati. Le regolarizzazioni degli immigrati in Italia*. Bologna: Il Mulino, pp. 19-45.

Pepino, L. (1999). 'Immigrazione, politica e diritto (Note a margine della legge no. 40/1998)'. *Diritto Immigrazione e cittadinanza*, 2(1): 11-27.

Piore, M.J. (1979). *Birds of passage: migrant labour and industrial societies*. New York: Cambridge University Press.

Reyneri, E. (2001). 'Migrants in irregular employment in the Mediterranean countries of the European Union'. *International migration papers*, 41. Geneva: ILO, at http://www.ilo.org/public/english/protection/migrant/download/imp/imp41.pdf, accessed December 20, 2008.

Reyneri, E. (2004a). 'Immigrants in a segmented and often undeclared labour market'. *Journal of Modern Italian Studies*, 9(1): 71- 93.

Reyneri, E. (2004b). 'Immigrazione ed economia sommersa nell'Europa meridionale'. *Studi Emigrazione*, 41(153): 91-113.

Ruggiero, V. (2008). 'Stranieri e illegalità nell'Italia criminogena'. *Diritto Immigrazione e cittadinanza*, 10(2): 13-30.

Santos, L. (1993). 'Elementos jurídicos de la integración de los extranjeros'. In G. Tapinos (ed.), *Inmigración e integración en Europa*, p. 111. Barcelona, Itinera Libros quoted in Calavita, K. (2003) 'A "reserve army of delinquents"', *Punishment and Society*, 5(4): 399-413.

Sassen, S. (2006). *Cities in a world economy*. Thousand Oaks: Pine Forge Press.

Sayad, A. (1996). 'L'immigration et la 'pensée d'Etat'. Réflexion sur la double peine?' In S. Palidda (ed.), *Délit d'immigration. La construction sociale de la déviance et de la criminalité parmi lés immigreiés en Europe*. Bruxelles: Communauté Européenne, pp.11-29.

Schuster, L. (2005). 'The continuing mobility of migrants in Italy: shifting between places and statuses'. *Journal of ethnic and migration studies*, 31(4): 757-774.

Sciortino, G. (2005). 'Le migrazioni irregolari. Struttura ed evoluzione nell'ultimo decennio'. In Fondazione ISMU, *Decimo rapporto sulle migrazioni 2004*. Milano: Franco Angeli, pp. 289-304.

Semi, G. (2004). 'L'ordinaria frenesia. Il processo di regolarizzazione visto dal "basso"'. In M. Barbagli, A. Colombo & G. Sciortino (eds.), *I sommersi e i sanati. Le regolarizzazioni degli immigrati in Italia*. Bologna: Il Mulino, pp. 167-185.

Sutherland, E. & Cressey, D. (1978). *Criminology*. Philadelphia: Lippincott.

Triandafyllidou, A. (2003). 'Immigration policy implementation in Italy: organisational culture, identity processes and labour market control'. *Journal of Ethnic and Migration Studies*, 29(2): 257-297.

Zanfrini, L. (2007a). 'Il lavoro'. In Fondazione ISMU, *Dodicesimo rapporto sulle migrazioni 2006*. Milano: Franco Angeli, pp. 103-128.

Zanfrini, L. (2007b). *Sociologia delle migrazioni*. Roma: Laterza.

The eligibility of work: some notes on immigrants, reputation and crime

Pietro Saitta[40]

INTRODUCTION TO THE FIELD: SICILY AND LE MARCHE

This paper discusses some of the findings of an ethnographic study I carried out in Sicily and Le Marche in the period 2002-2004.[41] In particular, I analyse the cases of Mazara del Vallo and Urbino, two areas characterised not only by different economies but by significantly different political and social fabrics. The former is situated in a relatively depressed area, and its economy is based on traditional activities and farming, a somewhat backward tertiary industry, and an underdeveloped tourist industry aimed above all at a local public; lastly, it is characterised by high levels of illegal work. Urbino, meanwhile, is distinguished by small and medium-sized enterprises, a medium-sized university which fuels the rented property market and by 'whistle-stop' tourism with a limited economic impact.

On the face of it, the two areas seem difficult to compare, but the reason they are put together in this comparative study is interest in observing the settlement models of two national groups: Moroccans and Tunisians, both foreign born, who are widely present in the areas and play a 'structural'[42] role for local economies. In particular, I compared the trajectories of these groups, and tried to understand if it is true, as suggested by certain commonly held beliefs and generalisations, that 'typical' cultural features influence settlement models[43] and if work really helps immigrants integrate in Italian society.[44]

---

40. This paper is derived from Saitta, P. (forthcoming), 'Il lavoro integra? Alcune note su immigrati, reputazione e crimine', *Studi sulla Questione Criminale*, 3.
41. The full results of the study are presented in Saitta (2007).
42. 'Structure' is a key-concept in economics and it has stimulated many nuanced analyses. With regard to the European labour market and the (structural) role played in it by immigrants, a simple but eloquent definition is provided by Hollifield (1992: 91), who defines foreign workers as '[A] necessary pool of surplus labor that could be more easily hired and fired in times of crisis'.
43. When I was planning this research, in the early part of the decade, it was not rare to hear public speeches emphasising the 'cultural' (or 'natural', no less) propensity of certain groups for certain activities. Typically, on the basis of these generalisations, the Chinese were shopkeepers; Filipinos, domestic staff; Albanians and Romanians, criminals. The habit of attributing 'cultural traits' or 'natural traits' to national individuals and groups (or to 'races') is deep-rooted, and is a tendency found in every historical period characterised by the movement of people. The fact that it was necessary to dismantle certain associations was something that had already appeared evident to Boas (1911) at the beginning of the last century. The historical material on these issues is vast. By way of example, I would merely like to mention here W.F. Whyte's introduction to *Street Corner Society* (1983) and his description of the anti-Italian climate in Boston in the 1930s and 40s.

In order to deal with the second point, classic theories such as those of Lewin (1951) on 'punishing socialisation' will be referred to. According to this theory, individuals who share risks and inferior social positions tend to develop bonds with each other which may help them deal with the difficulties encountered in a hostile environment. Even though Lewin's theory dates back to an almost extinct age – that of the Fordian factory, class solidarity, and mobilisation of the masses – it seemed worth dusting it off for various reasons. It in fact referred not so much to political and class aspects in the strict sense as to forms of 'natural' solidarity: those forms of closeness we can find inside a wide range of 'totalising' environments, such as boarding schools, clinics and, without doubt, factories. Not even the age of 'opulence' had affected these types of relations, as Goldthorpe et al. (1969) had observed. I thus thought it plausible that our own era, characterised by reduced guarantees, the increasingly precarious nature of work and growing insecurity,[45] could also be studied using Lewin's theory, since it referred to psychological and almost innate dynamics rather than to the 'spirit of the times'. The functionality of certain relations had more to do with nature than culture, so to speak. Hence, if forms of solidarity between national groups (Italians and foreigners) were found, this would demonstrate that the supporters of the 'integrationist theory of work' were right. Consequently, equipped with this tool, I went into the field to study the relations between North African and Italian workers. I first examined the situation in farming, fishing and other sectors of 'legal but illegally run' work in Sicily, and subsequently went to Urbino to observe social dynamics in an industrialised region where the foreign workers are mainly resident and in work, and where the presence of immigrants is unanimously acknowledged as 'structural' (Ambrosini, 1999).[46]

To summarise briefly, the conclusion reached whilst observing widely different working environments was that work has ceased to be a catalyst for integration. As we know, the contemporary ethic is no longer merely work-oriented, and does not attribute work with a central role in identity-creation processes. As Habermas (1972; 1986) has said, contemporary identity is generally fragmented, and this

---

44. The rhetoric of common sense, and social action by the third sector or local bodies, as well as the policies of immigration control implemented in Italy, emphasise the role of work in establishing the integration of foreigners and in limiting the phenomenon of crime (see, for example, the recent 'anti-Romanian' decree issued in the wake of the murder of Giovanna Reggiani in Rome; but this is a common feature of legislation in the field from the 1980s onwards). In brief, work would allow survival, generate processes of socialisation and encourage reciprocal acknowledgement (especially by Italians towards foreigners, who would finally be acknowledged as honest and 'equal' subjects).

45. There are many specific studies on the sense of insecurity and the consequences of these perceptions in Italy (see, for example, the periodical *Mappe* ('maps') by the sociologist Diamanti in the newspaper *La Repubblica*), but it is worth mentioning two general, and in their own way classic studies: those by Sennett (1998) and Beck (2000).

46. To avoid any risk of misunderstanding, it should be pointed out that the presence of employees is as structural in the north as it is in the south. However, the majority of studies in the field of economic and labour sociology dealing with immigration seem to have focused on the north. For this reason, I feel that there are unanimous views as far as regards central and northern Italy, but some uncertainty as far as regards the south.

means that a vast number of Italians who share working spaces and time with foreigners do not feel any affinity with these new members of the working class ('ethnic' workers). In general, Italians are by now unable to experience a sense of community based on the traditional values of the class, and do not see foreigners as 'comrades'. In other words, on the whole, the locals seem unable to go beyond the original images of otherness, i.e. those attributed to foreigners when the immigration phenomenon first began. The identities attributed to people – the images of the *other* – are usually dynamic, but as far as immigrants are involved, we witness a sort of jamming of those cognitive mechanisms which leads individuals and peoples to gradually transform their point of view with regard to the information at their disposal.

We thus find that work does not help determine a sense of belonging to the community for foreigners either. To be more precise, work fosters in them the conviction that they are 'subjects with rights', that they are earning credit within the overall system in which they live and work, and to which they actively contribute; but on the other hand, they do not often develop feelings of affection towards Italians. Basically, they do not feel part of the group. When we add to this perception objective conditions of exploitation and the impossibility of seeing work as a vehicle of promotion, then we have the basic conditions for involvement in criminal activities or in 'mixed' careers, which alternate or combine legal and illegal activities.

Work, crime

Originally the research dealt mainly with themes related to the labour market, to cultural and ethnic dynamics and to various methodological issues involved in ethnographic practice, but it is also correlated with a new direction in Italian research into immigration and criminality. In recent papers by Melossi (2007), Calavita (2007) and Sbraccia (2007) on the 'processes of criminalisation', the authors deal with the 'eligibility' of work. In particular, they ask whether working is 'more eligible' than committing crimes. To put it differently, is it true that through employment in legal activities, immigrants boost their status and self-esteem? Through extending my original field of research, this issue can be tackled, starting by looking at people employed in greenhouses, on fishing boats or in dangerous industries and through analysing the various structural and environmental elements which, like those examined by Sbraccia,[47] may lead many immigrants to abandon legal activities or commit crime episodically.

---

47. It is not easy to faithfully present here Sbraccia's complicated analysis. His investigation deals with 'oscillating' biographies: the life stories of the protagonists in his study oscillate between 'legal' and 'deviant' careers. The people he interviewed in prison pay the price of a 'flexible legality', which sees them move between different legal statuses, 'normal' and criminal occupations, between different forms of rationality, between good and bad fortune. Their relationship with work seems to me to represent the backdrop to this type of conduct, eternally suspended between will and passivity.

As I start to discuss the elements mentioned above, I should first mention that the elements I found in the field are not particularly original. In other words, I don't think I can add much to the long list of problems affecting the Italian labour market and the 'legal milieu' that serves as a backdrop to immigration (with legislation and government offices which are in general inefficient, slow and unhelpful). Luckily, the majority of the existing deformities have been extensively explored by scholars from a variety of disciplines, the media and many institutions from the public or third sector.[48] Similarly, the extent of the illegal labour market is well known,[49] as is the degree of exploitation to which immigrants are subjected (and not only them, as the recent deaths of Italian workers in a large factory such as Thyssenkrupp remind us) in small and large industries, building sites and greenhouses, where pesticides and poisons are extensively used with little or no consideration given to the health and safety of the workers.[50]

What, then, is the aim of my research? Above all, it focuses on relational aspects. In fact, one of the questions I raised at the beginning revolved around how work affects the 'social distance' separating native people and foreigners. To summarise, the issue is whether foreign and Italian workers start to 'share a world'[51] by virtue of the long hours spent together in the fields, on ships or in factories. Another way of putting the question is whether immigrants' reputations as workers and people is positively influenced by their employment in local labour markets.

I think that the answer to these questions is 'no'. With reference to the first point, the construction of a common universe of meanings, my impression is that the sharing of working hours and premises ('working together', in other words) does not generally lead to any closeness between the members of different national groups. Naturally, there are exceptions and, occasionally, Italians and foreigners can develop friendships or enjoy good relations with each other. Even so, the majority of the Italian and immigrant workers I interviewed agreed on the fact that they tended to have stronger relations with their compatriots. Personally, I tend to interpret this tendency as being correlated, we could say, with 'everyday' motivations. For example, many immigrants maintain that they tend to spend breaks in the company of their compatriots. In fact, they want to relax and the

48. Considering its vastness, it is impossible to give an overview of the critical literature on the issue. Here I would merely like to mention the reports by the Commission for the Integration of Immigrants edited by Zincone (2000; 2001) and the annual reports published by the charity organisation, Caritas.
49. According to the Italian statistical institute ISTAT, in 2004 the added value produced by the underground economy accounted for a minimum of 16.6% of GDP (around 230bn euros) and a maximum of 17.7% (around 246bn euros). According to the State Revenue Office, in 2002, 63.6% of companies illegally employed one or more workers. In 2005, also according to ISTAT figures, around 6 million illegal workers were recorded.
50. Sociological research on employment issues seems to have neglected to investigate accidents at work in detail and from a micro-sociological perspective. For some general, primarily statistical detail, the fundamental source of reference is the *Notiziario Statistico dell'Inail*, together with the other series of publications issued by this body.
51. The references to Husserl (1961) and his idea of 'worlds of life', and to Berger and Luckman (1966) should be clear.

ambient noise does not simplify dialogue with the locals (due to the language problems that slow down communication).[52] Consequently, the majority of these periods, during which people could potentially foster friendly relations, are not used for 'social' ends.

The same holds true for the other side. Just like the immigrants, the Italians also tended to talk with their compatriots during breaks. What did they talk about in these moments? Ordinary things related to life, naturally (family, football, children, girls, cars); but also problems regarding work, people's attitudes, tensions with colleagues. Foreign colleagues in particular, were often the subject of their complaints. More specifically, Italian workers accused immigrants (those belonging to certain national groups more than others) of being lazy, unproductive, arrogant, unprofessional, ignorant and of 'getting paid for slacking'. Asked explicitly, Italian employees could provide many examples of their foreign colleagues' attitudes. Obviously, the majority of these stories confirmed the point of view that Moroccan and Tunisian workers were unreliable and unprofessional ('I asked him to bring me 62 blocks, and they come in packs of 30. So the forklift truck driver, who is Moroccan, brought me three packs of 30. I told him I only needed 62, not 90, and to bring me two from open packs. So then he brought me five. He does this kind of thing because he doesn't count – maybe he doesn't know how to count! – or because he doesn't want to waste time. And I've never seen a Moroccan hurry!'). This type of comment was fairly common among Italian employees, and I heard similar stories when talking to people ranging from factory workers to engineers on fishing boats.

Whatever the case, these comments reflect the locals' perspective. The immigrants' point of view, however, was somewhat different. They maintained that they worked like slaves, that they were underpaid, that they were not respected by their employers and that they were asked to perform dangerous jobs or tasks for which they did not have particular skills ('I slipped into the engine of the machine... as big as a room ... and I had to pull the piece out. I didn't know what to do and a part of the machine could have come off and fallen on my head. I was afraid!'). They did not see themselves as unreliable workers: rather, they felt they were simply giving as good as they got.

One of the interesting results of this situation is the appearance of conflicts between foreign workers and employers.[53] A classic interpretation suggests that there is an ethics of the immigrant that dissuades foreigners from participating in public life (Portes, 1971; 1978). It does not seem to me that this model holds

---

52. Both factories and fishing boats are very noisy environments. As a Tunisian fisherman told me once: 'You don't talk on the boat. You scream all the time...!'. In a way, this condition makes these two milieux, boats and factories, very alike. At the other end of the spectrum, the countryside is certainly more silent, in spite of the tractors and the other machinery. But the workers there are mostly foreigners and natives of the same country (or linguistic area). Therefore, I argue that it may be interesting to observe the interactions among ethnic and national workers in a calmer environment: Results may be in that case slightly different.

true in the case of the Italian situation, and some recent studies, as well as data issued by the main trade unions regarding elected representatives, seem to support my point of view.[54] Moreover, I tend to think that some isolated and individual forms of protest may be read as political manifestations. In any case, what we are witnessing around Urbino and in many industrialised areas is the spread of displays of tension and malcontent, expressed both through trade union channels and in personal negotiations. The employers interviewed in Urbino said that immigrant workers were much more likely than Italians to ask for explanations regarding their amount of pay or the criteria used to establish shifts, and tended to consult the trade unions more often. In Sicily, at the time of the study, the trade unions were much less active than in the north on the immigration front, and illegal workers tended to turn to them less frequently. In any case, Sicilian employers of immigrants also recounted numerous anecdotes on arrogant and even violent workers who, instead of appreciating the opportunity given to them to make ends meet, were always complaining and demanding more.

I wonder then if this 'arrogance' so widespread among immigrant workers can be interpreted as a form of 'political resistance'; a form of resistance against their employers, Italian co-workers and also the surrounding environment that is often unorganised, chaotic and solipsistic, but which nevertheless displays some of the characteristics discussed in the classical analysis by Scott (1990). There seems to be a 'hidden transcript', namely the chatting between peers (essentially, between compatriots), and a moment of 'revelation' (the clash between parties, at times violent). Above all, I wonder whether 'arrogance' and 'violence' – elements which are part of the process of criminalisation and on which the 'fear of immigrants' is based – may be interpreted as a claim or as a demand to be compensated for damage suffered.

Recently, a few studies have analysed some of the 'ethnic' strains and riots which have occurred in Italy since the 1980s. By referring to these events and, especially, their follow-up, Sciortino (2003) has spoken of a process of 'organization of the immigrant proletariat in Italy' (resuscitating, in a very appropriate way, a lost concept from the dictionary of the Italian social sciences: the 'proletariat'). Deepening this analysis and discussing the revolt of the Chinese shopkeepers in a Milan neighbourhood, Borghi (2007) has employed Hirschman's concept of

---

53.　In reality, the relation between foreign employees and employers is much more complex than it might appear in this paper. What I would however like to point out is that, albeit tense, the relations between them are of a different conflictual quality than those between colleagues in the production facilities I studied (which represent, in fact, study cases and are not necessarily representative of Italian working life as a whole). Moreover, in the industrial districts in Le Marche, employers were admittedly critical – and generous with examples on the difficult characters of foreign employees – but, on the other hand, they were aware that they were indispensable, and often made efforts to settle disputes. This does not however prevent employers from making extensive use of dismissals, written warnings or 'dressings-down'; nor does it prevent, for their part, workers from abandoning the workplace without warning, exploiting 'making out games' as a vendetta tool, etc.

54.　See, for example, the recent paper by Mantovan (2007) on immigrants' forms of political participation and self-organisation. As far as regards union representatives are concerned, according to the CGIL trade union, in the early 2000s there were already around 160 foreign elected representatives.

'voice' and proposed that these riots were sound protests aimed at influencing not only the policies of the city concerning immigrant businesses but the general process of governance of immigration (in the aftermath of the riot, for example, the Chinese Ministry of Foreign Affairs complained officially to the Italian government, and the Chinese consul has met the mayor of the city). In sum, according to these and other authors (see Mantovan, 2007), the phase Italy is now witnessing consists of a pale shift from 'voice' to 'organization'.

Thus I ask myself whether those I have heard were in fact voices.

Suspicion and lack of confidence

The sensation or fear of being cheated characterises many immigrants and this suggests, from my point of view, the importance of suspicion as a relational practice. Relations between Italian employers or employees and foreigners are often characterised by reciprocal doubts regarding their real intentions. This appears clearly when we think of the relations between sailors, captains and shipowners in Mazara del Vallo. One might think that spending three weeks a month on a small vessel in the middle of the sea, in situations which are at times extremely dangerous, is something that requires unity and, perhaps, even friendship between the members of the crew. In reality, contrary to this expectation, the relations in this particular environment were usually founded on the premise that everyone else is a 'rogue'. Tunisian fishermen thought that the shipowner was only apparently friendly, but that in reality he was suggesting to the captain not to trust them. For their part, the Italian captain and engineers thought that Tunisian fishermen were unreliable, unprofessional and that their ultimate aim was to take control of the boat. Once they returned to port, every time there was an argument about the pay owed to the fishermen (under their contracts, this depended on the size of the catch and thus varied), since the fishermen thought that the shipowner, who is responsible for selling the fish, did not tell them the whole truth about profits. On the other hand, the shipowners said that the fishermen were impossibly demanding and resented the lack of trust displayed towards them. This model of interaction resulted in an extremely high staff turnover, with some fisherman working on up to seven different vessels a year (the average was 4-5 per person).[55] Lastly, the fact that the Italians hardly ever changed boat suggests that the relations within this group were essentially based on bonds of 'community' or trust and that the practice of suspicion did not influence its members.

The next issue we thus need to face is that of the impact that these relations have on the group of North Africans as a whole and on the members of the group. In this case as well, the analysis produces nothing but negative results. I am in fact convinced that some individuals may enjoy an excellent reputation among small but significant groups of Italians, composed of people able to supply help, work or provide other types of support. But when these 'good immigrants' leave their environ-

55. The data refer to 2002, and were collected personally after an attentive reading (and skimming) of the registers of the Mazara del Vallo Coast Guard.

ments to look for new opportunities, they tend to become part of a dark mass and have to deal with the same prejudices and obstacles encountered by the others.

It seems that on the basis of this picture the following conclusions can be drawn: for Italian society, work is not enough. Many foreign workers are 'inserted' into the system, but not included (or 'integrated').[56] The situations encountered during direct observation of two extremely different forms of provincial lifes lead me to affirm that, for Italians living in small towns, immigrants are essentially a foreign body. The commonplace comments widespread in these spaces leave no room for doubt: for the majority of Italians, foreigners employed in factories or other manufacturing sectors do not display any professionalism. Rather, they try to impose their own working style, but do not have the skills or talent necessary to transform ways of working or innovate. Immigrant workers are not humble enough and do not appreciate the efforts of employers. Moreover, the concentration of immigrants in the districts mainly occupied by the working class makes these areas less attractive and lowers house prices. Lastly, immigrants are 'different' and Italians do not feel they can forge friendships with the majority of them.

Judging by the existing literature and by systematic reading of the newspapers, I do not think that the situation in urban and metropolitan centres is in general much different. Referring particularly to northern Italy, I think that inter-ethnic relations in large cities are also more complicated than in small towns and in the South as a whole. In fact, while in the provinces the type of tensions described above generally cause social distance and 'ill feeling', and are expressed behind the back of those directly involved, in the large urban areas of the North, the presence of immigrants tends to be seen in terms of public order, and institutional campaigns for security replace private malicious gossip and disputes.[57]

---

56. I prefer to use the term 'inclusion' because, perhaps wrongly, I have the impression that in common usage its synonym 'integration' has become confused with the concept of 'assimilation'. On this point, see Mantovan (2007).

57. There is an extensive literature on these processes of criminalisation. However, we cannot say that there are unanimous views as to how to regard them. Some maintain that critical analyses of these phenomena often sound apocalyptic, and that Italy, despite everything, is the ideal country to attempt working on a wide-ranging multicultural project (especially due to its low degree of nationalist feeling) (Melotti, 2004). I believe that recent Italian history has also witnessed openly xenophobic groups, such as the Lega Nord and Forza Nuova political parties and the civic committees in the north of the country. There have also been the security drives of right-wing and left-wing political forces and the equally alarmist campaigns of provincial newspapers (which in my opinion have a greater impact than national papers because they are more immediate and reach wider sectors of the population). Above all, we need to take into account the transverse nature of racial prejudice among the population. Moreover, at the risk of sounding 'impressionistic', the tone of the discussions on the street and in a thousand local bars all over Italy sounds anything but amenable and non-nationalistic. The idea of the country as a national space – a territory which is the 'property' of those born there and who boast citizenship – is extremely widespread. On these themes, three works are representative: Dal Lago and Quadrelli (2003), Palmas et al., (2007) and Mezzadra (2007).

THE INELIGIBILITY OF WORK

Returning then to the initial question, can we maintain that work represents a good option? Is work 'more eligible' than crime? I do not think this is easy to answer. The question is in fact wide-ranging and any analysis should first clarify why some individuals commit crime and others do not. Certainly, however, if one of the reasons that dissuade people from committing crimes is the fear of damaging their reputation,[58] we could then maintain that the consideration in which immigrants are generally held is really too low to represent any inhibition to criminal behaviour. With regard to their public reputation, the majority of immigrants (especially if young and without immediate family ties) have nothing to lose should they decide to commit crimes. This is even more true if we take into consideration movement between the south and the north. Even if we know that not all immigrants resident in the south come from Mazara del Vallo, in other words from a small town where the majority of individuals share origins and provenance[59] and tend to be concentrated within a restricted urban area in which community control is fairly solid and extensive, we may maintain that as a consequence of moving to the large cities in the north, many immigrants begin to think that there is no longer anyone whose view they need to worry about. In other words, there is no longer anyone who thinks of them as 'good lads', and they may then stop thinking they need to prove anything (except for 'instrumental' reasons, related to the possibility of obtaining loans and not being excluded from the forms of mutual assistance and the alternative welfare state that the immigrants have managed to set up in the 'high concentration' areas, the contemporary equivalent of the working class districts of the past).[60]

In my opinion, the reduction of forms of community control and personal acknowledgement (which is another way of saying 'reputation'), together with the low level of salaries and the unprecedented opportunities to be involved in illegal trafficking, help make work less attractive than crime for some individuals. In order to understand this point we must accept that, from the perspective of many

---

58. Referring to 'reputation' might cause confusion. As suggested by Sutherland and Cressey (1974), reputation is enjoyed not only by the honest, interested in preserving their 'face' and their reputation as upright citizens, but also by criminals, interested in being considered 'hard' or 'bad', and simply by the 'respected' (the concept of 'good' is in fact extremely relative. Moreover, it would be interesting to deal with the theme of criminal nicknames, due to the insight they provide into values, but that is another matter). Here, as should be clear, I am considering reputation as far as it relates to the first group, the 'honest'. As far as regards the issue of reputation as a moral brake, no particular evidence should be necessary. With tools such as the 'pillory' of the public showcase trial to being pilloried in the media, not to mention the techniques of 'stigma' and 'labelling', the weapons of social reaction and state power clearly aim to compromise individuals' reputation (as well as causing fear).

59. The majority of Tunisian immigrants in Mazara del Vallo in fact came from Mahdia and La Chebba. According to unreliable data, which are however the only sources available to me, in the period during which I carried out my research around 900 out of 2,500 people came from Mahdia.

60. I am referring to simple, 'everyday' benefits, such as the chance of receiving a hot meal, small loans, favours and information (an extremely precious asset in general and of inestimable value in situations of deprivation).

Italians, the fact that a foreigner works is only just preferable to him being involved in crime. The desire to make the individual feel inferior and to devalue him, typically correlated with fear of the immigrant and the 'tautology of fear' (Dal Lago, 1999), will in fact find other ways to manifest itself, even when the foreigner is legally employed.[61] For Italians it is not enough that 'others' work and legally find a means of subsistence; rather, they are interested in the *way* in which they work, the *diligence* they express, and the *submissiveness* with which they accept their subordination. If this is plausible and if this perception takes root in the consciousness of an immigrant, what is irrational about choosing crime? In particular, what moral brake should dissuade him from undertaking a career in crime or, at least, from occasionally breaking the law?

CONCLUSIONS

What then is needed? I only have a few answers to give. The first are fairly obvious formulae, relating to national and local policies.[62] What is required, in my opinion, is: i) a reform of the legislation regarding access to Italian citizenship; ii) simplification of the legislation regarding obtaining residence permits and access to housing; iii) an extension of special programs for the qualification of workers (to be aimed at 'illegal immigrants' as well as legally resident immigrants); iv) the recognition of academic qualifications;[63] v) the abolition of the link between work and residence permits.

---

61. It is important to highlight the fact that due to the Italian law on immigration, the concept of 'legality' stumbles when referring to immigrants. The combination of bureaucratic inefficiencies, the vicious circles created by the requirements for permits (e.g., one cannot acquire a residence permit without a job, and cannot have a job without a residence permit: see: Art. 22, *Testo Unico delle disposizioni concernenti la disciplina dell'immigrazione e norme sulla condizione dello straniero*) and, finally, the intertwining of permits and work are only a few of the obstacles that make very difficult for an immigrant to acquire and retain a regular status. Thus it is better to interpret the above expression, 'legally employed', as a synonym for 'honest worker'. In fact, depending on the phase of their lives and available possibilities, immigrants in Italy swing between different statuses and are often honest workers but illegal residents. Yet, in everyday life the status of the immigrants does not seem to be very important for the Italians, unless they are employers (in this case they may take advantage of the foreigner in several different ways and may adopt strategies to hide illegal foreign workers, should an inspector visit the establishment). Interestingly, in public discourse illegal immigrants are strawmen, but in reality the status in itself usually does not affect interactions.
62. I believe that in the current situation of administrative and functional decentralisation, it is local policies that really affect citizens. Personally, I am not very enthusiastic about the results of decentralisation, which has led to the fragmentation of social policy and the welfare state (basically producing as many different situations as there are local authorities). However, seeing that there is no sign of a move towards centralisation, I feel we need to work on a local level and that this is the only possible antidote for the inadequacies of centralised immigration legislation. Among the many analyses available, a recent paper by Ferrari and Rosso (2008), focusing on immigration, comprehensively covers the issue both at the general and the specific theoretical level.
63. A necessary step, given studies such as those performed by Pisa-OECD (2007) which show how Italian students rank in terms of levels of academic learning well below those of people from the many developing countries which are the point of departure for migratory flows towards Italy.

Each of these points has a clear link with the question with which we are dealing. Together, they represent those structures of (lack of) opportunity responsible for the oscillation between legal and material statuses (legal/illegal, employed/unemployed, etc.). The flexibility of immigrants in Italy is in fact linked to the temporary nature of the benefits obtained. Of course, we should not make the mistake of only considering the mass of 'marginal' immigrants. In fact, concentrating solely on problematic cases prevents us from seeing that there is also a core of integrated immigrants, who obtain residence permits or citizenship, go into business and put down roots. However, the number of people forced to live a precarious and even 'redundant' existence is still extraordinarily high. Detaching the granting of residence permits from the need to have a job is an almost obligatory measure in an age characterised by the 'end of work'. Moreover, the dissuasive function of this association seems to be very limited, as demonstrated by the fact that individuals clearly do not decide to stay in the country because of their illegal status or due to their lack of legal employment.

Similarly, guaranteeing forms of access to housing is essential not only because this is a primary need, but also because people do not renounce living in our urban centres just because the buildings are practically uninhabitable. Moreover, worker qualifications are necessary, because it is wrong to think that a worker with few qualifications will only be asked to perform certain tasks and not others. Many employers in fact have no qualms about asking their employees to perform 'impossible missions', and the weaker immigrants have no choice but to try their hand, from time to time, at being machine tool technicians or workers specialised in dealing with the most unimaginable jobs and dangerous emergency situations. Investing resources in training workers, as well as those illegally resident, may be an important strategy not only to increase the chance for these individuals to find better jobs, but also to limit the daily massacre of workers and limit the costs of the national health system.[64] Lastly, we should not forget that the failure to acknowledge academic qualifications, due at best to reasons of a political-economic order[65] and, at worst, to boorish considerations about the adequacy of the university systems in countries of origin,[66] compromises immigrants' chances of success. This setback brings with it, in addition to dangerous sentiments of disappointment, frustration and lack of confidence towards our nation, also a significant loss of potential human resources.

---

64. Amounting to 45bn euros (3.21% of GDP), according to INAIL data (Ortolani, 2007).
65. The political-economic considerations are those which have to do with the regulation of professional markets and access to the professions. We should not forget the role played by professional bodies, which have even hindered mobility for European professionals (Olgiati, 1998).
66. Such considerations are boorish because they are fundamentally ethnocentric, and do not take into account the fact that in many developing countries university courses are based on European (French or English) and American models. Moreover, a significant number of university teachers in these countries also have a European or North-American educational background. To be frank, there are also doubts that the Italian university system can be considered competitive compared to its European and American counterparts. This does not however prevent us from having professionals who accompany us through our life and in whom, despite frequent statements to the contrary, we usually trust.

The other series of recommendations, difficult to implement, but in my opinion absolutely vital, is 'Gramscian' in nature. For some time I have been saying that 'critical scholars' must achieve access to public discourse and the media, and make an effort to dismantle perceptions which characterise society's views on immigration and immigrants (as well as on a whole wealth of other issues). In order to do this – I agree with Melossi (2007) – we must not deny that there is a problem or that immigrants commit crimes. Rather, I think we need to find ways to influence public discourse and public stereotypes, in turn connected with everyday practices (those performed by persons in everyday life). The academic world has extensively deconstructed concepts such as power, race, culture, identity, normality and many others which make up the 'marginalising discourse' in the West. As scholars, we rightly continue to keep on digging down to find the origins of exclusion, and to discuss the results obtained and new ideas. However, I believe that social investigation has provided a sufficient amount of evidence regarding the 'constructed' nature of certain phenomena and that the time is ripe to present these analyses to a wider public. Directing, or hoping to influence, policies is no longer enough. In order to work, policies must enjoy social legitimation (or deal with issues so important for the state agenda that they involve continuous surveillance, which does not seem realistic in this case). In other words, it seems to me that, in addition to dialogue with the political world, committed intellectuals active despite themselves in this celebrity society must necessarily learn to flirt with public opinion, journalists, scriptwriters and the media in general. No real transformation can take place without intervening to change the 'mental provincialism' which has its origins in the dark ages of the 'closed communities' of ancient times, with its asphyxiating ideology of nation and nationalism, and which remains fairly widespread in our villages and in our cities and makes our contemporary society suffocating.

Now, as in the past, the main problem of 'radical' democrats remains that of hegemony. The construction of a social bloc which respects minimal fundamental principles (those moreover expressed in liberal constitutions) should preferably be manifested through less ephemeral channels than those of the mass media, and especially television. However, we must acknowledge that the media as a whole has for some time represented the arena within which the fundamental issues of freedom are continuously questioned and threatened. There is then no doubt that this must become one of the venues of choice for communicating the results of research, since it is certain that, as Borgeois (2003: 18) put it, social science 'can be a site of resistance' and 'social scientists should and can "face power"' – providing, however, that they do not restrict themselves to self-referential babble.

REFERENCES

Ambrosini, M. (1999). *Utili invasori. L'inserimento degli immigrati nel mercato del lavoro italiano*. Milano: Franco Angeli, Fondazione Cariplo – ISMU.

Beck, U. (2000). *Il lavoro nell'era della fine del lavoro*. Bologna: Il Mulino.

Berger, P. & Luckman, T. (1966). *The social construction of reality: A treatise in the sociology of knowledge*. Garden City: Doubleday.

Boas, F. (1911). *The mind of primitive man*. New York: MacMillan.

Borghi, P. (2007). 'Immigrazione e partecipazione sociopolitica nei contesti locali. Dalla 'voice' alla rappresentanza'. In F. Grandi & E. Tanzi (eds.), *La città meticcia. Riflessioni teoriche e analisi di alcuni casi europei per il governo locale delle migrazioni*. Milano: Franco Angeli.

Bourgois, P. (2003). *In search of respect. Selling crack in El Barrio*. Cambridge: Cambridge University Press.

Calavita, K. (2007). 'La dialettica dell'inclusione degli immigrati nell'età dell'incertezza. Il caso dell'Europa meridionale'. *Studi sulla questione criminale*, 2(1): 31-44.

Dal Lago, A. (1999). *Non persone. L'esclusione dei migranti in una società globale*. Milano: Feltrinelli.

Dal Lago, A. & Quadrelli, E. (2003). *La città e le ombre. Crimini, criminali, cittadini*. Milano: Feltrinelli.

Ferrari, M. & Rosso, C. (2008). *Interazioni precarie. Il dilemma dell'integrazione dei migranti nelle politiche sociali locali: il caso di Brescia*. Messina: Cirsdig.

Goldthorpe, J., Lockwood, D., Bechhofer, F. & Platt, J. (1969). *The affluent worker in the class structure*. Cambridge: Cambridge University Press.

Habermas, J. (1972). *Cultura e critica*. Torino: Einaudi.

Habermas, J. (1986). *The theory of communicative action vol. 1*. Cambridge: Polity.

Hollifield, J. (1992). *Immigrants, markets and state. The political economy of postwar Europe*. Cambridge: Harvard University Press.

Husserl, E. (1961). *La crisi delle scienze europee e la fenomenologia trascendentale*. Torino: Einaudi.

Lewin, K. (1951). *Field theory in social science: Selected theoretical papers*. New York: Harpers.

Mantovan, C. (2007). *Immigrazione e cittadinanza. Auto-organizzazione e partecipazione dei migranti in Italia*. Milano: Franco Angeli.

Melossi, D. (2007). 'La criminalizzazione dei migranti: un'introduzione'. *Studi sulla questione criminale*, 2(1): 7-12.

Melotti, U. (2004). *Migrazioni internazionali. Globalizzazione e culture politiche*. Milano: Mondatori.

Mezzadra, S. (2007). 'Il nuovo regime migratorio europeo e le metamorfosi contemporanee del razzismo'. *Studi sulla questione criminale*, 2(1): 13-29.

Olgiati, V. (1998). 'Pilastri d'argilla a difesa della società europea'. *Stato e Impresa*, 46: 44-47.

Ortolani, G. (2007). 'Quanto ci costano i danni da lavoro'. *Notiziario Inail*, 12: 47.

Palmas, L., Cannarella, M. & Lagomarsino, F. (2007). *Hermanitos. Vita e politica della strada dei giovani latinos in Italia*. Verona: Ombre corte.

Portes, A. (1971). 'Urbanization and politics in Latin America'. *Social Science Quarterly*, 52(3): 697-720.

Portes, A. (1978). 'Toward a structural analysis of illegal (undocumented) immigration'. *International Migration Review*, 12(4): 469-484.

Saitta, P. (2007). *Economie del sospetto. Le comunità maghrebine in Centro e Sud Italia e gli italiani*. Soveria Mannelli: Rubbettino.

Sbraccia, A. (2007). *Migranti tra mobilità e carcere. Storie di vita e processi di criminalizzazione*. Milano: Franco Angeli.

Sciortino, R. (2003). 'L'organizzazione del proletariato immigrato in Italia'. In P. Basso & F. Perocco (eds.), *Gli immigrati in Europa. Disuguaglianze, razzismo, lotte*. Milano: Franco Angeli, pp. 376-405.

Scott, J. (1990). *Domination and the arts of resistance. Hidden transcripts*. New Haven: Yale University Press.

Sennett, R. (1998). *The corrosion of character. The personal consequences of work in the new capitalism*. New York: Norton.

Sutherland, E. & Cressey, D. (1974). *Criminology*. New York: Lippincott.

Whyte, W. (1993) *Street corner society. The social structure of an Italian slum*. Chicago: University of Chicago Press.

Zincone, G. (ed.) (2000). *Primo rapporto sull'integrazione degli immigrati*. Bologna: Il Mulino.

Zincone, G. (ed.) (2001). *Secondo rapporto sull'integrazione degli immigrati*. Bologna: Il Mulino.

The anti money laundering complex: power pantomime or potential payoff?

Perspectives on practices, partnerships and challenges within the fight against money laundering

Antoinette Verhage

> '*You can ask yourself whether they really want to achieve something. Instead of uniting forces and trying to obtain the same goal, it's every man for himself and even trying to stand in each other's way.*' *(cpl 12b)*

Introduction

Money laundering is the transformation of money in order to give illegal money a seemingly legal appearance. In a purely legal sense, money laundering 'can consist of nothing more than depositing the proceeds of crime in a domestic bank account' (Levi, 2001). This is one of the reasons why the financial sector is one of the main contributors in the battle against money laundering.

Money laundering takes place on the threshold between the legal and the illegal/ informal economy, although the boundaries between these two are partly artificial (Brown and Cloke, 2007; Vande Walle, 2008). After illicit money has passed this threshold, it will be 'formalised' and behave as 'normal' money. As such, money laundering is functional for both the formal and the informal or illegal economy; it allows for a legal use of money stemming from the informal/illicit economy in formal financial markets – stimulating precisely this informal/illicit economy – while the 'normal' behaviour of money results in financial flows in the financial market (Brown and Cloke, 2007). From an economic point of view, the battle against money laundering may be considered as unnecessary. However, as we live in a society that aspires to fight crime and to reduce opportunities for criminal activity, the motivation to fight money laundering does not solely derive from an economic perspective. After all, the fact that crime – in itself a 'condemnable' reality – should not allow for more opportunities for the launderer in legal spheres (which is what money laundering actually does) represents a normative standpoint.

Although the informal economy does not exclusively consist of transactions (illicit) money, some informal money flows are directed precisely towards the use of this money in the formal economy. The extent of access for illicit money flowing into the formal economy is to a large degree defined by legislation and the subsequent enforcement of this legislation. This also implies that the nature and extent of the informal economy is delineated by these factors. In the case of money laundering, this is the anti-money laundering (AML) legislation, which has focused on prevention of this flow from the illegal to the legal economy. AML legislation tries to achieve this both by making access to the formal economy more restricted and by detecting and reporting transactions that may be linked to money laundering. The philosophy behind this legislation is the assumption that (illicit) financial flows look for the line of least resistance – those areas in which access is least restricted.

One way of studying the informal economy and the impact of AML legislation on this economy is by making estimates of its size and subsequent changes to its size. Several researchers have attempted to measure the extent and size of the informal economy – based on, for example, the proceeds of crime or based on gross domestic product (Unger, 2006). However, these calculations remain rather vague and sometimes inconsistent. We therefore consider them as 'attempts' (Van Duyne, 2006), as conclusive statistics are lacking: we do not know how much money the informal economy represents, nor do we know what amounts of money cross the borders between illegal-informal-formal economies. This makes measuring the effects of legislation very difficult (Verhage, 2009); we lack both a pre-measurement and a measurement of impact.

This is why, in the research set out in this chapter, we have taken another approach in order to gain a perception of the effectiveness of the AML system. By studying the attitudes, relations and interactions of actors engaged in the implementation of anti money laundering legislation, we aim to deduce some conclusions with regard to their effectiveness and efficiency. Hence we will study the practical impacts of this legislation, its means of implementation, and the way in which institutions deal with this implementation. Based on this, we will describe their views about the operation of the system and how they assess its effects. After a short introduction to the principles of the anti money laundering system, we will discuss the results of a number of conversations with the institutions involved in the system. First, we will consider how AML legislation is experienced by banks and what consequences AML activities may have for compliance departments. We will do this by studying the ways in which banks position themselves in the anti money laundering complex. Secondly, we will consider the functioning of the complex and flows of information (or lack thereof) within the complex. We will reflect on the extent of the AML duty of commercial organisations and their own interest in implementing AML procedures. The focal point of this article, however, is the section in which mutual relations within the AML complex are discussed. In this section, we explain the experiences, opinions and mutual views of the participants in the complex. In the final section, we shall try to gain an overall view of the effectiveness of the AML system.

THE CREATION OF AN AML COMPLEX

Since the late 1980s and early 1990s – first in the US and UK, later on also in continental Europe – policymakers have warned and alarmed the public by proclaiming that money laundering poses a huge threat to the world economy at large and the integrity of the financial system (Stessens, 2000). Images of money laundering destabilising the economy and carried out by organised criminals that are planning to take over companies and financial institutions, thereby infiltrating the world of the formal economy are not only historical: today we still see this kind of argument (Aninat et al., 2002). These 'mirages' as they are sometimes called (Van Duyne, 2006), although contested on a regular basis, have served their policy-purpose and resulted in an impressive fight against money laundering, permeating not only the public sphere of justice, police services and regulators, but also the world of private corporations: banks, casinos, lawyers, notaries... Levi describes this approach as a 'global risk management process in which entrepreneurs are primarily responsible for implementing public policy goals and developing a "security quilt"' (Levi, 2002).

Today, a large number of (inter)national actors are united in the battle against money laundering, working on preventing, detecting, investigating and reporting potential money laundering cases. It is precisely this all-inclusive approach that characterises anti money laundering. This combination of all these actors within an AML complex (Verhage, 2008) proceeded with surprisingly little public disquiet; privacy issues were overruled in pursuit of the ultimate goal: fighting money laundering (Shields, 2005). Although the fight against money laundering seems to have united several institutions in this – what is considered as crucial – objective, we may question the extent to which fighting money laundering actually is the solitary goal of all 'partners' in this AML complex. After all, each type of organisation engages in this fight (voluntarily or not) from its own standpoint, striving for its own purpose. Private organisations – in this paper represented by the Belgian financial institutions, who are obliged to fulfil the AML-commitments, primarily have the interest of their organisation at heart: preventing any association with criminal activities, protecting the reputation of the company and avoiding regulatory fines or loss of confidence from other banks (Helleiner, 2000). Regulators have a more general interest: keeping the financial system's integrity safeguarded, resulting in a 'healthy' economy (although the events of the past year have shown that this is not exclusively related to the prevention of money laundering). Law enforcement (police, public prosecution and FIU), as a third associate, mainly aims to fight (predict) crime (possibly combined with the confiscation of assets deriving from this crime) (Gouvin, 2003). As each institution works from a different perspective, each partner in the complex will have his own interests at stake. These different interests need to be taken into account when trying to assess the effectiveness of the system. After all, to say something about the effects of a system, we need to know which goals are pursued by the system.

In this article, we will look more in-depth into this battle against money laundering through the eyes of the institutions that are working on the implementation of AML legislation. The article presents the results of an interviewing phase (2007-2008[67]) with compliance officers of financial institutions (responsible for implementing AML measures), police members, regulators and the financial intelligence unit. Within this phase, a total of 32 respondents[68] were asked for their opinions on the feasibility of the battle against money laundering, their practices, challenges and problems, and their views on, and interactions with, the other associates in the AML battle. Respondents were selected by making use of several methods. First of all, we wanted to make sure that there was an equal representation of different types of banks (large, medium-sized and small), based on the assumption that the tasks and views of a compliance officer vary according to the size of the bank. Secondly, as compliance officers are not that easy to contact, we asked our respondents after the interview if they could refer us to colleagues who would be willing to participate. The selection of regulatory and law enforcement respondents was based on their expertise in the subject. Both methods were applied simultaneously, which can be summarized as a combination of snowball or chain sampling on the one hand and purposeful sampling on the other hand (Patton, 2002). In the end, everyone who was contacted (both through referral and through spontaneous contacts) agreed to cooperate with this research. We conclude by discussing the AML-system and its performance, success or failure, explaining why we may describe the participants in this battle against money laundering not as 'partners', but as 'associates' – nolens volens.

THE AML COMPLEX

Its basis: legislation and regulatory action

The framework of the AML complex is constituted by the AML legislation and regulation. In Belgium, the AML legislation came into force in 1993. This AML legislation formed the starting point of the creation of the Belgian AML complex: it involved the establishment of an (administrative) Financial Intelligence Unit or FIU, that functions as a filter between reporting organisations and law enforcement. This obligation was combined with the introduction of the obligation to monitor and report potentially suspicious transactions or clients to this FIU for several (financial and non-financial) organisations. However, during the 1990s, the practice of reporting suspicious transactions remained rather arbitrary. For

---

67. As part of ongoing research: 'The anti-money laundering complex and its interactions with the compliance industry: empirical research on the private actors in the battle against money laundering'. UGent, funded by FWO Vlaanderen, 01/01/2006 – 31/12/2009.

68. The respondents were 23 compliance officers and 9 law-enforcement/regulatory officials. The compliance officers were working for large banks (11 respondents), medium-sized banks (7 respondents) and small banks (5 respondents). The law enforcement respondents mainly worked for police services (6), the regulator and the FIU (3). We would like to thank all respondents for their cooperation and their enthusiasm.

the financial sector, this gave rise to regulatory action. By means of a circular in 2001 (CBFA, 2001) – afterwards converted into a legal obligation in 2007,[69] the regulator for the financial sector (CBFA – or Banking, Finance and Insurance Commission) introduced the obligation to appoint a *compliance officer* within each financial institution. This compliance officer became responsible for the implementation of AML procedures and the execution of these procedures within the financial institution. The result of this regulatory obligation, in combination with the AML legislation and the obligations of public and private organisations within the battle against money laundering, is a chain of anti-money laundering (Figure 1).

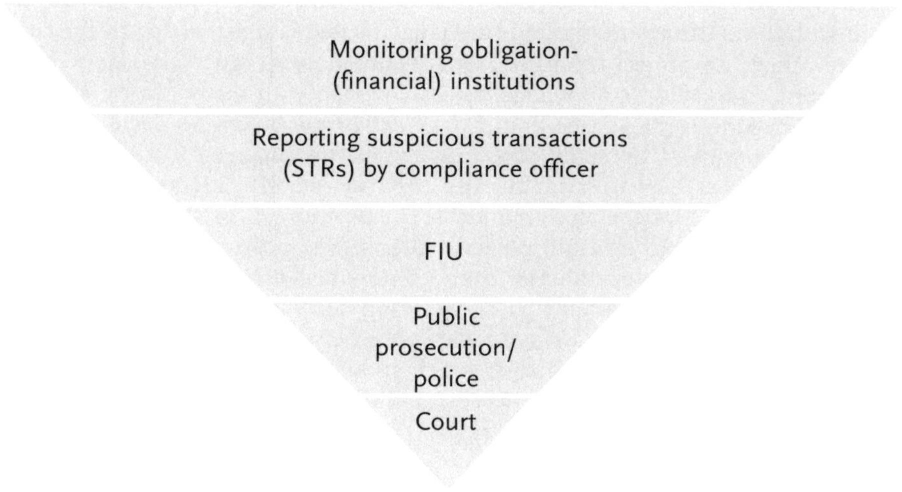

Monitoring obligation-
(financial) institutions

Reporting suspicious transactions
(STRs) by compliance officer

FIU

Public
prosecution/
police

Court

Figure 1   AML-Chain

The several phases in the AML-chain are carried out by different actors: the compliance officer in the financial institution (monitoring, preventing and reporting cases), the FIU (which investigates the report by making use of several official sources, and subsequently may report it to the public prosecutor), the public prosecutor (who can decide to carry out further investigations or prosecutions on receipt of the report), the police (who are ordered to investigate by the public prosecutor) and the court (if the case finally ends up before a judge, which occurs in a very small percentage of cases – 3.7% of all FIU-files[70]). This chain also explains why, in this chapter, the compliance officer occupies central stage: he or she is a key witness to the functioning of the AML chain. After all, because of their gatekeeper-position in the AML chain, they determine the input of the AML-system and have insight into the effects of AML for their daily practice in the bank.

---

69. By article 20 inserted in 2007 in the Law on the statute and supervision of credit institutions, *B.S,* 19th of April 1993.
70. For more statistics on the AML chain, see: Verhage (forthcoming).

The compliance function in theory

Arising from their function and duties within the financial institution, the compliance officer has a dual position. His or her first responsibility is to safeguard the 'integrity of the bank' by applying the policy on integrity within the institution (CBFA, 2001). This comprehensive job description results in compliance departments carrying the responsibility for an array of issues related to integrity in the broader sense (privacy regulation, insider dealing, prevention of fiscal fraud, conflicts of interests), among which anti money laundering is just one of the many other tasks to carry out (Nivra-Nyenrode, 2008, Verhage, 2008). The application of this integrity policy ought to enable the compliance department (the department within the bank working on compliance-related issues, headed by the compliance officer) to protect the bank from reputational or other damage. On the other hand, in practice, compliance tasks may clash with the commercial objectives of a bank: in certain cases, compliance departments have to make decisions that interfere with commercial objectives, typical of financial institutions. The regulator was aware of this duality and tried to establish a framework which should allow for an independent mandate. The position of the compliance officer should be supported by providing specific guarantees: a compliance officer ought to be able to work independently from commercial entities, 'monitoring and stimulating compliance with the rules regarding integrity of banking by the institution' (CBFA, 2001). Secondly, the compliance department has to be positioned directly under the board of directors, which should not only allow for free information flow between compliance officers and the higher levels within the bank, but also for an appropriate hierarchical position with regard to employees. Thirdly, the compliance department is obliged to write a compliance charter, containing the compliance tasks, powers and responsibilities, and the position of the compliance department. This charter must be approved by the board of directors (CBFA, 2001).

Although the regulator has taken steps in the right direction, these regulations do not exclude every contradiction or clash between compliance and commercial employees. After all, as the compliance officer is also a bank employee, it may be very difficult to act counter to the wishes of the directors and the bank's interests.

How does this work out in practice? Essentially, a compliance officer carries out governmental tasks, but is paid by the bank and works within the framework of the financial institution. It is precisely this duality that is studied throughout the interviews with Belgian compliance officers within banks and their law enforcement-associates within the AML complex. Starting from their experiences with anti money laundering and the difficulties of AML, through cooperation and interaction within the AML complex, we consider the question: what impact does the complex have in general on the effectiveness of the battle against money laundering? In the following paragraphs the results of these interviews will be reflected upon, by discussing both the views of the compliance officers and the opinions of law enforcement associates within the AML-complex.

BANKS AND THEIR POSITION IN THE AML COMPLEX

The reporting system in Belgium

The Belgian AML legislation is based on the principle of 'intelligent reporting': banks are supposed to report 'any transaction which they suspect of money laundering' (Spreutels and Grijseels, 2001). This implies that there are no objective indicators for reporting to the FIU: banks are supposed to develop their own standards on the basis of which they decide to report (contrary to, for example, the system that existed until recently in the Netherlands, where banks were supposed to report cases involving transactions above a specific amount (MOT, 2006)).

These AML obligations imply that banks need to install AML measures (such as monitoring systems and procedures for internal reporting) and that they subsequently investigate the results of these systems: the alerts. These alerts may either be an indication of something suspicious and therefore give rise to an investigation, or may lead to the conclusion that the alert was false after having studied the client and the context of the transaction. Compliance officers have to make sure that both parts of the AML system are functioning well.

The 'risk-based approach' to money laundering, on which 'intelligent reporting' is based, involves a number of problems for the reporting institutions: first of all, they have the difficulty of deciding – based on a limited amount of information – which cases to investigate. Secondly, they need to decide which of the investigated cases should be reported to the FIU. Adding to these problematic decisions is the fact that banks run the risk of being sanctioned for non-reporting (by the regulator, or by criminal law). The threat of this sanction even increases when banks are internationally active – especially when US regulation is involved. Not only are regulations stricter in the US, but also the sanctions from the US regulator – or ultimately exclusion from the US market or withdrawal of the US license – can have far-reaching consequences for a financial institution, as history has shown (Shields, 2005). 'The risk is bigger in US regulation. The consequences can also be greater. One specific procedure is the "look-back", in which the bank is forced to look back at all transactions for a number of years. We process millions of transactions each day, and when they ask to re-examine everything for 5 years, then you need an army' *(cpl 8)*.

The solution to this problem would seem to be to report as many 'potentially suspicious cases' as possible, to be on the safe side. 'You're only completely "cleared" of liability when you've reported the case. But even then. If you investigate and decide not to report... it's a matter of interpretation. You're safer when you report because normally the bank and its employees will be covered' *(cpl 12a)*.

However, excessive reporting also involves some dangers. After all, a bank's clients may reproach the bank for unnecessary reporting, leading to potential lawsuits or at least the loss of the client. 'One time a bank was sued for reporting a client and that bank was with its back to the wall. Because you are not allowed to tell the client that you have reported and on the other hand you are summoned by a client and you want to say: I have made a report in good faith, but you are not allowed to say that you have made a report. An impossible position' *(cpl 1)*.

Secondly, as we will discuss later, reporting may also expose the bank and its employees to other dangers. This difficult position for the compliance department causes a feeling of being torn between several interests that may surface at the same time. This is why compliance departments and banks look for some input during their decision making, input from the authorities who – according to the respondents – have obliged them to adopt the position of whistleblower, which should make deciding on the reliability and benevolence of a client less complicated. As we will see later, this input or feedback from the authorities is – much to the frustration of the banks – rather limited. This makes deciding on what should happen with the client relationship very difficult. As a result of the lack of feedback, banks are left with their own appraisal of the situation and have to decide on either ending or continuing the client relationship. This could result in respectively a commercial loss (and a possible complaint by the client), or, in the latter case, a reprimand by the authorities. 'But after you have reported, we will make an appraisal: will we continue the client relationship or not. Sometimes we explicitly decide to continue, because a client can be monitored intensively when you let him proceed his transactions. If you discontinue the client relationship, a client can go to another bank, or will be alarmed. But still, now and then we are reproached: you have reported to the FIU but why did you not stop the client relationship?' *(cpl 12b)*

Automatic reporting versus 'intelligent' reporting

Compliance officers have a number of critiques with regard to the feasibility of the current Belgian legal framework. As we will see, these critiques are dual: the lack of concrete rules is perceived both as a hindrance and as room for manoeuvre.

On the one hand, the large majority states that the guidelines are too vague, which results in the fact that the responsibility is placed with the reporting institutions: they have to decide which cases could be potential money laundering cases. It also takes a lot of time, as the lack of concrete rules more or less obliges banks to investigate cases rather thoroughly – in order to decide whether something is 'black' or 'white', a lot of information on the case needs to be gathered and analysed. 'The only aspect is... that regulation is not clear enough, it leaves too much room for bypassing. We really do not know concretely: this we should report, this we should not report' *(cpl 14)*.

On the other hand, none of the compliance officers openly said they were in favour of automatic reporting to the FIU; they appreciate the room for discretion and are aware of the fact that this also allows them to prevent bona fide clients from being reported for a strange transaction. After all, every report to the FIU may result in the blocking of the clients' accounts, which could have serious consequences for their business.

Taking this into account, the system that was implemented in the US (in which automatic reporting – the duty to report every case above a certain sum of money, for example – takes place) is appealing to some because responsibility for analysing and reporting stays at the level of the government. 'It could be very easy; you design a programme, scan autographs and let it run every night and the FIU will be flooded with 1.500 reports each day. Then we'll hear what they have to say. And when all banks do this, there will be 10.000 reports each day' *(cpl 11a)*. On the other hand, the Belgian system is regarded as more useful and functional. First of all, the Belgian FIU 'would never be able to process systematic reporting by the banks. It would be the best way to sabotage them' *(cpl 2b)*. Secondly, compliance officers consider blindly reporting customers or transactions to the authorities as useless, 'intellectually frustrating' *(cpl 6a)*, which will reduce the quality of the system. Furthermore, it would also imply that banks lose a lot of information on their clients: 'in the current system we need to investigate clients, which implies that we know the client better and we have to decide whether to keep the client or not. In a system of automatic reporting, this knowledge will disappear. It will all disappear (...) maintaining our client-database would become extremely difficult' *(cpl 6b)*. Automatic reporting (without previous investigation by the bank) also implies commercial dangers. After all, 'Banks are supposed to do business in the first instance' *(cpl 6b)*. Although the current system may cause dilemmas – 'either you report as much as possible in aid of the battle against money laundering, or you report specific cases – therefore too little – and the clients will be pleased but the public prosecutor can tackle you. It's a continuous field of tension for all reporting institutions' *(cpl 1)* – the overall impression is that this system is preferred to a process of automatic reporting. Many compliance officers state that they have built an expertise in AML matters and are best placed for carrying out the AML task. After all, even in case of automatic reporting, compliance officers will still need to investigate cases to prevent harm to their institution: criminal clients can also lead to commercial losses and therefore need to be detected. Furthermore, if an automatic reporting system is introduced, it could be very likely that files that have nothing to do with serious fiscal fraud or money laundering, fall into the hands of the authorities. This could be case for regular fiscal fraud-cases. Whether this is still a function for the bank, is up for discussion.

The feasibility of AML legislation for banks

Because of the fact that Belgian AML legislation leaves certain room for interpretation, this forces the banks to investigate cases and clients rather thoroughly. This subjectivity also implies that a large responsibility rests on the banks in relation to preventing and detecting money laundering. The banks are obliged to install certain measures (training for employees to detect money laundering, transaction monitoring systems that allow for a continuous check on all transactions and sets off an alert in case of suspicious activity, Know Your Customer- or identification- and acceptance policies, etc. (Shields, 2005; Levi and Reuter, 2006; Verhage, 2008)). Needless to say, compliance departments are characterized by a heavy workload: 'The problem is, add 10 people to the AML-cell and they can all work fulltime. Everything we do here, everything that approaches us, is priority and we need to put priorities before priorities' *(cpl 12a)*.

The extent to which banks are able to meet these demands is not only dependent on the willingness of the financial institution. Some of the compliance officers pointed out that there are also practical issues that need to be taken into consideration. 'In an institution like ours, we have several million clients only in Belgium, and over 1.000 branch offices, these offices have thousands of clients, they cannot know all these clients personally. That is impossible' *(cpl 9)*. 'Compliance implies checking, observing all legislation and regulation and examining whether it is executed by everyone within the company. That is impossible, you cannot do that' *(cpl 17)*.

The level of AML-compliance also depends on the type of bank involved. 'The level of complexity is also dependent on the clientele: the advantage is that we are a savings bank, aiming for families, with rather simple products, we don't have any dealing rooms, ... and on the level of financial instruments we don't give advice but merely provide information' *(cpl 17)*. Some compliance officers point out that even when AML is seen as a high priority within a bank and a professional compliance department is trying to implement an AML-philosophy, it is not that easy to expect the employees who are working at the desk to always be vigilant and alert. 'When they see a client enter the bank, the first thing they think will not be: ah here a criminal enters the bank, or a money launderer, or a human trafficker... I don't know whether you've ever been behind a counter, but when 15 clients are standing in the queue you don't start asking "sir, what are the origins of these funds". Furthermore, the people at the counter are often younger colleagues who just started working, they of course don't have the knowledge of that client of colleagues who have worked here for 20 years' *(cpl 9)*.

On a more general level, there are a number of objections with regard to the AML-legislation by compliance employees. These objections mainly relate to the feeling of being a 'whistle-blower', specifically coming from an institution that thrives on its image of trust and trustworthiness towards their clientele. 'We have to carry out the job of the police, the public prosecutor, but we don't have their powers – fortunately – but for me there's a problem with regard to the client relationship based on trust. How can a client be able to trust us when we have to report him in so many circumstances?' *(cpl15)*. Some of them emphasise the intrusiveness of the system, affecting privacy and potentially harming the relationship between a bank and its clients. '...the legislator has implemented a system with reports, behind a client's back, who is by definition not informed. This is a true Stasi-situation, going against all healthy principles of law. Unless in this case, when it is carried out with the consent of the government and the public, because of the huge dangerous consequences it may have for the country – organised crime, serious crime' *(cpl 7)*.

FEEDBACK WITHIN THE AML COMPLEX

Information provision as a one-way street

To a certain extent, the associates within the AML complex need to co-operate and exchange information. Evidently, compliance officers are obliged to provide information to all associates: the FIU (reporting), the police (during investigations), and the regulator (during audits). Information provision is crucial in both the reporting and the investigation phase. However, this information stream only flows in one direction: from the reporting institutions (i.e. the compliance officers) to the authorities. Much to the frustration of the compliance officers, information the other way is very limited.

According to the compliance officers, feedback from the regulator or the FIU on reporting activities of banks is completely lacking. Apart from quarterly feedback on dismissed cases and incidental information on convictions (often many years after the initial report was made), formal feedback is absent. Because of the fact that they are bound by a duty of professional confidentiality, the FIU states that they are not in the position to give much information on cases or clients. This results in the FIU functioning as a black box: compliance officers make reports, but do not have a clue what happens with their report after they have sent it. This not only complicates the decision on what to do with a client once he or she has been reported by compliance, or trying to assess whether the reporting duty is carried out in compliance with the expectations of the authorities, it also impedes future reporting.

After all, when compliance departments have no idea of the outcome of their reports, this makes building AML-expertise very difficult as they cannot learn from previous cases or reports. 'To refine your system, more feedback would be useful. If only a small percentage of your reports are transmitted to the public prosecutor, you may ask yourself whether you are doing a good job. If ten out of ten are "bingo", you need to ask yourself whether you should report more cases' *(cpl 16)*. Furthermore, the lack of feedback and, more broadly, the lack of provision of official information and typologies, forces compliance officers to rely on the limited official information that is available on money laundering activities in Belgium. The majority of compliance officers state that they base themselves on the annual report of the FIU, in which a number of typologies are also published. However, this information is not very diverse, and not always concentrated on Belgian or smaller scale banks. 'The only thing we get is an annual report, which also includes typologies. But that is of little use for us, because many of those typologies include international transfers, while we, as a local bank, have hardly any transfers outside Europe. How are we supposed to make an assessment?' *(cpl 14)*. This annual report is also used for self-assessments by compliance departments to check how they compare to the total of reports. 'I keep track of our reports and the annual report of the FIU. Then I see that, based on these statistics, our reports ought to be of good quality' *(cpl 2c)*.

Compliance officers consider that the lack of transparency has a negative effect on the effectiveness of the AML chain. One of the examples was referred to by a number of respondents and relates to information questions from the FIU. When the FIU asks for information on a client, they will not explain why they have requested this information. However, the compliance officer will be alerted and will try to find out why this client is investigated by the FIU. After all, it is in the interest of the bank to exclude criminal clients from their clientele. 'When the FIU asks us for information on a client, they give us no information on the reasons why they ask for this information. "It is a question in general". But we cannot ignore this, because it may lead to a serious file. And if we do not investigate this, we will hear: you have an indication from the FIU and did nothing with it!' *(cpl 11b)*

This lack of information provision can have other counterproductive effects. In order to cover themselves against potential sanctions, banks may decide to play it safe and report more cases than necessary (defensive reporting). 'Sometimes you hear banks state: it's so vague, we simply report anything' *(cpl 14)*. But this is not the most distressing result. More problematic is the fact that – as the FIU's typologies are used as the main basis for reporting policies – this might hinder the detection of new types of money laundering and result in simply finding the same type of money launderers that were found in earlier years. As the FIU's annual report is based on the reports made by banks and other reporting institutions in previous years, this leads to the AML system continuously repeating itself and confirming earlier 'suspicious activities'. In this sense, the AML system is a self-fulfilling prophecy: when you look for a specific type of activity, you will find a specific type of activity. 'We ought to be investigating continuously how money launderers work. Now we base our actions on indicators that we read in annual reports of the FIU, common sense, the regulator, seminars... but these are cases that were discovered. Criminals find new ways. And if you publish indicators in the *Staatsblad*,[71] then you know that people will pay attention to them and try to avoid them' *(cpl 2b)*.

The same lack of information provision applies to the content of 'the 13 indicators'. In 2007, an article was added to the AML-law[72] and introduced 13 indicators for serious and organised fiscal fraud. These indicators are supposed to enhance the reporting of these types of cases.[73] However, there is no explanation accompanying these indicators and the FIU does not explain itself further: 'we have asked the FIU, who has written the indicators, to give their definition. But they say: ah no, we have written them on the basis of your reports' *(cpl 15)*.

---

71. Belgian Official Journal
72. The indicators can be found in the Royal Decree of 3 June 2007 – Koninklijk besluit tot uitvoering van artikel 14quinquies van de wet van 11 januari 1993 tot voorkoming van het gebruik van het financiële stelsel voor het witwassen van geld en de financiering van terrorisme, 3 June 2007.
73. Examples of indicators are: the presence of international transactions (indicator nr. 9) or the absence of documentation to justify bonds or savings (indicator nr 10).

An urgent plea for feedback

The frustrations regarding the lack of information exchange would not be very significant if the position of the compliance officer (and in general, the bank) were balanced more easily on the tight-rope. However, it now seems as though the sword of Damocles continuously hangs over their heads: if they report too few cases, this will result in problems with the authorities, while too many unnecessary reports leads to dissatisfied clients. Accordingly the compliance officers (and specifically those of small banks who have fewer contacts in the sector and less access to the FIU or the regulator) feel left to their own devices. This forces some of them to seek refuge with the large banks who have more means at their disposal and often more international experience in AML, but most importantly, large databases on money laundering cases. 'What is atypical? What is a sector that is susceptible for money laundering? Now we have no information on this, everyone needs to figure it out for themselves. So what do we do: we go to the large banks for help, they have more experience, large databases, they will know better than us. And they give us that information. But is that the way to do it?' *(cpl 14)*

This observation makes it clear that banks are emphasising the need for information, both on reporting in general (typologies) and on their reporting behaviour. 'When do we have to report? There has to be a suspicion. But what is a suspicion? It is very subjective. Depending on how a file is presented, a decision may vary between black to white, and that is what is so frustrating: it is not an exact science. And in that respect feedback from the FIU or the public prosecution would be very helpful' *(cpl 6a)*. When they get in touch with the authorities such as the FIU with questions on specific cases or reporting policy in general, the majority say that they are referred to the legislation in question. 'The FIU will never tell you: that should be reported or that case should not be reported. They say: it's up to you to make the decision. Very little information is given. They refer to their annual report. The regulator will ask questions during a check, and ask why, but the regulator will always put up their umbrella, they will not help you any further. They will not give you concrete criteria: do it like this... because.... on that issue, the authorities are of very little help. We try to exchange information between ourselves, but the authorities only provide information through their annual reports' *(cpl 17)*.

'It should not be excessive, but the legislator needs to realise that he has passed on one of his responsibilities to the banks, namely the detection of money launderers. Then we need to have minimal assistance and means' *(cpl 6c)*.

We must note however, that the level of information provision by the FIU also seems to depend on the scale of the bank. This might be due to the fact that large banks have more regular contacts with the FIU and probably have had more time to build up connections; as a result, large banks are often more satisfied about their contact and information exchange with the FIU compared to smaller banks. Here we must also note the importance of personal relationships: knowing the investigators who are working for the FIU can also be helpful. 'We have informal contacts with the FIU and we can ask questions. We don't have precise feedback, apart from the official questions they ask us. But when we invite them, we also ask "would you like to have more information on..."' *(cpl 4)*. 'It has changed. In former years, we would contact the FIU to ask: do you know this client. And they would sometimes answer: yes, probably. But now they say: make a report' *(cpl 7)*.

All things considered, it may be no surprise that banks develop reporting strategies and policies and base these strategies on how to best protect the interests of the bank. After all, the AML complex is composed of a continuous shirking of responsibilities onto other associates in the complex. Compared to the situation within the banks, where desk employees are answerable to the application of AML rules, we see that responsibility within the whole of the AML complex is also shifted towards the base of the complex.

By providing a limited amount of information, the authorities force the reporting institutions in charge of making reporting decisions to do so based on partial and incomplete information. This results in a system in which everyone puts up his or her umbrella, trying to push accountability towards the others. 'It is possible that an inspector from the regulator comes here and says: I would certainly have reported that file. While we say: we will not report, because it fits into the profile of the client. While a third party, in all subjectivity, says: why did you not report this? For us it is incomprehensible that not everyone understands that we have an obligation to perform to the best of one's ability, not to a specific result' *(cpl 6a)*.

'They ask the banks to be gendarmes, and therefore an extension to the Ministry of Finance. But we still do not have the instruments: we have to rely on what the client asks us. And we can ask for documents, but not for everything. We cannot ask for copies of bills or fiscal declarations. Banks would no longer be able to function. There is limited information and it would be helpful to have official information' *(cpl 4)*.

AML AS A TASK FOR COMMERCIALLY ORIENTED INSTITUTIONS

Governmental or corporate responsibility?

To what extent is AML implementation a government task? Is this something we can expect from private organisations? Compliance officers state that compliance and AML can be seen as a type of outsourcing by the government. Many of them emphasise that this outsourcing implies that not only the practical execution of the AML-system is left to the bank, but that also the responsibility for anti money laundering rests with the financial institution. According to the compliance officers, the government has simply stated: this is now your responsibility. 'In this system, the legislator has passed the responsibility to the society – the banks' *(cpl 6a)*, while most of the police-respondents simply take it for granted that the private sector carries out these tasks. Several compliance officers however, are not convinced of the fact that AML is naturally a task for the private sector and question the range of the requirements that need to be met by the banks 'We are evolving towards undertaking debt collections for the government' *(cpl 7)*. This quote makes it clear that banks also have doubts about their function within the AML chain and ask themselves how far this should go. Some of the respondents point out that future developments might lead to an even more intrusive monitoring role for banks. Currently, banks are obliged to report only *'serious and organised* fiscal fraud' to the FIU. 'Regular' fiscal fraud is excluded from the reporting obligation. However, there is a new legislative proposal, aiming to make fiscal fraud or tax evasion one of the specified crimes under the AML legislation.[74] This would imply that banks will be obliged to report any customer they suspect of committing fiscal fraud, which, in Belgium, could mean that 'there will be huge problems for our clients, they will no longer want to come to us' *(cpl 6a)*. This could cause many clients great concern and they would be much less inclined to do business with that specific bank. 'It would be against business. The socialists want the economy to function, but when they block it like this, it doesn't work either' *(cpl 6a)*. And, even so: 'How will we check that? It could have enormous consequences. The AML law should not be abused by adding all kinds of problems that will ultimately overrule the initial issue' *(cpl 6b)*. These concerns that banks will be mobilised as tax officers, indicate the worries banks have in being used for tasks far beyond the range of organised crime control.

Reasons for banks to invest in compliance

In spite of these concerns, banks have shown their willingness to invest in anti money laundering (Harvey, 2007), which leads to the question: what are the incentives for banks to make these investments? On the one hand we observed the reservations of banks regarding the effects of their input in the AML system and the problems and dilemmas they encounter during their reporting activities. On the other hand, it is also clear that banks are making enormous investments in anti money laundering, both at the level of personnel and at the level of technology (mainly software). Considering both of these findings, one could wonder why banks are willing to invest this amount of time and effort in implementing AML legislation and thus investigating clients and cases. We therefore asked the compliance officers what reasons and motives there are for banks to engage in the AML complex. Are the interests for the bank motivated purely by 'loss-prevention' and are they – according to economic theory – therefore solely focused on company interests, overruling criminal law objectives (Hoogenboom, 1988)?

Compliance departments reacted diversely in relation to this question. The first reaction of a few respondents to the question 'what is the goal of compliance?' is 'to fight crime'. This more idealistic point of view however, only represents a minority of the compliance officers interviewed. 'We try to avoid thinking that we

---

74. Belgian House of Representatives, *Bill for the reform of the law of 11 January 1993 on the prevention of the use of the financial system for the laundering of money and financing of terrorism with regard to funds and assets that are considered as illegal.* 12th December 2007, DOC 52, 0549/001.

do all of this to avoid penalties or sanctions and keep out of range. We try to think that we do this because it has a value, that's idealism. Maybe that is true. If you would allow dangerous crime to take over your economy then it becomes impossible to deal with society in a healthy way' *(cpl 8)*.

Some respondents adopted a more general approach and referred to the integrity of the economic system. According to them, it is also in the interest of the bank to fight crime, because financial institutions can only function optimally in a healthy economic climate. 'They take over your economy. What would it be like to be a bank office at the corner of a street in Palermo? Not so simple!' *(cpl 8)*

Other compliance officers emphasised the need for banks to be profitable in the first place, while supporting legislation took second place. 'Compared to other legislation, AML is special, because for a bank it is purely self-interest to protect yourself from the outside world, secondly it should have a preventive result and thirdly it is an enormous whistleblower's arrangement' *(cpl 3)*. Some of the compliance officers also referred to the sanctions that are given by the regulator in case of non-compliance. 'I say: if you think compliance is costly, then try it without compliance. Compliance needs to cover two risks: the risk with regard to the regulator and the reputational risk' *(cpl 15)*. Surprisingly, banks most fear the effect on their reputation with regard to other banks. Not many respondents worried about the effect of money laundering scandals on their clients. 'When it's an isolated incident, it's different. But you also need to consider professionalism, the image towards other banks and what image you want to radiate. Do you consider the integrity of banking as important or not' *(cpl 16)*. In this sense, compliance investments serve to enhance the competitive position of a bank, supporting the reliability and professionalism of a bank in relation to other financial institutions.

Taking all the answers together, protection of reputation remains the most mentioned motive for investments in relation to AML. We must note here that, as in any group of respondents, the diversity of compliance officers should be taken into account. Each compliance officer has a personal view on AML and personal motives for carrying out his or her job. In studying the different motives that compliance officers suggested for the fight against money laundering, we can discern several characteristics that may be a prelude to a typology (Micucci, 1998) of compliance officers, reflecting different styles of 'policing the bank': 'the crime fighter', 'the reputation guardian', 'patron of the economy', ... This is not the place to enter at length into this typology, but the differences in viewpoints are remarkable.

But do money laundering cases lead to reputational damage? It is difficult to translate reputational damage into financial terms. Several compliance officers referred to the ABN-Amro case,[75] in which fines of 80 million dollars were imposed, and that the financial costs of this sanction do not end with paying the

---

75. ABN-Amro, a Dutch bank, was sanctioned in 2005 by the Dutch and US regulators for a total of 80 million dollars for, among other things, negligence regarding AML procedures, lack of monitoring and failure to report certain transactions.

fine, but also imply huge investments in compliance personnel and software. Furthermore, the additional reputational damage is said to be much more important that the financial damage. 'We would not like to see our logo worldwide in the press because we have assisted in handling criminal money' *(cpl 1)*. It may also be the case that reputational damage is dependent on both the extent of support given by the bank and the crime that a bank is suspected of. To be caught having supported the financing of terrorism is unlike any other type of crime, and one to which the public reacts excessively. Within the financial sector, every bank is perfectly aware of the level of law-abidance by other financial institutions. 'It depends on which level. In Brussels, there used to be an exchange office, a stock broking firm that only performed exchanges. In the financial world they were known for their money laundering activities. And when they got arrested, nobody was surprised. In the world of finance, it is known who is strict and who is not' *(cpl 16)*.

Earlier research has shown that the level of compliance is not linked to reputation per se. On the contrary, the fines imposed on non-compliant banks seemed to have very little impact on customer perceptions or the image of the bank (Harvey and Lau, 2009). A small-scale analysis of Belgian newspapers during the past 15 years showed us that very little attention is paid to banks' association with money laundering cases, and if attention is paid, banks are mainly perceived as victims of money laundering rather than as perpetrators. But even when we take this into account, there is still another reputational impact: although the first interpretation of 'reputation' may suggest that this is aimed at protection of reputation vis-a-vis clients, many compliance officers specify that the most important impact lies in 'interbank' reputation protection.

The AML-benchmark – finding the centre of the playing field

Another interbank phenomenon that was described in the interviews relates to the level of AML investment. The supply of services, advice, software, training etc that is available for AML compliance and other compliance-related issues, is very extensive. Banks have to decide how much they are willing to invest in AML regarding means, people and effort. The workload of compliance departments today also demonstrates the fact that resources are limited. 'It's a matter of finding the balance between the means we invest and what we should do as a bank. In the end a bank should also be profitable at the end of the financial year, have equity capital, make profits, that is also part of the deal. Which implies that banks will invest in compliance and AML, but also say: we want or can spend this amount of means' *(cpl 2b)*.

Because of the fact that banks lack clear guidelines from the regulator or the FIU on the extent of AML investments, they need to look for other criteria. After all, compliance is also costly, specifically because there is no direct return on investment. 'That is added value, which is vague and difficult to quantify and not so easy to justify the investments' *(cpl 8)*.

How do banks decide on the degree of AML investment and how far do they need to go in their investigations? What are the criteria they use in assessing their level of AML compliance? According to the majority of compliance officers, banks look to each other for the assessment of the level of AML investment. This is not a surprise, given the value that is attached to interbank relations. 'The domain of AML prescribes that you keep within the pack, it's not interesting to break away from the pack. That may be a minimalistic approach, but who breaks away, pays over the odds on investments – often without obvious added value – that is the drama' *(cpl 8)*. 'The benchmark is what happens in the market. We always attend the compliance forum and there you also hear how others function, which allows you to check if you're doing a good job or not' *(cpl 7)*. This makes it clear that banks exchange information on compliance matters, and try to look for a central position: if they make their AML procedures too strict in comparison with other banks, this could scare clients away, but if they are too lenient, they are at risk of a regulatory sanction. 'The system is based on an intelligent duty to report. And every bank wants to be the most intelligent' *(cpl 6a)*. This, in accordance with the remarks made regarding the image banks want to present to other banks, supports the idea of compliance investment as a means of competition.

Information on the level and content of AML investments and procedures is exchanged between banks, within large or smaller groups, on compliance gatherings and in more structural consultation, for example between banks in the same group. Most of the respondents emphasised the need for this information exchange. This need is even stronger as a result of the lack of feedback by the authorities in the complex. After all, interbank information exchange allows for some insight into the functioning of the compliance department in comparison with other banks. 'I think that all banks look at each other to see how it's done, how do they interpret this. Many banks think I don't want to be number one but not the last one neither. The middle group moves in a certain direction, which balances one another out' *(cpl 16)*. As such, information exchange is helpful for gaining expertise and building knowledge.

Banks are also alert to the need to limit costs, as clients will eventually be charged for these costs. Some compliance officers warn against potential contrary effects: 'Then we enter an Adam Smithian analysis: I raise my pricing for risky clients because I have to protect myself from potential risk. If you are very good at assessing the risk of your clients, you have a competitive advantage in relation to your competitors in the market, who cannot assess the risk precisely and therefore need to overprice their fares. I'm purely reasoning Kafkaesque now; it is very absurd, but actually, this is the direction in which we are strolling now' *(cpl 8)*.

Other ways of determining this benchmark is by means of information from the regulator. 'We also ask the regulator how we are positioned within the sector. We check with other banks of the same size how they do it and when these parties confirm our practice, it is ok' *(cpl 14)*. Then again, not all compliance officers have this kind of positive experience with information provision by the regulator: 'I've also asked: how do we compare to other banks? Ah, we don't know. So they will not examine the money laundering reports' *(cpl 2a)*.

The market remains the major benchmark for AML investments, although information from the regulator is important: 'There are a number of stakeholders, such as regulators who say: it needs to be stricter, legislation should be stricter and then we state: we also should take account of the fact that a number of money launders find the loopholes. To find the balance is difficult. But that balance will not be found in legislation, the balance is found in the fact that banks keep looking at each other' *(cpl 3)*.

There are limits to the degree of information exchange. First of all, some of the smaller banks say that they do not know how strict the large banks' AML procedures or policies are. Secondly, in spite of everything, each bank and each compliance department is responsible for managing its own risks. Even though compliance officers state that AML is not an issue on which there is a direct competitive aspect, every bank chooses its own path and tries to prevent its own losses. 'At the end of the day it's about your own company. And no one will come and save me' (cpl 9). Another restraint in AML-cooperation is the fact that it is practically impossible to design a system that suits all banks at the same time: 'there are different clients, different business lines, different risks to manage... There are many different organisations, it's not possible to attune this to each other' *(cpl 9)*. We can therefore conclude that there is an exchange of information between banks regarding the level of AML, but the information that is shared is limited (which could be due to the importance of AML with regard to its impact on the competitive position) and concrete cooperation is difficult.

MUTUAL RELATIONS WITHIN THE AML COMPLEX

Mutual relations within the AML complex are important with regard to the proper functioning of the AML-chain and may add to (or downgrade) effectiveness. We therefore asked all respondents – compliance officers, regulators and law enforcement representatives – for their opinions on the interactions between the associates in the AML complex. It soon became clear that some of the respondents still have (reciprocally held) prejudices towards the other parties. The relationship between law enforcement and compliance departments, for example, is not an easy one, partly due to incidents in the past. Compliance officers are, in their daily AML-activities, frequently confronted with the regulator, the FIU, and the police, which is why these actors are discussed here.

The compliance function: gatekeeper to the AML chain, actor in the AML complex

Eight years after the introduction of the compliance function, after a period of evolution and growth, both the compliance officers themselves and the authorities state that a professional sector has emerged in which banks have invested money, time and effort. Not only has the function of the compliance officer progressed, the attitudes of banks and bank employees have also evolved towards a higher awareness of the risk of non-compliance. Banks now realise that a compliance function is needed. 'In 1996 "compliance" meant: make sure that there are no huge transactions of drug money, but the last ten years this has grown considerably' *(cpl 7)*.

This, however, does not imply that all banks adopt a cooperative or even pro-active attitude. In a minority of small financial institutions, the compliance function still needs attention. A very small number of compliance officers are still in the process of struggling for the creation and/or the scope of their position within the bank. 'It is new, from 2001, and needs to grow, continuously evolving, which means that we are up to our necks in work. That is normal for a new function that is very focused within a highly regulated environment' *(cpl 2a)*. Although none of the respondents applied this to their own position, they noted other compliance officers who were having difficulties: 'I can imagine that in some banks it is different; that compliance is just advisory or stands less firm and has to carry out what the board of directors prescribes. Or that someone writes a policy and that the board of directors says: withdraw that document and write this or that' *(cpl 14)*. 'For some compliance officers this is the case: out of fear for keeping their jobs they will represent certain things differently than in reality' *(cpl 14)*.

In relation to specific cases or clients, compliance officers sometimes still seem to be confronted with reluctant directors or colleagues, as a result of conflicts between commercial goals and compliance-objectives. The difference in attitude towards compliance issues between commercially oriented employees on the one hand and compliance-departments on the other hand mainly surfaces in discussions about specific cases. It can be difficult to explain to colleagues why a client-relationship should be terminated, whilst this client is very profitable for the bank. 'One of the challenges or dilemmas is to reconcile the commercial aspects and compliance aspects. It is a matter of short, medium or long term policy. Commercial employees mainly think on a short term, while we – as compliance – think on the medium- or long term' *(cpl 6c)*. Compliance departments see themselves as those who draw the lines and define the boundaries for commercial activities. 'People are never satisfied because there are always little rules that are not respected or we ask too much information from the clients, service is not quick enough...etc. This is also the case with the branches who say to us: you always need to authorise everything or more documents and that takes time. Our job is to say what the laws are and how far they can go, while respecting the laws and doing business' *(cpl 4)*.

On a more general level however (a non-case specific level), most banks are convinced of the usefulness of compliance, specifically when it comes to protecting the bank's interests. Generally speaking, we can say that banks recognise the importance of the formal creation of a compliance function, responsible for AML-implementation. This view is supported by several authorities within the AML complex (the regulator, the FIU and the police): 'I would describe it as a very professional sector. It has become one of the core-activities of a bank' *(FIU)*. 'I have the impression that banks are imbued with the necessity of the law, and that they report when they have to. They know that if they do not report and we can prove that they should have, it will have consequences for the bank' *(pol 1a)*.

The regulator

The regulator carries out inspections with regard to the functioning of the compliance department. The inspections by the regulator seem to be mainly aimed at procedures and processes, and are less focused on an in-depth review of the AML system. 'They do ask: do you have a system, how does it work, are there scenarios... but they have not really concretely....' *(cpl 2b)*. Nonetheless, all banks state that the regulator knows what they are doing and how. Inspections or audits are carried out on a structural basis, and many banks express a need for more feedback on the quality and functioning of their compliance departments. The level and depth of monitoring by the regulator also varies according to the type of financial institution and the associated risk. The regulator has adopted a 'risk based approach' in their evaluations.

The regulator's opinion on how compliance departments currently work is rather positive. After an adjustment period in 2004, everything now seems to be functioning well: there were compliance charters put in place, and banks were well aware of the necessity of compliance. This is also illustrated, according to the regulator, by the fact that Belgian institutions are rarely mentioned with regard to money laundering, in, for example, the US. 'I have the impression that we are rather careful' *(REG 1)*. Furthermore, it could well be the case that the largest impact of AML is not so much in detection, but in its preventive activities (such as identity checks, and so on): 'I personally wonder whether it is not the preventive effect that is more important than the cases they (the banks, cfr) actually detect' *(REG 1)*.

A number of banks say that there is structural and constructive contact with the regulator, while others state that cooperation is limited to audits and the recommendations that follow from these audits. The majority of the compliance officers would welcome more specific information on how they assess the quality of compliance practices by the bank, and support in case of problems. Others wish to have more training or education on compliance matters, as the regulator now only takes up a monitoring role, not an educative role. Compliance departments do express the hope that the regulator will treat them as a discussion partner in the future, for example when new regulation is imminent.

While banks are looking for more contacts, so is the regulator. The regulator emphasises that they are open to more structural consultation with the compliance sector, but that they lack a contact person for the whole sector. At the moment, they state that they have no overview of how many people are working on compliance and how compliance is organised within the bank. As such, a compliance association would be very helpful to structure consultation between compliance and the authorities, and the regulator is hopeful that periodic – and closer – contact will be the result.

The FIU

With regard to the FIU, we must first note that there is a level of appreciation by compliance officers as to the way they position themselves in the AML chain. Although sometimes referred to as 'an ivory tower', it is precisely this position in the AML chain that enables the FIU to play an independent role, which is reassuring for compliance departments. The FIU performs a filtering function, acting as a barrier between the financial institution and the public prosecutor. This implies that it is 'safer' for banks to report because files do not directly fall into the hands of the police or public prosecutor (and hence, the press). Some compliance officers remark that the reporting system would not function if they were obliged to report directly to the police or public prosecutor. The FIU itself underlines the good relations with the banks in money laundering matters: when information is needed, banks are very willing to provide this. This information flow has been stimulated by the recent introduction of an online-reporting system. Financial institutions are responsible for the majority of the reports that the FIU receives, and also qualitatively (as regards the content of the reports) banks represent the best reporting group (CTIF-CFI, 2008).

Although banks are in favour of the filter function of the FIU, there are some critical remarks. Examples of matters broached for improvement are the time the FIU takes to investigate cases and the level of information provision and feedback. Some compliance officers experience very long processing times. 'My experience is that the FIU transmits a file rather quickly to the public prosecutor in the case of files in which other banks have reported or when the client involved is known at the FIU. But sometimes we get a phone call or a fax about a report that we have made a year ago, which has been sent to the prosecutor a few weeks ago. Apparently a number of files take a long time to arrive' *(cpl 1)*. There are some explanations for this delay, such as for example, the workload of the FIU: 'the inspectors of the FIU have a mass of files and when there is no indication that a file is urgent, it will end up on the bottom of the pile. And they will be processed at the same pace, which can take a few months' *(pol 1)*. Furthermore, when international information gathering is needed and other FIUs need to be contacted, this may also take a long time.

The slow working processes of the FIU are also mentioned by the public prosecutor's office, as in many of the FIU-files that reach the public prosecutor's office, there has already been a financial investigation making the FIU report redundant. Furthermore, the police services state that the preventive AML system does necessarily not result in criminal charges, as it is sometimes easier to start from the instant crime than it is to start from money laundering and look for a connection to a crime. 'For the police, this is more successful in terms of results, and the criminal justice method will therefore be carried out more often' *(pol 4)*.

Relating to feedback to the compliance departments, a considerable concern for compliance departments, the FIU itself points out that their duty of confidentiality does not allow for more information exchange and that that the secrecy of investigation also forbids this. 'It would give a wrong signal if we would say to the banks: we have reported that person. Because an indication does not equal evidence' (*FIU*). Concerning feedback on the quality of cases, they also signal problems: 'It would give them no information: whether we transmit files to the public prosecutor's office has nothing to do with the quality of the report by the bank, it has everything to do with the results of our own investigation' (*FIU*). This is confirmed by the police services: 'this could lead to blacklists and the principle of "once a criminal, always a criminal", which is not a good development. We don't want to end up in a police state' (*pol 1*). But we must note here that, whilst the lack of feedback can be explained by referring to confidentiality, the lack of information provision cannot. When we see this within the framework of the current philosophy within the Belgian police – as one of the police services noted – this method of working is not very productive. After all, the fact that banks need to establish their reporting policy on – basically – their own reports, can be considered more as a type of reactive policing; instead of using the available data and information to gain a better, more profound insight into the phenomenon, based on an analysis of a combination of sources (intelligence-led policing), this same information is recycled.

Although the police and the FIU work closely together, information management by the FIU still needs some work and could be refined. One of the police respondents gave the following example: 'annual reports of the FIU more or less remain in the same framework. When we make suggestions they interpret this as criticism, while other possibilities would give richer information. With the sources they have now, they could be able to retrieve more information' (*pol 4*). Further criticism by the police is mainly aimed at the position of the FIU in the AML system, stating that FIUs are expensive organisations ('with no police skills on investigations whatsoever' (*pol 1*)) that have grown out of proportion ('creating their own economy' (*pol 2*)) and hinder a quick flow of files through the system, completely surpassing the goal of the AML-chain: 'This while the philosophy of the system is based on a continuous flow of these reports: you cannot demand from the banks that they report within a certain time span, if you know that from the time you push "send", a time span develops of not just days, but years. If you want to relate this to preventing abuse of the financial system, there should be a time limit. You cannot oblige the banks to train people, to develop infrastructure, to comply with all kinds of legislation under penalty of whatever ... and then fall into a system in which we have 14 months to deal with this report. The seriousness and logic is completely missing' (*pol 2*).

These issues raise important questions with regard to the effectiveness of the current AML chain. When both police and compliance departments have these kind of reservations towards the operation of the AML chain, this calls for a more in-depth study of the problems related to the execution of anti money laundering legislation and the position of the FIU in all this.

The public prosecutor

Direct contact between the public prosecutor's office and compliance departments is very limited, as these contacts often pass through either the FIU or the police. Nevertheless, a number of compliance officers remarked on the manner in which investigations are carried out. A comment that was frequently made, for example, concerns the fact that during investigations by the public prosecutor's office, the suspect is told (in most cases by the police) which bank has made the report. This is not an isolated incident, but was quoted repeatedly by different banks. 'The client came to us and said: you have reported me, I was invited to the public prosecutor's office and before me, on the table, I saw faxes with your bank's letter heading' *(cpl 14)*. Clearly these practices are not very helpful in developing good relations within the AML complex. Not only does this have an effect on the relationship between the bank and the client, it may also result in dangerous situations for bank employees. 'I know there are banks where – luckily we have not experienced this until now – the employee had to act as a witness. Those kind of things are not good for a point of sale ... sometimes they are also threatened by clients "you have refused this transaction" or "you have reported us to the FIU"' *(cpl 4)*.

Certain banks have therefore pleaded for the possibility of anonymous reporting, to protect their employees, but also to prevent jeopardizing the AML system within their bank. After all, once an employee has been threatened or intimidated after reporting a suspicion, the will to report other cases will disappear. 'If an employee gets into trouble or is hurt because of a report, no employee will ever report a case any more. And in such circumstances I would not be able to oblige them to report any more either' *(cpl 15)*. And as the financial world is a small world, this news will spread, which could affect the willingness of desk employees within the financial sector. 'In one of the banks where the point of sales was assaulted and the day after, 90% of the offices knew about this' *(cpl 4)*.

The police services, who have practical experience of the functioning of the public prosecutor's office, state that there is a lack of personnel working in the financial crime departments of the public prosecutor. Some illustrate this by referring to the fact that the court in Brussels only accepts three financial files each month. According to the police service, another reason why files are dismissed at the public prosecutor level is the delay in the system: 'a number of magistrates, when the file is too old and there are no Belgian perpetrators, in which the money just passed through Belgium, will dismiss the case' *(pol 1)*.

The police services

Compliance's perception of the police

The most problematic relationship within the AML complex is that between the police services and compliance departments. In some cases relationships with the police are strained, as a result of prior cooperation (or the lack thereof) and difficulties in specific cases. On top of a number of negative experiences, this situation is even more complicated because of traditional prejudices that still exist between both worlds. One of the examples of bad experiences with police investigations is related to the problems described above on informing the client about the 'whistleblower'. Other points of criticism are mainly related to the attitude of police services, for example during investigations. Compliance officers often feel judged by the police and state that they are treated more like a suspect than as a partner in (anti) money laundering. 'You get the feeling as if you're being a target. The basic assumption is that we're accomplices and that we do everything to enable the launderer. That is just too crazy. And if you see which investments and efforts are made here, and then you still have to justify yourself...' *(cpl 12b)*. The fact that, even after years of investment in compliance and AML, they are still not treated as partners in the battle against money laundering, but more as the usual suspects, is very frustrating and can lead to a resigned attitude. 'How many banks worldwide are paying for the battle against money laundering? You would be flabbergasted. Then why don't they consider us as equal partners? Because in anti-money laundering, there is no competition' *(cpl 12a)*.

The delicate relationship between compliance on the one hand and the police on the other, is illustrated by the compliance respondents who state that they are sometimes doubtful about whether or not to report a case. As stated before, each choice (making a report or not) may have negative consequences for the bank. Some of the compliance officers feel as if they should be constantly watchful and that both the regulator and the police are stuck in their negative perception of banks in general This results in heavy workloads as more cases than necessary need to be investigated, to enhance compliance: 'We investigate too many cases. But it is very delicate to exclude certain categories of transactions, because if years later it becomes clear that these categories covered a type of crime, the government will return to the bank and say: didn't you see that? (...) And by means of a government and police or judicial services who try to prove their usefulness with regard to society, by throwing it to the media or whatever. "We have dealt with a bank". Afterwards, it could well be the case that the bank wins the procedure, but you will never hear that from the media' *(cpl 8)*.

This tendency of law enforcement officials to present themselves as crime fighters against banks, is cited by many compliance officers: 'Just to show you: we are not regarded as an equal partner, we are regarded as accomplices or.... we're responsible for everything that goes wrong. "C'est la banque!"' *(cpl 12a)*.

Next to the perceived negative attitude of police services, the compliance officers' impression of police capability to investigate fraud or money laundering cases is rather pessimistic: the police have too little expertise for complex financial investigations. 'Swift, international payments, sheets on the opening of accounts, history of an account, documents of specific transactions... often you see that they look flabbergasted, that they do not know the subject. So I hereby plead for specialised departments in the federal police' *(cpl 9)*.

Many compliance officers still feel that police and compliance still live in completely different worlds, which may result in communication problems: police have little insight into the tasks of compliance officers, while compliance officers on the other hand, sometimes perceive police activity as patronising and even naive. 'I'm going to give you an example. We were invited by the police services for a meeting on terrorist financing. They say to us: you need to check all your non-profit organisations because they are used for terrorist financing. So we look at each other: we have hundreds of thousands of non-profit organisations in our database .... they say that we need to look at certain small amounts of money that are deposited which are transferred abroad. But a youth football team, also a non-profit organisation, also receives small sums of money and may pay for their tournament abroad. How can you check all this?' *(cpl 11a)*

Obviously, these mutual perceptions are a hindrance to developing constructive working relationships between police and compliance departments. The prevalence of negative perceptions and attitudes towards other associates in the complex – sometimes based on impressions that were developed years and years ago – cannot be adding to the effectiveness or efficiency of the AML chain. It could for example result in banks developing strategies to prevent potential sanctions by the regulator or the police, whilst losing track of the 'real' objectives of the AML implementation. 'We only get hit on the head. And what you do is cover yourself against everything and try to have an audit trail so you can state: this is what we did' *(cpl 12a)*.

Police perceptions of compliance
From a police point of view, however, we hear a different story. Although some police officers do mention the possibility of banks as perpetrators ('cooperation becomes very difficult when someone is implicated as accomplice' *(pol 4)*), we noticed a relatively high level of appreciation towards compliance and AML activities. The negative attitude towards banks, as described by compliance officers, was not made explicit during conversations with police respondents. On the contrary, in general, the police were relatively positive about the AML efforts by banks, and stated that the attitude of banks has changed tremendously in the past ten years. The police also noted that banks are carrying out their reporting duties very conscientiously, in contrast with other organisations under the AML law.

The overall impression after the interviews is that police services lack a clear idea of what compliance officers actually do and represent, regarding both their expertise on (anti-) money laundering, and the efforts that are made in controlling money laundering. The police are therefore asking for more insight into compliance tasks and their knowledge of the phenomenon of money laundering, to learn from each other's knowledge and tools. 'It's the private sector and specifically banks, institutions that have more means to develop software and other tools... whereas the police is a little behind concerning equipment' *(pol 4)*. The police are willing to have a more active cooperation with compliance departments, and some have – contrary to the constitution of the current framework – even asked compliance departments to report suspicious activity to them. It seems that the police are asking to receive information on reports earlier than is the currently the case. Some compliance officers have pointed out that although the police have requested more information exchange between banks and themselves, they are not inclined to do this, not only because this type of information exchange is not allowed, but also for other reasons: 'the federal police have asked for more interaction, but we cannot do that, for reasons of privacy, but also because of the fact that the Belgium system functions through the FIU. So we make reports to the FIU and not to the police. (...) We notice a sort of competition between the FIU and the police' *(cpl 1)*. Other compliance officers welcomed closer cooperation, as it could help protect the bank's interest: 'I really think they do not know which efforts are made to guard that risk as much as possible. Because for me the principal part of our job is to safeguard our bank's name and integrity. We are working very hard with the means available. And we should have many more means, also from the outside world; liaison officers, for example: you might create a relationship based on mutual trust with one or two persons, with whom you can exchange information on a formal basis' *(cpl 11a)*.

In cases in which there is ad hoc cooperation, the police state that in large banks, compliance departments are well structured and expertly handle anti money laundering. In small banks, cases may sometimes result in problems: 'we once had a case in which we needed to freeze the safe on the day of a police operation. And two days later, we come there with the suspect and the safe is not put under seal, and the bank manager says "but I know everyone who comes here"... ' *(pol 1)*. Apart from ad hoc cooperation, there are some structural contacts between police and compliance officers, in which information is exchanged. These interactions are dependent on personal contacts between police and banks, sometimes based on years of cooperation in money laundering cases. Within these relationships, some of the compliance officers stated that the police are willing to provide information on an informal basis. 'We sometimes also exchange information with the police, practical information, but of course that is confidential and only by telephone' *(cpl 2a)*. Conversely, others refuse this kind of cooperation and state that there are no contacts with the police services prior to a report to the FIU.

We must note here that our results differ from results among French compliance officers. In one of the very few studies in this area, close cooperation was observed between compliance officers and police services in France (Favarel-Garrigues et al., 2008). The fact that the French study came to contrary conclusions

can, in our opinion, be explained by the fact that in France the majority of compliance officers are former police officers, whereas in Belgium compliance officers
are mostly economists or lawyers. The Belgian compliance officers are therefore
unable to rely on their 'old boys' network.'

Partners or associates?

We can discern a diversity of perceptions on and appreciations of each contribu-
tor to the anti money laundering battle. Mutual relations within the complex are
sometimes difficult because of problematic experiences in the past (such as
police-compliance cooperation) or because of lack of transparency (such as the
ivory tower mentality of the FIU). Important to note, however, is that some of the
difficulties are also caused by a lack of open mindedness with regard to 'other'
sectors (public versus private) or a lack of willingness to adopt another viewpoint
and try to put themselves in the position of the other parties.

We can divide the remarks that were made into two levels: a level of principle and
a practical level. On the level of principle, predominantly the problems regarding
feedback, provision of information and the position of the FIU are discussed.
These are issues that are partly due to the legislation surrounding AML, although
should the FIU have more personnel and more means at their disposal, they
would probably be able to provide more (non-case related) information.

On a practical level, relations are more problematic, as these are built on years of
frustration and mutual misunderstandings. Most of the contacts within the AML
complex take place between compliance and police officers. Compliance departments think in relatively pejorative terms about policing and their know-how,
while they experience a deprecating attitude from the police. Banks, as institutions that are burdened with the paradoxical duty to report their own clients,
while not having law enforcement as their core business, feel as if they are more
sabotaged than supported by other associates in the AML complex. This is particularly galling because in fact, anti money laundering is not something that is
needed to protect their purely financial interests. After all, banks are not victim-
ised by money laundering, the government is. The result of detecting money
laundering is profitable for governments, who have shifted this duty to the banks.
And banks are very aware of these economic forces behind anti money laundering: 'At the time of the introduction of new guidelines, the government predicted
a sum of 35 million euros of proceeds as a result from the higher amount of
reports. This makes you wonder: what does the legislator want, what is the goal of
an AML-cell? Is it about money laundering or something else?' *(cpl 6b)*. Perhaps
it is time that these joint negative perceptions are discussed openly. More transparency between all associates within the AML complex could help transform the
current associates into partners and stimulate effectiveness.

VIEWS ON THE EFFECTIVENESS OF AML EFFORTS BY BANKS

As the views of law enforcement agencies on effectiveness were discussed in the previous paragraph, here we focus on the compliance officers' perceptions of the effects of their own work. A number of compliance officers cast doubts about the actual effectiveness of this system. They wondered whether the AML systems essentially fulfil the goals that were presupposed at the time of the introduction of this system. 'In the first place, this is to suppress serious gangsterism. And I think it has an effect, at least in the financial sector: people cannot go anywhere with their money. Drugs, human trafficking, illegal weapons, we will fight this with the greatest enthusiasm. But when we see which types of transactions we also have to investigate ... that has almost nothing to do with those crimes' *(cpl 7)*.

Besides pointing out the fact that the financial sector was and still is the most targeted sector in terms of anti money laundering efforts and demands, some of the compliance officers are aware of their limited ability to detect the sophisticated criminal structures which are in part the goal of the AML legislation. 'Of course, banks are capable of seeing things. But you cannot expect a bank to find every money launderer in his database. Because the ones you find are the bad launderers, the bunglers or the amateurs ... The typical cases, everyone spots them. A homeless guy who comes into the office and hands you a sum of money .... everyone has noticed that: "this is an a-typical transaction". But when it's more sophisticated, it's not so easy' *(cpl 9)*. This also emphasises the *relativity* of the efforts and investments by the financial institutions. While millions of Euros are invested in anti money laundering activities by banks, there is a chance that the criminal groups that are actually targeted by the AML complex remain largely out of sight. One of the compliance officers stated: 'How many drug dealers have we had as a client? It could happen, and we are very careful, but this much effort for which result?' *(cpl 15)*.

The doubts with regard to the effectiveness of AML within the financial sector do not only relate to the type of crime that is targeted, but also to the (in)ability of the financial sector to exclude money launderers. 'As a compliance officer, you might say: at least you protect yourself from the outside world. But when you take all the banks of Belgium and measure the impact, you might conclude that money laundering has shifted to real estate or to offshore countries. Then you have to ask yourself how effective this is. It will only be effective if you forbid all banks to bank' *(cpl 3)*.

CONCLUSIONS

Through the introduction of anti-money laundering legislation and by making private corporations responsible for the detection and reporting of crime, governments have contributed to the *'multilateralization'* of policing (Bayley and Shearing, 2001). Compliance officers have been forced to take up a role in policing the enterprise and the client, which – contrary to private security – not only suits the purposes of the corporation, but focuses on meeting the wishes of the authorities. Financial and other institutions under the AML law were gradually urged into a framework on anti money laundering, by making governmental problems into corporate problems. After all, when banks do not comply with legislation or regulation, they can be sanctioned by the regulator, their colleague-banks and, finally, by their customers. Today, this has resulted in a very uneasy position for compliance officers, in which uncertainty and a continuous awareness of risk prevails. Immobility or at least loss of effectiveness can be the result.

Although this was not initially the objective of the research, we cannot avoid the question of effectiveness. However, none of the respondents were clear about this point, because they have no insight into the results. There are, apart from the views of the respondents, some conclusions we can draw with regard to the functioning of the system that, by its very nature, may affect effectiveness.

Within the anti money laundering complex, relations between different parties are constructed in such a way that responsibilities and liabilities are shifted mainly towards the base of the complex. Whilst the government states that the financial sector is the key to the problem, the financial sector points to their compliance officers, and they on their part, refer to the desk employees. The perception of who is in control and which party is most powerful in convincing others of their ideas, shapes the complex and hence its effectiveness. This deduction can also be made from the statements of compliance officers. They say that, with very little support from the authorities with regard to not only the provision of information that ought to feed into anti money laundering tactics and money laundering identification, but also regarding their appraisal of how banks actually fulfil their obligations, looking at relations within the complex, an outsider starts to wonder whether this complex is actually striving to fight crime. A system in which the base of the chain – responsible for the input of the system – is not supplied with information, forcing them to rely on their own information sources, on informal information exchange with other banks, or on annual accounts from their own reports, functions as a self-fulfilling prophecy as institutions are obliged to continuously confirm their own analyses. This might lead to banks using either the wrong criteria for reporting ('defensive reporting'), or those criteria that are most suitable within their commercial setting. All things considered, we cannot then be surprised that banks develop reporting strategies and policies, and base these strategies on how to most favourably protect the interests of the bank. In these contexts, 'blaming the bank' is rather easy.

A number of problematic relationships occur within the AML complex. One of the examples is the position of the FIU towards all other associates. Its role as a black box has pros and cons, but is interpreted by some as a way of providing for its own reason for existence. The FIU becomes a mystic part of the AML chain: you know the input, but not the outcome, nor what happens in between. Another example is the interaction between police and compliance employees, dominated by misunderstandings, negative experiences in the past, and relatively unconstructive attitudes towards each other. Compliance officers also finds themselves divided between a law-enforcement role on the one hand and a commercial responsibility on the other. The combination of these conflicting interests and attitudes can make the functioning of a system rather complex.

However, we should not judge the anti money laundering system by its cover. Fighting crime is not the only outcome of the complex; the prevention of criminal elements entering the financial system is also an important concern. The preventative effect of the system is probably obvious, but the problem is that there is no way to prove it (Hoogenboom, 2006). We do not know how many 'criminal entrepreneurs' have turned away from the official financial system and turned towards other channels. Clearly, it may be that there are numerous other methods to launder money, and the number of methods will probably only increase as 'formal' methods become more and more limited. We can only guess that there are certain displacement effects of the AML policy, but we have no insight as to the impact of this policy on the scope of the informal economy. With regard to activity within the informal economy, however, there are some suggestions. Van de Bunt, for example, describes how Hawala-banking can be used for the transfer of illicit funds, which may increase as a result of stricter formal economy rules (Van de Bunt, 2008). One of the police respondents for example, signalled the rising popularity of travelling with suitcases of money. Others state that offshore and tax havens constitute important 'nodes' for these kinds of illicit transfers (Brown and Cloke, 2007). The possibilities are numerous. What we do know is that the number of suspicious transaction reports made by banks in Belgium remains at a high level (CTIF-CFI, 2008), which might suggest that at least not all criminals have turned their back on the banks.

In conclusion, we should add that the power-relations between the actors may result in a system that purely functions as CCTV without the roll of film: it provides a feeling of safety, reassures the public that 'something is being done', whilst behind the cameras, when we look more closely, we don't know if anybody is watching or whether the camera is aimed at the right places. We do not know what the effects of the system are, or whether the feeling of safety is legitimate. One could wonder whether a society is willing to sow this much while not knowing what they may reap. Or are others harvesting?

REFERENCES

Law of 11 January 1993 on the prevention of the use of the financial system for the laundering of money financing of terrorism, *B.S.*, 9 February 1993
Aninat, E., Hardy, D. et al. (2002). *Finance and development*. IMF vol 39.
Bayley, D. & Shearing, C. (2001). *The new structure of policing. Description, conceptualization and research agenda*. Washington, D.C.: National Institute of Justice.

Brown, E.D. & Cloke, J.O.N. (2007). 'Shadow Europe: Alternative European financial geographies'. *Growth & Change*, 38(2): 304-327.

CBFA (2001). Bijlage aan de circulaire D1 2001/13 van 18 december 2001 over 'compliance'. CBFA.

CBFA (2001). Circulaire D1 2001/13 aan de kredietinstellingen.

CTIF-CFI (2008). *Activiteitenrapport 2007*. Brussel.

Favarel-Garrigues, G., Godefroy, T. et al. (2008). 'Sentinels in the banking industry. Private actors and the fight against money laundering in France'. *British Journal of Criminology*, 48: 1-19.

Gouvin, D. (2003). 'Bringing out the big guns: The USA Patriot Act, money laundering, and the war on terrorism'. *Baylor Law Review*, 55(101): 956.

Harvey, J. (2007). 'Just how effective is money laundering legislation?' *Security Journal*, 21(3): 189-211.

Harvey, J. & Lau, S. (2009). 'Crime-money, reputation reporting'. *Crime, Law and Social Change*, published online 25 November 2008.

Helleiner, E. (2000). *The politics of global financial reregulation: Lessons from the fight against money laundering*. Working paper 15. Centre for Economic Policy Analysis and New School of Social Research.

Hoogenboom, B. (1988). 'Commerciële misdaadbeschrijving. Over de rol van de particuliere beveiligingsindustrie'. *Justitiële Verkenningen*, 14(2): 83-107.

Hoogenboom, B. (2006). 'Voorbij goed en kwaad van witwassen'. *Justitiële Verkenningen*, 32(2): 76-86.

Levi, M. (2001). Money laundering: Private banking becomes less private. *Global Corruption Report 2001*. Transparency International.

Levi, M. (2002). 'Money laundering and its regulation'. *The Annals of the American Academy of Political and Social Science*, 582(1): 181-194.

Levi, M. & Reuter, P. (2006). *Money Laundering*. Chicago: University of Chicago.

Micucci, A. (1998). 'A typology of private policing operational styles'. *Journal of Criminal Justice*, 26(1): 41-51.

MOT (2006). Jaaroverzicht 2005 en vooruitblik 2006 Meldingen ongebruikelijke transacties.

Nivra-Nyenrode, Capgemini, Nederlands Compliance Instituut (2007). *Compliance Survey 2007*. Breukelen: Nivra-Nyenrode Press.

Patton, M. (2002). *Qualitative Research and Evaluation Methods*. Thousand Oaks: Sage.

Shields, P. (2005). 'When the "information revolution" and the US security state collide: Money laundering and the proliferation of surveillance'. *New Media Society*, 7(4): 483-512.

Spreutels, J. & Grijseels, C. (2001). 'Interaction between money laundering and tax evasion'. *EC Tax Review*, 10(1): 3-12.

Stessens, G. (2000). *Money laundering: A new international law enforcement*. Cambridge: Cambridge University Press.

Unger, B. (2006). *The amounts and effects of money laundering*. Report for the Ministry of Finance. Ministry of Finance: Den Haag.

Van de Bunt, H. (2008). 'The role of Hawala bankers in the transfer of proceeds from organised crime. In *Organized Crime: Culture, Markets and Policies*, pp. 113-126.

Van Duyne, P. (2006). 'Witwasonderzoek, luchtspiegelingen en de menselijke maat'. *Justitiële Verkenningen*, 32(2): 34-40.

Vande Walle, G. (2008). 'A matrix approach to informal markets: towards a dynamic conceptualisation.' *International Journal of Social Economics*, 35(9): 651-665.

Verhage, A. (2008). 'Between the hammer and the anvil? The anti-money laundering-complex and its interactions with the compliance industry'. *Crime, Law and Social Change*, published online 26 November 2008.

Verhage, A. (forthcoming). 'Compliance and AML in Belgium: a booming sector with growing pains'. *Journal of Money Laundering Control*, May 2009.

Corporate security and private settlement: an informal economy of justice

Nicholas Dorn and Clarissa Meerts[76]

INTRODUCTION

Whilst policing is conventionally considered to be led by public agencies, there is wide recognition of the ways in which local communities and private entities are recruited as partners in the 'ownership' and delivery of policing in its wider sense, as an aspect of governance (Garland, 2001, Simon, 2007). Within that context, there is ready recognition, and sometimes criticism, of the 'police-like' roles played by private security – sometimes supporting or complementing public enforcement and sometimes serving purely private/corporate interests (see Cools, 2002; Jones and Newburn, 1998; South, 1998; Wakefield, 2003; Johnston, 1999; Stenning, 2000; and other work mentioned below).

What, however, about the activities of private companies and public bureaucracies that produce forms of informal and private discipline and justice for their staff – including for their mid-level and high executives when they are seen to act against the interests of their employers – as a substitute for formal and public justice through the formal justice system? What of the role of corporate security companies in facilitating such private settlements? And what might be the eventual consequences of such internal and informal settlements for other private sector actors and indeed for the wider public interest? These are the concerns of this paper. The following two quotes, derived from our interviews, point to a potential contradiction in the private settlements that are brokered by corporate security.

> *'Private settlement does occur under certain conditions. This is [for example] when fear for the reputation of the victim company is present.'*

76. The authors express their gratitude to anonymous interviewees, not all of whom would necessarily agree with every interpretation made here. This paper arises from the research programme 'Regulating Corporate Crime', funded by the Executive Board of Erasmus University Rotterdam. The authors thank the University, the School of Law and Henk van de Bunt for making the research possible. The first author also acknowledges earlier, broadly related work carried out with Mike Levi at Cardiff University and funded by the European Commission (Sixth Framework Programme and DG-Justice, Freedom and Security).

'It depends on the contract the client has with its employees whether or not the reason for resignation is to be made available to future employers and thus whether the employee can repeat the behaviour when working for a different employer in the future.'

On the one hand, as will be discussed, corporate security provides valuable services to the private sector, while on the other hand, some negative consequences of the use of corporate security and private settlement seem to exist.

Exploration of this question requires an acknowledgement of the limits to much of existing scholarship on private security. There is an impressive amount of research and theory building on the subject of private security within the public sphere (for example, within local communities), however the field of corporate security within the private sphere (for example, within companies) is less discussed in academic circles. Examples of well-known and much celebrated work on private security in the public sphere include Shearing and Stenning's (1981) and Johnston's (1992) work on the upsurge and benefits of private security – and Loader and Walker's rejoinder (2006) on the necessary place of the state in the production of security, 'anchoring' private interests within a shared polity. Such work is locked in a debate on the proper balance between public and private policing within the public sphere of life (see also Button, 2002; Rosenthal et al., 2005; Cools et al., 2005). Furthermore, it is implicit in most such work that, when the security agents (be they public or private) have identified and captured serious wrongdoers, the latter would be candidates for some form of public, formal and state-provided adjudication, redress and/or punishment – typically provided by the courts (or some form of prosecutorial diversion). In other words, justice would be public even if the policing that preceded it were to be partially or predominantly private.

However, as is most persuasively illustrated by the work of Williams (2005; 2006) security as practised within the private sphere of medium-sized to large companies typically excludes not only public policing agencies but also the other institutions of criminal justice – prosecutors and courts. This non-recourse to the criminal justice system is not captured by forms of organised crime research that have an implicit or explicit criminal law and policing perspective (see for example Van Dijk, 2007; Kugler et al., 2005). Nor is it captured by a more recent tradition that places organised crime issues in the context of administrative cooperation (see for example Neelen and Huisman, 2008; Van de Bunt and Van der Schoot, 2003; Levi and Dorn, 2008). There is however a well-established stream of work on 'white collar crime' that notes its effective decriminalisation, resulting from policy ambivalence, low police prioritisation and/or judicial deference (Sutherland, 1945; Pearce, 1976; Box, 1983; Levi, 2002; see also Verhage, 2009). Yet, even there, the focus remains on forms of malfeasance by companies and/or their managers that impact externally: that is to say, upon other companies or upon the public. The present paper, by contrast, looks at how corporate actors, aided by corporate security, deal with problems internally – within their own social boundaries – and at what seems to be a silence on that topic within the public policy discourse. We would like to try to make a contribution to filling this (relative) void in scientific work on corporate security.

The paper focuses upon the ways in which in-house security departments and contracted-in corporate security services meet clients' concerns about reputation. Recently collected interview data from the Netherlands are utilised. Private investigation of those suspected of acting against companies' interests, typically followed by private settlement, serves companies' needs for maintenance of privacy, discretion and reputation (Williams 2005; 2006). Our work confirms for the Netherlands these tendencies. However, previous analyses may have taken insufficient account of some longer-term dangers implicit in private settlement, and may have engaged insufficiently with the question of why the public authorities allow corporate security such a high degree of autonomy.

Talking with corporate security practitioners

Loosely structured, lengthy and confidential interviews were conducted, primarily in the Netherlands but also in Belgium, between November 2007 and May 2008, with eleven senior persons active in or well-informed about the role of the private security sector in protecting private companies and public agencies from a variety of threats, particularly economic crimes against the companies/agencies involving their own staff (cf. Williams, 2005; 2006, more generally Van Outrive, 1999). By 'loosely structured' is meant that, although the researchers had a set of concerns, the approach taken to these concerns and their depth of coverage depended on the interviewee and his or her background and presentational style. By lengthy is meant a minimum of one and a half hours and a maximum of two and half hours. By confidential is meant that we respect the sensitivity of data concerning specific cases: we focussed on general themes, no attempt being made to obtain information about specific cases where information was not already in the public realm.

The persons interviewed were senior figures, in the sense that they either had many years operational, management and/or consultancy experience in the provision of corporate security services, or (as in the case of our public sector and academic respondents) they had closely observed it; the majority had worked both in the public and the private sector. Most have international reputations within their field, the remainder having name recognition within the industry in the Netherlands and also Belgium. Eight of the eleven interviewees were currently primarily working in the corporate security sector, while three worked primarily in the public sector; however it would sometimes be the case that interviewees, or their firms, would be providing consultancy and/or investigative services in both the private and public sectors. Thus what was discussed in interviews was provision of services to both public and private sector organisations. The span of activities ranged across international, national and local security issues faced by private companies (and in some cases by public officials). The majority of the respondents were Dutch, but two Belgian nationals were also interviewed. Most of those currently working in the corporate security sector previously worked in the police or other public security agency. Services offered included forensic accountancy (for example in relation to fraud against companies), crisis management (including anti-extortion and anti-kidnap), specialised technical services (surveillance of suspects, information technology in the case of cyber-crime), private investigation more generally, and the formulation and implementation of integrity codes. (Static guarding, visual surveillance and physical patrolling are of course also required as part of corporate security, however these relatively unskilled activities are not at the heart of the higher-level corporate security services of concern in this paper.) Our public security respondents worked in the public prosecution and in the police.

As none of the interviews were audio-taped, 'quotes' in the current paper represent the spirit of the words of the respondents, as captured from contemporaneous notes, and are not in every case the exact utterances of respondents. It is for this reason that they are presented between single quotation marks.

A VARIABLE GEOMETRY OF PUBLIC-PRIVATE DISTANCE

The appeal of corporate security

In his path-breaking work about the FACI (forensic accounting and corporate investigations) industry, James Williams claims that three factors limit the involvement of public security (the formal criminal justice system) in relation to economic crimes[77] within companies and stimulate the involvement of corporate security (Williams, 2005: 326). The first of these is 'the framing of economic crime', meaning that security providers are contracted by companies to control activities that are harmful to them, whether criminal or not (while the public security actors are only interested in activities that are criminal according to the law). This also implies that activities that are criminal but not harmful to the client may be reported to the client company but, if the latter does not see them as a priority, it may instruct its security provider to take no further action. Corporate security can adapt to this framework of its clients, as it is not necessarily bound to the legal framing of the conduct (although, where non-disclosure could later be found out and seriously embarrass the company, it may result in defensive reporting).

Likewise, some of our corporate security respondents mentioned 'conflicts of interest' as an important harmful situation for a company or organisation. While it is not a crime *per se*, conflict of interest can be very damaging to the organisation and may eventually amount to a criminal offence. Other respondents men-

---

77. We focus here on economic crimes originating within companies – by managers and other employees – and running against the interests of the same companies (as does Williams 2005; 2006, see also Karpoff et al., 2008). We are not concerned here with crimes against a company that are exclusively committed by perpetrators from outside that company, therefore we do not discuss questions related to reporting and victimisation surveys concerned with actions by outsiders.

tioned the 'shadowy area' between legal and illegal in business practices, 'especially abroad' (such as the 'smoothing along' of business through 'gift giving'). Corporate security is centrally involved in the prevention of activities that are harmful to the company, but only contingently involved in prevention of activities that, whilst they may be criminal, are beneficial to the company.

To take an example: if security providers become aware that the company hiring them is befriending local politicians or public officials – perhaps arranging opportunities for advancement by their relatives, or helping them with planning their retirement by smoothing the path to seats on company boards, all this being done to encourage a certain planning or investment decision, for example – then the security provider that turns that information over to the police or prosecutor may not get much follow-on business.

Thus the focus and activities of corporate security are at the same time broader and more narrow than that of the public sector. As Williams puts it, the FACI industry and its clients perceive the matter as follows: '(...) one of the key problems with the police is that their organizational framing of economic crime is both excessively narrow and unjustifiably broad' (2005: 326). Our Dutch (and Belgian) respondents underline this observation, pointing to corporate security's understandable tendency to protect clients' interests.

The second aspect of the FACI industry that Williams mentions is its promise of secrecy, discretion and control (Williams, 2005: 327). Of great importance for corporations in dealing with crime within and around their own perimeters, is control over the process and the outcome of investigations. This control is lost when public security actors handle the investigation (Gill and Hart, 1999: 252). As one of our respondents stated:

> 'In the private sector, control is very important and companies will try to control everything. This is a problem when a company that has been victimised goes to the police because in that case there is only one possible way to handle the matter. The big advantage of the private security sector is that the client can retain more control over the case.'

Corporate investigators can maintain secrecy and confidentiality, whereas openness and visibility are key features of public security, at least once the investigation establishes or constructs its facts and moves towards a resolution (Williams, 2005: 332). As one of our respondents stated with regard to private settlement:

> 'Information can be kept confidential. In that case the private investigation company makes a full inquiry and confronts the suspect with the findings, who has some possibility to defend himself. When it involves an employee, he or she is then given an option to resign/be fired or to have to face a civil suit.'

As the above quote shows, in its investigations and the conclusion of the case, corporate security can adapt to and respect the need for confidentiality. Our respondents confirm that secrecy is very important, since openness can lead to difficulties for the victim company, for example through damaging its reputation, which is a valuable resource (Braithwaite, 2005). In research by Karpoff et al. (2008: 582), it was found that 'reputation loss exceeds the legal penalty by over 7.5 times', which implies a significant influence of reputational issues on the preference for secrecy. Although the research by Karpoff et al. focuses on situations in which the company itself has committed the crime, it could be argued that in cases where a highly-placed executive commits the crime, this will also bring disgrace to the company and as such companies would want to keep these matters a secret.

The last of the three aspects that Williams posits as central to the appeal of corporate security is the legal flexibility of the private security provider (2005: 329). In this context, 'legal flexibility' refers to corporate security's freedom to choose which legal alternative to use (while public security actors usually are obliged to aim at criminal prosecution). The main objectives of a victim company do not revolve around punishing the offender, but '(...) (1) stopping the bleeding; (2) recovering the losses; and (3) establishing programs to minimize future losses and financial risks' (2005: 329). This is supported by our interview data. One respondent stated that the way corporate security reacts depends on the case: for example, in responding to a kidnapping of a company employee, the priority is to get the kidnapped person back safely, with money and prosecution being secondary priorities. 'Catching and trying the bad guy' is not a key objective and so responses other than criminal justice are commonly used, such as negotiating ransom money after kidnapping of executives in a foreign country. However, if the client company considers that unacceptable, or the security provider considers it could be a slippery slope to further demands, then the local police may be asked to take the lead in a joint quasi-military rescue operation.

A further example mentioned frequently by our respondents concerns suspicion of a crime by an employee against the client company. If an investigation confirms the grounds for suspicion, then the employee involved is generally fired and *may* be sued (in the civil courts) to 'get the money back'. In other cases – the majority of cases according to our respondents – the company does not want the publicity of a court case, a quiet dismissal being preferred, possibly accompanied by a written settlement. In the latter case, the (often phoney) threat that the company will bring a criminal and civil case against the employee, backed with evidence from the corporate security investigation, is enough to ensure that the employee goes quietly and on terms set out by the employer (see below).

In summary, all of the alternative legal solutions mentioned by Williams – informal settlement, firing of the employee, recovery and restitution through civil charges (2005: 329) – were spontaneously referred to by our respondents, who indicated that in the Netherlands too the majority of cases are settled in a different way than through the criminal justice system. And thus, so far, we find grounds to agree with Williams that corporate security is 'custom made justice' for companies, allowing them to 'keep the authorities out of their business' (2005: 330). According to our respondents, fear that the publication of the information will lead to damage to the reputation of the company is one of the most important motivations (see also Levi, 2002). Reasons for the clients of our interviewees to want to keep such matters out of the hands of public authorities include the loss of control over the proceedings and information, shame in relation to shortcomings of management, the need to keep customers and competitors ignorant of such embarrassments, and a low level of faith in the public authorities (similar arguments are put forward in Benson, 1998: 70-71).

However all our respondents indicated that there are circumstances in which they would suggest to their clients that they should consider reporting matters to the police (e.g. when the damage to reputation would be serious, were the issues to become public despite the existence of a private settlement).

Variations in public-private security distance

In his work on corporate security, Williams focuses on one end of the scale of public-private cooperation/isolation: that of no involvement by the public sector in the activities of the FACI industry. Interestingly, our Dutch interviews seem to indicate that this approach towards involvement of either the public or the private sector in the policing of crime is too 'either/or', in that it fails to capture a middle ground in which corporate security keeps up a dialogue with the public police, *negotiating the extent* of the privacy of its clients, rather than taking it as total and as a 'given'. Williams' statement that corporate security acts in the interest of its clients is supported by our interview data. However our respondents also suggested that corporate security can often persuade its clients that keeping open the lines of communication with the police is wise – it does not have to mean revealing a lot of information or opening the door wide to public scrutiny.

The interviews reveal a 'scale' of public police knowledge of and involvement in corporate security investigations. At the one end of this continuum is policing without any involvement by the public sector (the police being unaware that corporate security is working on a case on their 'patch'), while at the other end the public sector may be invited to take over the investigation (leaving the corporate security provider as an assistant). In between these extremes there are various modes of 'cooperation' between the public and private sector.

For instance, the police regularly hire corporate security firms to perform some activities for which they themselves lack sufficient resources, for example to provide technical services in the context of a police-led investigation of crimes against a company. It also often happens that the public authorities are informed about the existence of a private investigation, either while still in progress (giving just an outline, not necessarily the identity of the client company) or at the end of the investigation (either saying that the matter has resulted in internal company discipline or, more rarely, seeking a prosecution). This notification can either be an official report of an alleged crime (necessary if the company is seeking insurance money and/or prosecution, see below); or alternatively an 'off the record' informal notification. The latter is likely when the client company wants to deal with things itself, with the assistance of corporate security, but the corporate security firm considers it prudent to assure colleagues within the police that all is well, thus keeping them 'in the loop' and 'on-side'. Also, in the event that the internal settlement should fail and that the company feels it has to fall back upon the police, it is easier to do so if police officers already have some background information.

In general, our respondents agreed that many crimes (we have insufficient information to speculate whether a minority or majority) against companies are not formally reported to the public authorities. Interestingly, this also holds true for governmental organisations that have become the victim of certain crimes, even though there is an obligation for organisations in the public sector to report crimes (although in the Netherlands and common law countries, unlike those operating under a Napoleonic code, the police have discretion as to the extent to which they investigate).

In which circumstances, then, might companies and their security providers forgo all those advantages and decide to go to the police and prosecutors? One important reason, according to our respondents, is violation of trust.

> 'The most important drive to report a crime is the violation of trust, both in the internal form (the trust inside the organisation is breached) as the external form (the trust of e.g. the voters, clients or society as a whole is breached) depending on the situation.'

For companies in the private sector, this violation of trust manifests itself as a feeling of a moral duty to report, in order to prosecute and in order to show its social responsibility.

> 'It sometimes happens that the company is so shocked that it wants to report the crime(s) and set an example for the rest of the company.'

> 'Sometimes they feel it is their moral duty to go to the police. Furthermore it shows that the company is dealing with it, which can be good for the reputation. The company is showing its responsibility towards society.'

Another reason to make a formal report to the police is that such a report is a necessary prerequisite to any insurance claim, which becomes a consideration if a loss has occurred and if it is large in relation to the organisation's budget (source: several interviewees).

So far, our research in the Netherlands largely supports Williams' contention that public and corporate security move in different jurisdictions, defending different interests and following a different logic (2005: 330-332). Williams points out that it would be nonsense to talk about privatisation in these circumstances, since such crimes are not publicly handled in the first place: the two forms of security move in a different jurisdiction and are not 'fishing in the same pond'. This is borne out by our respondents' observation that, even when corporate security gives the police or prosecutors some information on crimes that are of considerable concern to private companies (for example on intellectual property theft), often the public authorities seem to do nothing. This suggests that these are not the crimes that interest the criminal justice system most. As Gill and Hart (1999: 252) claim, 'there is supporting evidence that the public police regard crime within the workplace to be of secondary concern (...) and that they prefer to concentrate their resources on dealing with offences against the general public'. Williams explains this by stating that, in the light of the high political risks and the low symbolic rewards associated with these crimes, the criminal justice system is willing to 'cede its jurisdiction and responsibilities for financial crime to the private sector' (2005: 333). One of our respondents furthermore elaborated this normative conception, saying that public and private security have differing interests, with public security investigating for the 'public good' and corporate security investigating 'private troubles'.

SOME WEAKNESSES OF PRIVATE SETTLEMENT

'You [may] amplify the problem by keeping it a secret and removing restraints for the potential perpetrator. The wish to keep things secret often results in non-adequate sanctions.' (Interviewee)

We come now to the question of whether, in the private settlements that typically make up the final phase of corporate security/FACI investigations, it is possible to discern elements of, on the one hand and for a temporary duration only, gross inequality of resources and possibly unfairness in the relationship between the client company and the person who has been investigated (an 'inequality of arms', in legal terms); and, on the other hand, for the future, complete freedom of the person accused to go forth and do elsewhere what he or she has just been investigated for.

The power imbalance in the private settlement process

We start by acknowledging the power imbalance that exists between those who can afford to hire corporate security (the client company) and those who generally cannot (persons under investigation – the company's employees, for example). This quite normal information and power imbalance is increased through the use of corporate security, which collects information about the less powerful party and gives it to the more powerful party. The company can then 'negotiate' with the suspected employee. Typically, some alternative outcomes are presented, from which the employee can 'choose': (voluntary) resignation, a civil suit or criminal charges (or possibly a combination of these alternatives).

This can fairly be characterised as 'negotiation under duress'. One of our respondents used the term 'soft blackmail' for these kinds of situations. When private sector 'negotiation' takes the place of public sector criminal justice processes, then the procedural guarantees that are present in criminal procedure, such as the right to defend oneself and the presumption of innocence, are at best somewhat diluted. In most cases, our respondents told us, they would suggest to the client company that nothing is lost by giving the accused person an opportunity to explain him- or herself; and that the client company would be wise to follow its established disciplinary procedure, remembering that not to do so would look very bad in the small number of cases that fail to be resolved by private discussions and which become public.

However, the power imbalance clearly remains – for as long as the employee remains in that relationship.

A crime skills-learning and displacement scenario

In some of our interviews with corporate security providers and public integrity advisers, we asked about the longer term consequences of dealing with problems in this manner. We started by asking about the presumed crime prevention potential: that persons investigated receive a nasty scare and decide to do nothing questionable in the future. However, from the hesitations of some respondents – and then from some direct statements made – we began to pick up the fact that at least some of our respondents had serious doubts about the longer-term consequences of private settlements.

These doubts fall into two categories, the first of which is displacement: persons investigated and their dubious skills are displaced to other companies. Secondly, our respondents refer to crime-facilitation: a learning process could occur on the part of persons investigated and accused, leading them to become more aware of how they had come to be investigated and hence of how to avoid that in the future. By the end of the research we began to wonder if some of those who might have been falsely accused, and who might have accepted termination of employment because of a mixture of shock and inability to present proof of innocence, might turn to crime subsequently; however we have not researched that question. We did not ask all our respondents about these possibilities, because the themes emerged only tentatively from some of the interviews – and we had not been alerted to it by our reading of the published literature. We became alerted to the issue little by little.

To give an example of these issues, one of our respondents mentioned that private security does not always take the longer term (or the bigger picture) into account when providing for a solution in a particular situation. In responding to most instances of employee crime, secrecy is maintained – other companies and the authorities are not informed – leading to a situation in which an employee who has committed a crime against his or her employer can repeat the act at his or her next job. An agreement not to disclose the reason for resignation, which is common according to our respondents, prevents disclosure in an employment reference. In this way, the use of corporate security could allow company employees and others to build up a criminal career, learning from how they had been caught, taking safeguards against making the same mistakes again, and developing their skills in another company or market.

We were alerted to the possibility that informal transmission of information to other companies might occur, regardless of a non-disclosure agreement. This possibility and the conditions under which it might occur – e.g. in a local context, which implies that the informal system would not operate when the ex-employee moves further afield – deserves further attention in future research.

It was suggested to us by some respondents that learning and deepening of criminalisation may be more likely for those relatively high up in the organisation, for the following reason. When a person with high standing defrauds the company, disclosure of this would be particularly bad for the company's reputation. An agreement on confidentiality is therefore likely to be actively sought by the company, and in pursuit of this it may be prepared to forego attempts to retrieve any money lost and even give quite generous severance payments – anything as long as the matter is brought to a quiet conclusion. By contrast, if a person who is of a low rank inside the company 'goes public', this will not damage the company very much, as it can more easily claim that the person was fired because that kind of behaviour cannot be tolerated by the company (which might even strengthen the reputation in this case).

As we have seen, while providing a short term solution in a specific case, corporate security might actually through its use of private settlement create, reproduce and amplify the problem in the longer term (this is what we mean by 'the contradiction in corporate security'). The bottom line is that there is a hardly-touched research agenda here, concerning the wider criminal consequences of private settlement, and the ways in which these processes and consequences may be shaped by the economic and social level of the persons who are investigated and quietly displaced to new pastures. In this paper we do not claim to have answers to these questions but we do draw attention to them, believing they deserve more research attention than they seem to have attracted so far.

SPANNING MULTIPLE LEGAL ORDERS

In terms of broad distinctions between public and private, Williams' work focuses on private sector providers of security services to the wider private sector, who employ these services: a system of 'private legal orders' (Williams, 2006; Shearing, 2006; Shaffer, 2008).

One query and possible extension of that thesis is whether public sector organisations – state entities and agencies at federal, regional or local levels – might also have an interest in acquiring such services from private providers. From the limited work undertaken in the Netherlands by the present authors, the answer to this appears to be an affirmative, implying an extension of 'private legal orders' into the state.

Why does such private policing exist? Williams rejects the answer of what he calls the 'shift thesis' – the widely accepted notion that some functions of the public police force have become privatised because the public sector could not cope with the growing demand for these services (Williams, 2005: 323). One can, for instance, find the shift thesis in the work of Benson (1998), who claims that what he calls 'private justice', is a natural reaction to the failing of the criminal justice system to prevent and repress crime adequately.

Instead, Williams states that the public police and corporate security actors move in entirely different jurisdictions, because they have fundamentally different interests and mandates. Williams' 'juridification thesis' states that it is not possible to speak of 'privatisation'. The activities of the FACI industry are inherently different from those of the police, who have never been much involved in this area of crime control – echoing observations made in the classic work of Sutherland (1945), in contemporary work by fraud specialists such as Levi (1992) who remark on fraud being 'under-policed', and the claims of critical criminologists that 'crimes of the powerful' are left unpoliced (Pearce, 1976), whilst crimes of the powerless are focussed upon by the criminal justice system (Box, 1983). Corporate security offers companies faced with problems of financial loss and reputational risk an opportunity to deal with these matters in a way that is compatible with their specific interests and needs. By employing corporate security services, companies maintain control of investigations and of any actions taken (whilst by contrast the public police might 'take over'). Furthermore they keep embarrassing matters private, thereby safeguarding their public reputation, consumers' loyalties and managers' career chances (Williams, 2005: 325; 2006: 219).

In short, Williams' answer to the question why the state allows corporate security to function autonomously, helping private sector companies to keep their 'dirty washing' out of the public view – and out of the criminal justice system – is limited to his historical observation that the state never did have much of an interest in policing within the corporate sphere. That might be so, however it remains at a descriptive level and does not explain the 'why'.

One possibility might be to think more broadly about multiple legal orders – here we mention four (there could be, of course, other legal orders, depending on how they might be defined, but for our purposes the ones mentioned are most relevant). The first of these is public sector law, for example criminal law. The second is private sector law, such as that regulating labour relations. These first two can be seen as 'formal justice systems', as they come forth out of formal (state) channels (Wojkowska, 2006: 9). Community based regulation, such as (informal) conduct norms in a neighbourhood, can be seen as the third legal order of importance here.

Finally, Mafia-like organisations, providing their own internal regulations, form a fourth possible legal order. These last two can be seen as 'informal legal orders', not originating from state agencies, but from informal channels such as communities (whether these are 'legal' or 'illegal' communities) (ibid., p. 9).

Williams sees the FACI industry as a 'private legal order', performing 'ordering functions [in] regulatory spaces between states and markets' (Williams, 2006: 210). We prefer to refer to *multiple* legal orders, in order to differentiate the corporate security sector from other legal orders that are strictly private. As Williams (2006: 219) himself also states, corporate security or FACI actors move in a space that is hybrid, in that it incorporates elements of both the public as the private sphere. Furthermore, as explained above, we see legal orders in a different light, dividing them into *formal* and *informal* justice systems, not merely following the *public* and *private* divide.

As we have seen above, private settlement has elements of both formal and informal justice systems. We suggest that private settlement through corporate security 'floats' between, or alternatively forms a bridge between, formal and informal justice systems. This is schematically presented in figure 1 below: private settlement uses elements of private or civil law in its agreements to 'settle' the matter with the suspected person. Furthermore, both private and public law can be used as a 'stick behind the door' against a suspected person, to enhance the incentives for them to cooperate with the form of settlement preferred by the clients of corporate security firms. In this sense, private settlement has one foot in the formal justice system. On the other hand, private settlement as used by corporate security and its clients is also community based, insofar as it involves informal bargaining, and an element of coercion, without direct public oversight.

It could be argued that this hybrid character is appealing both to clients of corporate security and the state. The widely acknowledged impossibility for the state to handle all crime related matters itself[78] makes the use of other elements of the formal justice system than that of the criminal justice system (such as civil law) 'the next best thing'. However, as both Williams' and our own work shows, seeing corporate security as being just another part of state control would be too simplistic a view. We suggest that there is a need to develop an analytical framework that integrates parts of formal justice systems with parts of informal justice systems – not favouring a state-led over a private sector-led system, nor a 'formal' over an 'informal system', but rather integrating both into a hybrid system. To make a hybrid system flexible enough for it to be advantageous to companies, it includes elements of informal justice systems, as we have seen. As stated above, clients highly value a settlement that is both non-state and professional, which implies some measure of formalisation. The professionalism and flexibility of corporate

---

78. This reasoning forms the basis for e.g. the principle of opportunity that is used by the Dutch criminal Prosecution Office to decide which cases to prosecute (Groenhuijsen, 2002: 437).

security secure the most beneficial traits of both formal and informal justice systems for victim companies.

Figure 1   Private settlement as a bridge between formal and informal justice systems

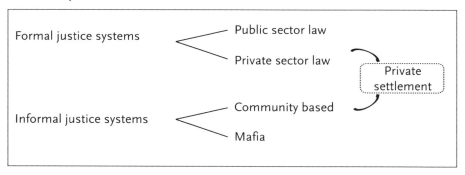

Whilst further work would be needed to determine why the state allows this hybrid, formal/informal and largely private arrangement to continue, our hypothesis (in line with the general thrust of Williams' juridification thesis) is simply that, historically, the state always had conceded to market participants the responsibility to settle their disputes. Only when private settlements seem unduly coercive does the state directly take a hand – and corporate security firms provide a professional framework of working within which such overt abuses are reduced. Whether or not this arrangement is satisfactory, in the light of the possibility of crime displacement and facilitation over the longer term, is a rather provocative policy question.

CONCLUSION

Criminology generally and this edited volume specifically focus on illegal activities by individuals and enterprises on the one hand, and enforcement agencies and criminal justice systems on the other hand, and on interactions between these actors, within wider political, economic, social and cultural environments. In short, the focus of dramatic encounter is between the state and informal economies. By contrast, a study of the role of private security firms in facilitating private settlements in corporate settings concerns activities within the formal economy, but outwith the state. In the formal economy, the state cedes direct control, allowing private entities and public organisation to 'police' their internal economies. This is justice as the formal economic actors prefer it: quick, quiet and (at least in its immediate, short-term aspects) cost-effective for corporate entities. As Williams (2005; 2006) clearly pointed out, this informalisation of justice within the formal economy does not mark a retreat of the state, since the state never took direct command of such issues.

This paper has explored the involvement of corporate security in the control of serious economic crimes against companies or organisations in the Netherlands, especially those crimes involving (sometimes exclusively) managers or other senior staff within the organisation. The points of view engaged with here are those of some providers of security services and some observers from the public sector. Our respondents, read against the existing literature, justify a conclusion that the 'policing' (investigation) of these matters, and the settlement of them, typically without direct involvement of the public police, constitute an arena of informal justice.

Analytically, corporate security and private settlement amount to an informal economy of the machinery of justice: what might have been expected to be a realm of public, formal justice, turns out to be informal, non-transparent and privately governed. Justice here is an aspect of the economy, not of the state. How this is to be evaluated in policy terms depends, of course, on the perspective adopted. On the one hand, these procedures offer considerable advantages for the public and private organisations involved; on the other hand, there are risks for other organisations and potentially for the wider public interest.

For private sector companies (and sometimes public sector organisations) who experience crime or integrity problems that may have an internal dimension, the private, confidential and controllable nature of corporate security has certain strategic advantages over a public security sector solution, and in this respect this work broadly replicates for the Netherlands some observations made for other countries. In line with Williams' (2005; 2006) remarks about the FACI industry, our interviewees agree that involvement of corporate security is generally accepted by public security actors, even if that acceptance may be sometimes 'rather ambiguous' (private sector interviewee). Although the notion of 'public-private cooperation' has become something of a political totem (Dorn and Levi, 2008), it would be wrong to regard corporate security and the public authorities as always having a close relationship outside matters of contract. The private sector and also many public sector organisations purchase specialist services from corporate security providers in order to safeguard their own economic and reputational concerns.

However, finessing previous research, our work suggests that contacts and cooperation between corporate security investigators and public police agencies vary along a continuum: sometimes no contact, sometimes keeping the public police informed in broad terms, and (rarely) drawing them into the action. Our respondents suggest that this is most likely to occur in cases of a serious breach of trust and/or when a large economic loss can be offset by an insurance claim.

Finally, and breaking new ground, we point to certain possible dangers inherent in the private settlements that are made possible by corporate security investigations, calling for further research on criminal displacement and on the potential for development of criminal careers amongst at least some of those who are 'let go' by private settlements. We claim that the tentative advances made by this research merit attention in future, more extensive work.

REFERENCES

Benson, B. (1998). *To serve and protect; Privatization and community in criminal justice*. New York: New York University Press.

Box, S. (1983). *Power, crime and mystification*. London: Routledge.

Braithwaite, J. (2005). *Markets in vice, markets in virtue*. Sydney and New York: Federation Press and Oxford University Press.

Bunt, H. van de & Schoot, C. van der (eds.) (2003). *Prevention of organised crime: A situational approach*. Den Haag: Boom Juridische uitgevers.

Button, M. (2002). *Private policing*. Cullompton: Willan.

Cools, M. (2002). 'Onderstromen in de private veiligheidszorg'. In J. Mulkers (ed.), *Ontwikkelingen inzake private opsporing*. Antwerpen: Maklu, pp. 41-64.

Cools, M., Ponsaers, P., Verhage, A. & Hoogenboom, B. (2005). *De andere rechtsorde: Demonopolisering van fraude-onderzoek*. Brussel: Politeia.

Dijk, J. van (2007). 'Mafia markers: assessing organized crime and its impact upon society'. *Trends in Organized Crime*, 10(4): 39-56.

Dorn, N. & Levi, M. (2008). 'Private-public or public-private? Strategic dialogue on serious crime and terrorism in the EU'. *Security Journal*, Available at: http://www.palgrave-journals.com/sj/journal/vaop/ncurrent/full/8350086a.html.

Garland, D. (2001). *The culture of control: crime and social order in contemporary society*. Chicago: Chicago University Press.

Gill, M. & Hart, J. (1999). 'Private security: enforcing corporate security policy using private investigators'. *European Journal on Criminal Policy and Research*, 7(2): 245-261.

Groenhuijsen, M. (2002). 'De dreigende verdachtmaking van het opportuniteitsbeginsel in het Nederlandse strafprocesrecht'. *Delikt en Delinkwent*, 32(5): 437-445.

Johnston, L. (1992). *The rebirth of private policing*. London: Routledge.

Johnston, L. (1999). 'Private policing in context'. *European Journal on Criminal Policy and Research*, 7(2): 177-196.

Jones, T. & Newburn, T. (1998). *Private security and public policing*. Oxford: Clarendon Press.

Karpoff, J., Lee, D. & Martin, G. (2008). 'The cost to firms of cooking the books'. *Journal of Financial and Quantitative Analysis*, 43(3): 581-612.

Kugler, M., Verdier, T. & Zenou, Y. (2005). 'Organized crime, corruption and punishment'. *Journal of Public Economics*, 89(9-10): 1639-1663.

Levi, M. (1992). 'Policing the upper-world; towards the global village'. In D. Evans, N. Fyfe & D. Herbert (eds.), *Crime, policing and place; Essays in environmental criminology*. London: Routledge, pp. 217-232.

Levi, M. (2002). 'Suite justice or sweet charity? Some explorations of shaming and incapacitating business fraudsters'. *Punishment and Society*, 4(2): 147-163.

Levi, M. & Dorn, N. (2008). 'Public-private security cooperation'. In E. Savona, (ed.), *Organised crime in the EU: A methodology for risk assessment*. A study financed by the European Commission – DG Research under the Sixth Framework Programme. Rotterdam: Erasmus University Rotterdam, pp. 204-231.

Loader, I. & Walker, N. (2006). 'Necessary virtues: the legitimate place of the state in the production of security'. In J. Wood & B. Dupont (eds.), *Democracy, society and the governance of security*. Cambridge: Cambridge University Press, pp. 165-195.

Neelen, H. & Huisman, W. (2008). 'Breaking the power of organized crime? The administrative approach in Amsterdam'. In D. Siegel & H. Neelen(eds.), *Organized crime: culture, markets and policies*. New York: Springer, pp. 207-218.

Outrive, van L. (1999). 'Morphologie des agents et agences privées dans six pays'. In J. Shapland & L. van Outrive (eds.), *Police et securité: Contrôle social et interaction public/privé*. Paris: L'Harmattan, pp. 179-194.

Pearce, F. (1976). *Crimes of the powerful: Marxism, crime and deviance*. London: Pluto Press.

Rosenthal, U., Schaap, L., Riessen, J. van, Ponsaers, P., Verhage, A., Mechelen, P. van and Cools, M. (2005). *In elkaars verlengde? Publieke en private speurders in Nederland en België*. Politiewetenschap no. 24, Programma Politie en Wetenschap. Zeist: Uitgeverij Kerckebosch.

Shaffer, G. (2008). *Business and law: A theory of dynamic interaction*. Minnesota Legal Studies Research Paper 08-48 (December 5), available at SSRN: http://ssrn.com/abstract=1312062. Forthcoming in D. Coen, W. Grant & G. Wilson (eds.) (2009). *The Oxford handbook of business and government*. Oxford: Oxford University Press.

Shearing, C. (2006). 'Reflections on the refusal to recognise private legal governments'. In J. Wood & B. Dupont (eds.), *Democracy, society and the governance of security*. Cambridge: Cambridge University Press, pp. 11-32.

Shearing, C. & Stenning, P. (1981). 'Modern private security: Its growth and Implications'. *Crime and Justice*, 3: 193-245.

Simon, J. (2007). *Governing through crime: How the war on crime transformed American democracy and created a culture of fear*. Oxford: Oxford University Press.

South, N. (1998). *Policing for profit: the private security sector*. London: Sage.

Stenning, P. (2000). 'Power and accountability of private police', *European Journal on Criminal Policy and Research*, 8(3): 325-352.

Sutherland, E. (1945). 'Is white collar crime crime?' In P. Bean (ed.) (2003), *Crime: critical concepts in sociology*. London: Routledge.

Verhage, A. (2009). 'Corporations as a blind spot in research: explanations for a criminological tunnel vision'. In M. Cools, S. De Kimpe, B. de Ruyver, M. Easton, L. Pauwels, P. Ponsaers, G. vande Walle, T. vander Beken, F. vander Laenen & G. Vermeulen (eds.), *Governance of Security Research Papers Series I: Contemporary issues in the empirical study of crime*. Antwerpen: Maklu, pp. 79-108.

Wakefield, A. (2003). *Selling security – the private policing of public space*. Cullompton: Willan.

Williams, J. (2005). 'Reflections on the private versus public policing of economic crime'. *British Journal of Criminology*, 45(3): 316-339.

Williams, J. (2006). 'Private legal orders: Professional markets and the commodification of financial governance'. *Social and Legal Studies*, 15(2): 209-235.

Wojkowska, E. (2006). 'Doing justice: How informal justice systems can contribute'. UNDP Oslo Governance centre, Oslo.

Intertwining between state and economy – state capture

Bojan Dobovšek

INTRODUCTION

Post-modern society is characterized by unpredictable and explicitly contradictory economic, political and social developments. Capitalist society today is characterized by economic and political globalization,[79] which is supported by the grey economy and tax evasion. One of its effects is the appearance of new and complex forms of extremely intensive and far-reaching threats to individual and collective security. State capture is one of the new complex threats to individual and collective security and is the subject of this chapter.

'Inefficient', 'contradictory', 'legally and morally controversial' are apt descriptions of the increasingly global and intensive threats posed to security in the present world, namely organised crime. Official security discourse has focused largely on the abstract security of the international community and international organizations/institutions or individual states/state institutions. These discourses therefore highlight issues of security with regard to elites and their members and challenges to security through 'internal' and 'external' threats which are widely held to be rooted in culturally, economically and socially deprived environments (Meško, 2004). Official 'understanding' of security problems and the means of resolving them have obviously been biased towards the interests of the 'civilized' world, and its elite groups and individuals. As elites are formed by politicians and the bosses from the economic sector, we will focus on the notions of state capture and abuse of state power with the purpose of gaining more money legally or illegally.

In the context of security policy, crime – particularly in its most dangerous forms, including state capture – is not being analyzed as a phenomenon rooted in state social processes and structures. Economic and political elites, which manage the mechanisms of public decision-making at the global and local level, have consciously, or unconsciously, overlooked the fact that 'society' is not only the victim of crimes, but also plays a part in the causes of these phenomena and therefore shares some responsibility for them. Phenomena such as organized crime, capa-

---

ble of influencing the political process, are rooted in an unjust social order, an extremely unbalanced distribution of material sources and goods, exploitation, isolation (for example by means of an 'efficient' immigration policy), poverty, unjustified deprivation (for example, to deny such basic rights as the right of a nation to independence), discrimination and marginalization (Kandu, 2003).

Economic exploitation (usually with the consent of the exploited), poverty, indirect discrimination, having an unprivileged status, lack of access to society's decision-making mechanisms and actual deprivation of rights for the majority of the world's population are all circumstances which explicitly demonstrate – despite the ignorance of economic and political elites – that the actual political system is quasi-democratic and the economic system (i.e. the neo-liberal capitalism) amoral, unjust and exploitative. Such processes cause antagonistic human relations ('social Darwinism' or the 'homicidal war of everybody against everybody') and are therefore, in essence, criminogenic, i.e. a security risk.[80] The post-modern capitalist 'risk society' thus facilitates the 'culture of fear'. This is due partly to an artificial fear of 'terrorism' and 'crime', fear which has its own ideological background, but which is primarily caused by ever greater economic and social insecurity. Its main features are economic violence based on the fear of unemployment, fear of losing existential security, social security and material comfort, and fear of foreigners, immigrants, and others who are regarded as un-socialised, undisciplined and non-conformist individuals and groups (Kandu, 2003). Economic problems and the grey economy have particularly been exposed in countries in transition in the EU recently. Typically various anomalies and corrupt activities arise. These activities are hard to explain using classic criminological etiology. The problem occurs especially when no clear boundary between public and private codes of action or interests are established within the state (due to the collapse of the former system and no completely defined new system), or in other words, when the executive branch of power (the state) and the economy intertwine. It often happens that one side prevails over the other in such a situation. It is not necessary that the state be the one that dominates the economy; it may be completely the opposite. Some industrial moguls can acquire influence over the state using various non-transparent means, through co-operation between high-up state representatives and wealthy businessmen.[81] This can lead to non-transparent decisions that harm the public interest, but are difficult to prove. Using the concept of state capture one can try to establish a defined framework for these very hard to prove corrupt[82] acts. Due to these problems, efforts are being made

---

80. Some researchers taking a critical position on society point to the inadequacy and questionable legitimacy of the existing social and economic system, which is clearly failing to facilitate balanced economic and social development. They see such 'dysfunctions' of the current system as indicative of an inevitable downfall of the liberal capitalist economy. Others, however, take exactly the opposite position, by claiming that the world is about to reach 'the end of history'. According to them, the capitalist market economy (and parliamentary democracy) represents the last stage of history.
81. This co-operation takes place on different foundations: a state representative can be superior to a business representative. A businessman can hold a state representative in check, or they can be equal.

to develop a methodology that will help to define precisely the content of these phenomena.

Any analysis of the literature in this area shows that numerous definitions of corruption exist – it is therefore impossible to enumerate them all. In order to set up a basic understanding of the concept of state capture, the following definition is important, stating that we are dealing with corruption when: '1. a public official[83] (A), acting for personal gain, 2. violates the norms of public office and 3. harms the interests of the public (B) 4. to benefit a third party (C) who rewards A for access to goods or services which C would not otherwise obtain' (Philip, 2001: 1-2). However, it has to be pointed out that a certain activity may be defined as corrupt even though not all four criteria are met.

Sometimes the activities of A may include a change in an administrative procedure so that the results of this process benefit C more than B. It cannot be said that A is violating the law, but A is still responsible for committing a corrupt activity in a broader sense. There are also cases where A and C work together to bring such laws and other regulations into the political process that enable A and/or C gain benefit. This shows that sometimes the legal definitions of corruption sometimes do not encompass some of the worst forms of corrupt activities. Thus, corrupt transactions can become institutionalized in the state and the economy (Philip, 2001: 3). Such a situation is already very close to the phenomenon called state capture. Here it has to be stressed that the concept of state capture refers especially to institutionalised corrupt activities.

Corruption not only distorts the economic system of a country, but also has a negative impact on its political system. Informal networks become a problem when members of such networks choose to ignore rules and legislation and focus on those actions that only benefit themselves and/or fellow members (Rose-Ackerman, 1999:3). As pointed out by Rose-Ackerman, cross-country empirical work has confirmed the negative impact of corruption on growth and productivity – even when corruption and economic growth coexist, payoffs introduce costs and distortions.

DEFINTION OF THE CONCEPT OF STATE CAPTURE

Many economists think that the major cause of corruption is ineffective regulation, but ineffective regulation and corruption are quite often the two sides of the same coin. Often corruption causes ineffective regulation, and not the other way around (Lambsdorff, 2007: 9-11).

---

82. This is not the classical form of corruption described in penal laws against, for example, bribery, but similar definitions which include patronage, nepotism, informal networks etc. Corruption in short is abuse of public office for private gain, according to Transparency International.
83. Meaning civil servants at all levels, including those in the political sphere (including judges). This term is used to avoid enumerating all those employed in the name of the state at every stage.

When defining the concept of state capture, we need to ask ourselves how various corrupt activities influence the formation of laws, rules and general regulations. This includes such phenomena as buying votes in parliament, bribing parliamentarians to adopt certain government regulations, bribing judicial decision-making and illegal financing of political parties. The European Bank Business Environment and Enterprise Performance Survey (BEEPS) distinguishes between the concepts of administrative corruption and state capture. Administrative corruption includes the activities of firms which provide illicit or non-transparent private benefits to public officials in order to change the prescribed procedures defined by administrative state regulations that govern business operations. State capture, on the other hand, denotes a situation when firms intend to influence the formulation of laws, regulations and decrees introduced by state institutions by means of illicit and non-transparent provision of private benefits to public officials (Hellman, Jones and Kaufmann, 2000: 5). Thus, we can distinguish between a corrupt activity aimed at distorting the implementation of rules, procedures and practices (administrative corruption) and a corrupt activity that distorts the basic rules of the political system (state capture) (Hellman, Jones and Kaufmann, 2002: 6).

Researcher Mark Phillip distinguishes between the concept of state capture and that of regulatory capture. 'The term capture denotes a transfer of control from A to C' (Philip, 2001: 6). We speak about regulatory capture when the regulations governing the industry and the persons implementing or issuing these regulations are subordinate to the interests of the industry. Consequently, the legislation is designed in such a way to primarily function for the benefit of the industry. Let us take the example of A (a regulatory unit), which is established to regulate and control the operation of industry in the public interest. We speak about the capturing of A when its activity is dependent on groups or individuals inside the industry which it is supposed to regulate. Regulatory capture is not necessarily illegal, nor is it necessarily corrupt. An activity is corrupt when due to a bribe, other illicit inducements or threats to public officials such as regulation that serves the interests of the industry (C) is adopted (Philip, 2001: 3). The concept of regulatory capture must not be confused with legitimate political processes such as lobbying,[84] negotiation and compromise making. For example, there are many laws which regulate relationships within industry and refer to special groups (e.g. people with disabilities). The process of passing such laws demands a great amount of consultation with representatives of these groups. These special groups try to influence the legislator in such a way as to ensure that legislation which will protect their interests will be adopted. In these cases we cannot speak about corruption, since means such as bribe or threats were not used to reach one's interests. We also cannot speak about capture, since the concept of capture,

---

84. Lobbying can be defined as a type of influencing directed at decision makers who are part of the legislative or executive branch of authority. Igliar (1996: 36) for example defines lobbying as: 'Lobbying denotes special ways of enforcing interests within the processes of political decision-making that take place in legislative and executive authority. Lobbying is unique in the fact that it is used by interest groups and not political parties as the main subject of political processes in modern society.'

if we are precise, means that, due to the influence from the industry, state institutions lose their independence in their decision-making and operation processes (Philip, 2001: 3).

The concept of state capture on the one hand widens the concept of regulatory capture as the controlling of state institutions is not necessarily done by the industry, but can be done by individuals and groups in pursuit of their own personal interests. On the other hand it means a narrowing in the sense that it refers to illicit provision of private gains to public officials through informal, non-transparent and highly preferential channels of access, or through blurred boundaries between the political and business interests of public officials. State capture refers to the influence of individuals, groups or firms (which are part of the private or public sector) on the formulation of laws, regulations, decrees and other government policies (i.e., the basic rules of the game) by means of illicit and non-transparent provision of private benefits to public officials and functionaries with the intention of gaining a certain advantage (Philip, 2001: 4).

To summarize, the concept of state capture encompasses three entities. The first entity is the 'captor' (which can be in the private sector or in the public sector), the second entity is the 'captured' (captured entities are usually laws and decrees, or to put it shortly, the state), the third entity is represented by the members of the public who are aggrieved (although usually not directly). The concept of capture denotes a situation when someone uses (abuses) the state (laws and other regulations) for personal benefits instead of in the interests of the public. Given the framework of this concept, this has to be done with illicit and/or non-transparent means.

State capture and countries in transition

'Transition' is a synonym for many negative phenomena that trouble modern society. Corruption is certainly one of these phenomena and according to many the Achilles' heel of transition countries. Due to the possibility of making fast and easy profits, corruption has global dimensions. Therefore, the conviction that it is something which concerns only poor and post-socialist countries is a misconception. However, there is no doubt that it has truly ideal conditions for development in a typical transition environment because of the many legal vacuums, the undefined relationships between individual public institutions and bodies, the loss of old values which have not been replaced by new ones, and many other unregulated areas.

A question which occurs is to what extent and why, if at all, transition countries are more susceptible to corruption than those countries that have had a system of parliamentary democracy for a longer period. The latest findings show that corruption has taken a new form in transition countries – so-called state capture. The question is whether this is a new phenomenon that has appeared in post-socialist countries only now because of transition, or whether it was already in existence and we have only now became aware of it. Most researchers studying the phenomenon of state capture have focused on examining transition countries (Lambsdorf, 2007). The question needs to be asked whether it is true that this phenomenon is connected only with post-socialist transition countries or whether it is just as typical for countries with long parliamentary traditions.

Processes known under the common name of 'transition' are not limited only to the period between 1989 and 1993 or to the continent of Europe, but are at the moment still taking place across the world. Thus, the beginning of the transition process can be seen today in many other countries in Asia and Africa (Freedom House, 2004). Transition is a term that can be understood as a transition from one system of social organization and industry to another, or from one stable phase of social development to another potentially stable phase. Some authors understand transition as a change in one and the same system and thus indicate the extent of variety in transition types. According to Leszek Balcerowicz, transition can be divided into the following types: 1) 'classical', which denotes the expansion in progressive capitalist countries between 1860 and 1920; 2) 'neoclassical', which denotes the democratization of capitalist countries after the end of World War II; 3) 'market-oriented reform' of non-communist countries from 1960 until 1990; 4) the 'Asian post-communist tradition' and 5) 'post-communist transition of European countries' at the end of the 1980s and the beginning of the 1990s (Švob-Dokič, 2000).

Although many transition types exist, we will deal with the transition type that has been marked by the events that happened 15 years ago, which drastically changed the geo-political map of Middle and Eastern Europe. The break-up of the Soviet Union, the decline of central planning economies and the formation of new independent states caused, together with the fall of the Berlin Wall, an insecure historical period of transformation (Derleth, 2000: 4). The fact is that transition, understood as a change in the system, presupposes the transformation of social parts as intentional and desired. At the same time, it is a process of changing that cannot be confined within one area and therefore always encompasses various social areas of activity. From a practical and functional point of view, the concept of transition influences the increase in market integration between supply and demand, and decreases the significance of the state, especially the classical national state, which is based on the territorial loyalty of citizens and a monopoly on the use of force (Freedom House, 2004).

According to data provided by the non-governmental organization Freedom House, there are 72 countries which can be classified as transition countries. As already mentioned, we will examine post-socialist European and some Asian countries, which have formed the territory of the former Soviet Union. The World Bank BEEPS survey from 1999 included the following countries: Albania, Armenia, Azerbaijan, Belarus, Bulgaria, Croatia, the Czech Republic, Estonia, Georgia, Hungary, Kazakhstan, Kyrgyzstan, Latvia, Lithuania, Moldova, Poland, Romania, Russia, Slovakia, Slovenia, the Ukraine and Uzbekistan.

Countries that used to have a similar social system now face similar problems. In the economic field they have had to deal with a high unemployment rate, which has created a big social problem, then with economic transformation and adapting to a market economy, as well as closing factories that have not been profitable. Political stability has been shaken by newly formed institutions that have had no legitimacy or authority for their operation (Derleth, 2000: 9). Economic anarchy and transition processes create unimaginable opportunities for corruption. The fact is that 'organized crime with corruption as a method is especially dangerous for countries that are only adapting their economy to market economy' (Pear in Ministry of the Interior, 1999: 8). Such a situation is also the basis for grand corruption, a special form of corruption, which is called state capture (Hellman, Jones, Kaufmann and Schankerman, 2000: 20).

STATE CAPTURE

Hellman indicates that, in transition economies corruption has taken a new shape – the so-called oligarchic manipulative political formation that even formulates the rules of the game according to its wishes and thus gains decisive advantage. Such behaviour is understood as state capture.[85] Although the concept of state capture presupposes a strong oligarch, it is interesting that captor firms come from a very wide area and from very different sectors. It is surprising that such companies are most probably new on the market. 'Many countries began transition as weak states unable to provide basic public goods and with a set of powerful incumbent firms (these were predominantly state owned or newly privatized) dominating their respective markets without having to resort to bribery payments' (Hellman and Kaufmann, 2001). This is precisely the reason why new firms need to use the strategy of state capture if they wish to be competitive. Individual firms adopt this strategy and create a zone of relative security and advantage for themselves, which on the other hand means significantly larger costs for others.

Regardless of various differences and particularities between various transition economies, we can define and at the same time distinguish between firms that capture (firms that want to influence the rules of the game by means of illicit and non-transparent provision of private benefits to public officials and functionaries), and firms that influence (firms that influence the rules of the game without using the means of illicit and non-transparent provision of private benefits). There is a clear division between the profits of these two groups of firms. The group of firms called 'companies with an influence', usually comprises companies originating from the former communist regime. These are generally big state-owned companies, with a larger than average market share in their sector, relatively secure ownership rights and tight formal and informal contacts with the

---

85. This statement needs to be questioned since there is no evidence that corruption does not appear in a similar form also in other countries.

state. Companies that capture have just the opposite profile. Typically these are private new[86] companies, with less secure ownership rights and weaker contacts with the state (Hellman, Jones and Kaufmann, 2000: 3).

The World Bank BEEPS survey speaks about administrative corruption and state capture (see above), and about a third phenomenon, which it calls 'influence'. The concept of influence is defined as the extent to which firms have an influence on the formation of laws, regulations and decrees set by state institutions, without using the means of illicit and non-transparent provision of private benefits to public officials (Hellman, Jones and Kaufmann, 2000: 6).

The Business Environment and Enterprise Performance Survey

The BEEPS has been carried out in three rounds in 1999, 2002, and 2005 and covers virtually all the countries of Central and Eastern Europe and the former Soviet Union. The surveys have been based on face-to-face interviews with senior managers and company owners. The first survey was undertaken on behalf of the EBRD and the World Bank in 1999-2000, when it was administered to approximately 4,000 enterprises in 26 countries. In the second round of the BEEPS, the survey instrument was administrated to approximately 6,500 enterprises in 27 countries. In the third round the BEEPS instrument was administrated to approximately 9,500 enterprises in the 28 countries covered by the second round of the BEEPS plus Turkmenistan (Albania, Armenia, Azerbaijan, Belarus, Bosnia and Herzegovina, Bulgaria, Croatia, Czech Republic, Estonia, Serbia and Montenegro,[87] FYROM, Georgia, Hungary, Kazakhstan, Kyrgyzstan, Latvia, Lithuania, Moldova, Poland, Romania, Russia, Slovak Republic, Slovenia, Tajikistan, Turkey, Turkmenistan, Ukraine and Uzbekistan). In seven of the countries (Armenia, Azerbaijan, Hungary, Kazakhstan, Moldova, Poland, Romania) the survey also included an additional sampling overlay of the 1,700 manufacturing enterprises in addition to the main BEEPS sample.

The main survey was conducted from 10 March to 20 April 2005. To maintain as much comparability with the BEEPS 2002 data and congruence with EBRD as possible, the BEEPS 2005 sample for each country was based on the achieved sample distribution of BEEPS 2002 (Synovate, 2005).

---

86. By the concept 'new' is meant those firms that have not been established on the basis of former state firms or corporations from the communist system.
87. The State Union of Serbia and Montenegro does not exist any more. On 3 June 2006 Montenegro declared independence. In response Serbia declared itself the legal and political successor of Serbia and Montenegro. On 17 February 2008 Kosovo seceded from Serbia. So the geographical area of the former State Union of Serbia and Montenegro now consists of three different countries: Serbia, Montenegro and Kosovo.

The survey focuses on four summary measures of corruption:
- the extent to which firms see corruption as a problem for business;
- the frequency of bribery;
- the amount of money paid in bribes;
- the impact of state capture on firms.

The first summary measure is meant as a composite, while the second and the third focus on administrative corruption and the fourth on state capture. Administrative corruption refers to bribery by individuals, groups, or firms in the private sector to influence the implementation of laws and regulation. State capture refers to bribery to influence the formulation or content of laws and regulation. Both administrative corruption and state capture can have pernicious effects on economic competition by restricting market entry and distributing economic preferences to influential elites.

Corruption as a problem for business

The indicator of corruption measured by the BEEPS focuses on the bottom line for firms: How much of a problem is corruption for the operation and growth of firms? We can say that there was a generalised improvement across transition countries.[88] Firms in the Slovak Republic, Georgia and Byelorussia reported the largest improvement. To a lesser extent firms in Bulgaria, Ukraine, Bosnia and Herzegovina, Moldova, Croatia and Romania, reported corruption to be a much less of a problem, although levels in Romania and Bosnia and Herzegovina are still high (with nearly 50 percent of firms saying corruption is a problem). The largest deterioration of the problem was reported in Russia, Azerbaijan, Kyrgyz Republic, Serbia and Montenegro and the largest of all in the Czech Republic, which is now among the half-dozen transition countries where business perceives the most significant corruption problem. Albania remains the worst performer among all transition countries. The finding that many firms see corruption to be less of a problem for business in 2005 than 2002 is good news, but however corruption as a problem for business is the most subjective off the assessments covered by the BEEPS.

The frequency of bribery

This indicator of corruption focuses on what firms said about the extent of firm-level bribery. Transition countries as a whole showed a decline in the frequency of unofficial payments, with the strongest improvements in the new members of the European Union (Slovak Republic, Bulgaria, Romania, Latvia, Hungary) and the countries in the southern CIS[89] (Moldova, Tajikistan, and especially Georgia, all from relative high figures in 2002).[90] The countries with the worst deteriora-

---

88. For a figure that shows corruption as a problem for business, by country, in 2002 and 2005 see Anderson and Gray (2006: 8).
89. The Commonwealth of Independent States (CIS) is a regional organization whose participating countries are former Soviet Republics.

tion, despite the previous high level of perceived bribery problems, were Serbia and Montenegro, Albania and the Kyrgyz Republic. In spite of the trends, firms in many transition countries report a high frequency of unofficial payments. About one half the firms in the Kyrgyz Republic and Albania, and more than a quarter of firms in Russia, Serbia and Montenegro, Ukraine, and Azerbaijan, said that bribery was frequent.

The amount of tax paid as bribery

This indicator of corruption focuses on the percentage of annual firm revenue paid in bribes, as reported by the firm themselves. Across all the transition countries, the average percentage of revenues paid in bribes declined from 1.6 percent in 2002 to 1.1 percent in 2005.[91] The largest declines in tax bribery occurred in Georgia, Romania, Tajikistan, Albania and the Kyrgyz Republic. Albania, the Kyrgyz Republic and Serbia and Montenegro showed improvements in tax bribery even whilst the frequency of bribery generally was increasing. While the results regarding tax bribery are encouraging, one fact should be kept in mind. 'Declines in the average bribe tax do not necessarily mean that the absolute amount paid in bribes has fallen, since the bribe tax is measured as a share of firm-level revenues. The size of the economy in every transition country grew rapidly, by an average of 63 percent in nominal terms, and the amount of money changing hands in unofficial payments could well have increased even as the share of bribes in total revenues fell (Anderson and Gray, 2006: 16-17).

State capture indicator

The indicator of state capture focuses on the impact of state capture on firms.[92] Major improvements were reported in Bulgaria, Latvia, the Slovak Republic, Ukraine, Georgia, and Slovenia. Significantly worse results were in Albania, Armenia, Russia and Azerbaijan. The highest level of state capture were perceived by firms in Bosnia and Herzegovina, Albania, FYRM and Serbia and Montenegro.

Considering all the results it appears that corruption has declined dramatically from 2002 to 2005 in Georgia and the Slovak Republic, and to a somewhat lesser extent in Poland and Latvia. The results also point to improvements in Bulgaria and Romania, and to significant improvements from relatively high levels in Ukraine, Moldova, Kazakhstan and Tajikistan. For other transition countries the results were more mixed.

---

90. For a figure that shows the frequency of bribery, by country, in 2002 and 2005 see Anderson and Gray (2006: 11).
91. For a figure that shows the amount of tax paid as bribery, by country, in 2002 and 2005 see Anderson and Gray (2006: 16).
92. For a figure that shows changes in the impact of state capture, 2002-2005 see Anderson and Gray (2006: 18).

The largest reduction in corruption among all transition countries between 2002 and 2005 occurred in Georgia. The main reason for that reduction is probably the fact, that in Georgia in 2003 the 'Rose Revolution' removed Eduard Shevarnadze from power. Since then in Georgia significant economic and institutional reforms have occurred. The reason for the reduction in corruption in Ukraine is probably the same. The 'Orange Revolution' in 2004 that removed Leonid Kuchma from power, was similar to the 'Rose Revolution' in Georgia, powered by citizen anger about corruption (Anderson and Gray, 2006). But on the other hand it has been argued that only the BEEPS shows a dramatic improvement in Georgia between 2002 and 2005 and no other source has corroborated it (Knack, 2006: 45).

Targets, agents and means of capture and administrative corruption

Politicians and public officials can be both agents and targets of state capture. They are targets of capture when they occupy a position within the civil service, the operation of which others wish to undermine. They are agents of capture when they undermine their own role or use illicit means to put others in a subordinate position, with the purpose of influencing legislation to ensure indirect or direct personal benefit. We distinguish between institutions that are captured or influenced (executive, legislative and judicial state bodies) and institutions that carry out this capture or influence (e.g. private companies, interest groups, political leaders etc.). Moreover, there are different means through which capture or administrative corruption can be achieved or carried out (bribes, threats, lobbying etc.). It has been proved that combinations of threat and offer (do X and you will get Y, and if you do not do that, we will impose sanction Z) – the so-called 'throffers' – are some of the most powerful and often highly successful type of incentive for groups working in areas where they control the law. This is particularly true for environments where there is confusion.

Capture can also take place across state borders by foreign companies and investors or even through participation from foreign governments. There are also differences between the duration and depth of penetration into the institutional structure of the state. Concerning the depth of penetration, it can be said that it is less harmful if someone buys parliamentary votes on a single issue than if someone is able to design a complete piece of legislation. As far as duration is concerned, it is for example more harmful if someone always has the opportunity to buy parliamentary votes than if someone has the opportunity to do that once (randomly). These are the distinctions between deep and shallow, and entrenched and occasional capture. When dealing with deep and entrenched capture, it is less likely that any substantial direct payments to officials will be involved; it is more probable that the capture will occur as part of informal networks and exchanges among them, in which monetary exchange does not play an important role.

The term 'capture' is meant to express a transfer of control from A to C, as we saw above. However, it is not entirely clear what or whom is captured. Formally, the objects of the capture are laws, policies or regulations, and not the persons who design these laws or regulations. The stress is on the artefacts and not the agents who produce the artefacts. At the same time public officials are the agents, insofar as their behaviour is undermined. Nevertheless, this is not a sufficient condition to speak about public officials as components of capture. C may ensure the compliance of numerous agents in the law-making process with bi-lateral (symmetrical), one-off financial transactions. In such cases capture is limited to the artefact produced. On the other hand, experience shows that in many states capture takes place on the basis of asymmetrical relationships between A and C. A, for example, is acting in a predatory manner in relation to the public who uses the services of A's office, or C controls A's continuing activities, or A and C lock themselves into a more permanent and stable relationship. We speak about deep and entrenched capture when a national service and its legislative power are completely subordinate to the private interests of individuals, groups or organizations.

Table 1   Mechanisms of corruption, capture and influence

Targets	Agents	Means
Media	Leaders of private companies	Free-riding
Voters	Officials	Influential lobbying
Political parties (national, local)	Politicians	Negotiation
Political parties leadership	**Intra-state:**	Regulatory capture
Public officials	Criminal corporations	Corruptive bribery
Politicians (national, local)	Companies	Blackmail
Legislation	Political factions	Threats
Regulations	State-based factions	Threats connected with provision of benefits
Inspectors	Political parties	Briberies for state capture
Judiciary	**Inter-state:**	Violence and intimidation
Legislative, executive and judicial institutions (national, local)	Foreign companies Foreign governments	**International state capture:** Bribery Military threats Trade threats Aid Sanctions

Source: Philip (2001)

Relationships in which corrupt demands meet corrupt supplies, and where, subsequently, informational symmetry between A and C (both have proof of illegal activities of each other) governs, and A and C have different possibilities of influencing other dimensions of the political process (such as the media, police, prosecution or judiciary) and/or have different possibilities of threat and the use of violence, which can dramatically deform the symmetry of exchange and only the price of goods and the ease with which they can be obtained, lead to a systematic pattern of domination (Philip, 2001).

These findings indicate that the current concept of state capture has certain drawbacks and needs to be further developed. Especially in transition countries where there is no clear boundary between private and public activities, it is hard to define who is capturing whom.

The question needs also to be asked whether such activities or the omission of governments is the result of state capture or an unintentional consequence of insufficient legislation; and if state capture really occurred the next question that needs to be answered is who captured whom? According to the state capture model given by the Word Bank, it can be said that in the case of planned efforts by politicians to support allies in conquering the economy the agents of capture are: 1) members of the government and its employees (who use their position for personal benefit at a cost to the public interest), or 2) individuals – tycoons (who offered members of the government or public officials certain benefits in return for influence). It is through the examination of transition economies that certain deficiencies of the current state capture model appear. This model insists on a clear division between the one capturing and the one being captured. The Word Bank overlooked two important factors that are typical of transition countries:
- those doing the capturing and those being captured can originate from the same social network. Public officials and politicians can do favours for their friends as part of complicated and complex mutual relationships, but do not have any direct personal benefit for doing so;
- members of the government and public officials seldom distinguish between private and public.

As we saw, the state capture model is not the most appropriate for studying transition processes and examining which government allies profit. Two factors show that individuals in transition economies do not have to use the strategy of capture or administrative corruption. Firstly, the legal vacuums and ambiguities were such that certain informal networks easily used them for their own benefit. Secondly, tycoons did not have to capture state leaders, since leaders were already interested in helping them (Barret, 2004).

It appears that in the future more time will have to be spent on the examination of informal networks to explain the negative effects of transition in post-socialist countries. This does not mean that the state capture model developed by the Word Bank cannot be put to use. It should be applied in more developed democracies where an appropriate legal system is in force and where it is clear who sets the law and how one can influence those setting it.

MEASURES TO LIMIT THE OCCURRENCE OF STATE CAPTURE

Previous repressive measures used by law enforcement authorities when they discovered corruption produced few results. Therefore, preventive measures which involve disrupting informal networks and corrupt activities should be increased. Lately, prevention has been the focus of modern criminality policies, which strongly strive to prevent the harmful effects of corrupt activities.[93]

With the highest form of corruption, called state capture, prevention is even more necessary due to the nature of the phenomenon (it is hard to discover, even harder to prove). The two main mechanisms that need to be established to fight state capture are transparency and competition. Transparency means an environment in which all information is open and available to all; an environment where the public is regularly informed; where an increased number of citizens participate in decision-making processes; where the financing and operation of political parties is transparent; and where civil society controls conflicts of interests and the connected provision of benefits. Competition denotes an environment in which monopolies are prevented and competitiveness and market economy are encouraged, and where the environment is favourable for entrepreneurship (Anti-Corruption Resource Centre, 2003: 3).

The effects of transition demand that the state adopt a new role. The state has to give up central planning and direct control over production, which requires reforms in many areas. The first measure implemented by states was price liberalization. After that an appropriate response to budgetary constraints was necessary with a decrease in state subventions. Banks had to take on the role of channelling capital from savers to investors. Due to the fact that the economy was relatively closed in the former system, states had to increase international competition and ease access to export markets. Due to undefined regulations, these extensive changes during the time of transition provided great opportunities for those who at a given moment had the power to use the strategy of state capture to bring them great benefits.

Reforms can be considered partial in two dimensions. They can be partial on an actual level measured by the reform index, or they can be assessed in relation to their extent in all areas. For example, a country may reach a high degree of reform in one or two areas, but achieve only small or no progress in other areas. Reforms are also considered partial, if they achieve a medium (average) level of progress in all areas.

The EPRIEE Project group[94] has analysed the correlation between partial reforms and the occurrence of state capture occurrence for each individual

93. See Dobovšek (2005).
94. Newcastle University, Newcastle Upon Tyne Department of Economics, EPRIEE project, http://www.ncl.ac.uk/search/advanced.php?q=state+capture&qq=&nq=&collection=&within=&go=Search.

reform variable (Barlow and Buckley, 2004). The analysis particularly examined countries with a high and low level of capture in their economy. Six key reform areas were taken into account: privatization on a small scale, privatization on a large scale, commercial and international exchange, bank reforms and price liberalization. The analysis carried out in the project, which was based on data from the first BEEPS survey, showed that the occurrence of state capture can be the consequence of reforms that were not comprehensive enough. Data from the Anti-Corruption Resource Centre (2003) are presented in Table 2 below and indicate how countries were classified as having a high or low level of capture economy. Table 2 presents for each country the share of firms that responded and admitted that a certain degree of state capture occurrence had significantly influenced their businesses. The capture economy index is defined as an average of the six indicators. The authors establish the correlation between the occurrence of state capture and reforms is a reverse U curve. Countries having a capture economy index of 18% or more are classified as highly captured. Reforms in these countries are usually slow or partial (e.g. Russia, Romania). Low capture economies are those with an index below 18%. This group comprises countries that were undertaking wide-ranging reforms and those countries that have not started with the implementation of reforms at all. The latter include for example Belarus and Uzbekistan, which have remained dictatorships in all aspects. In these two countries there have not been many opportunities for state capture, since the private sector, which would be the agent of the capture, does not exist. It has hence been discovered that the correlation between capture and reforms runs in both directions, which causes many problems with breaking out of the vicious circle of conspiracy between the financial moguls and the state (Anti-Corruption Resource Centre, 2003).

However sometimes corruption cannot be addressed by reform, at least not in the short or medium term. There are cultural causes of corruption. For example countries with a large share of Protestants, are perceived to be less affected by corruption and at the same time they have little inspiration to reform (Lambsdorff, 2007: 28-29).

But it is hard to argue that the press can not deter corruption. Brunetti and Weder (2003), show that a free press effectively deters corruption (see also Lambsdorff, 2007: 46). To deter grand corruption, which is called state capture, probably needs not just a free press, but also a very 'skilled' press.

Table 2   Measuring the capture economy (percentage of firms affected in business by corruption in each of the dimensions[95])

Country	Parliamentary Legislation	Presidential Decrees	Central Bank	Criminal Courts	Commer-cial Courts	Party Financing	Capture Economy Index	Classification
Albania	12	7	8	22	20	25	16	Low
Armenia	10	7	14	5	6	1	7	Low
Azerbaijan	41	48	39	44	40	35	41	High
Belarus	9	5	25	0	5	4	8	Low
Bulgaria	28	26	28	28	19	42	28	High
Czech Republic	18	11	12	9	9	6	11	Low
Croatia	18	24	30	29	29	30	27	High
Estonia	14	7	8	8	8	17	10	Low
Georgia	29	24	32	18	20	21	24	High
Hungary	12	7	8	5	5	4	7	Low
Kazakhstan	13	10	19	14	14	6	12	Low
Kyrgyzstan	18	16	59	26	30	27	29	High
Latvia	40	49	8	21	26	35	30	High
Lithuania	15	7	9	11	14	13	11	Low
Moldova	43	30	40	33	34	42	37	High
Poland	13	10	6	12	18	10	12	Low
Romania	22	20	26	14	17	27	21	High
Russia	35	32	47	24	27	24	32	High
Slovakia	20	12	37	29	25	20	24	High
Slovenia	8	5	4	6	6	11	7	Low
Ukraine	44	37	37	21	26	29	32	High

CONCLUDING THOUGHTS

There is no immediately apparent solution to the economic crisis in which post-modern capitalist society finds itself, particularly as all of the bodies determining global and regional political and economic issues (G8, the World Bank, the International Monetary Fund, the UN, the EU, and, in the security field, NATO and the OSCE) claim that the current 'world order' should be preserved. They support this claim by appealing to 'peace and stability', national sovereignty and integrity, economic and political modernisation, democratisation, the rule of law and, above all, human rights. It has to be stressed that in addition to economic security, the rule of law represents another issue that is being discussed lately. It is no exaggeration to claim that the rule of law, which during the previous century became the central stimulus for economic progressive development, currently

---

95. Firms were asked to what extent corruption on each dimension had an impact on their business: no impact; minor impact; significant impact; very significant impact.

constitute a legal and political doctrine; which, as a primary legal mechanism, can be abused. That is why the concept of state capture should be analysed closely.

As we have seen, the concept of capture denotes a state where someone uses (abuses) the state (laws and other regulations) for personal benefit instead of in the interests of the public. This has to be done using illicit and/or non-transparent means. Findings indicate that the current concept of state capture has certain drawbacks and needs to be further developed, especially for transition countries where there is no clear boundary between private and public activities, so that it is hard to define who is capturing whom.

When examining post-socialist countries, the question needs to be also asked whether non-transparent activities of governments or states are the result of state capture or an unintentional consequence of insufficient legislation. There are two factors that indicate that individuals in transition economies do not have to use the strategy of capture or administrative corruption. Firstly, the legal vacuums and ambiguities can be such that certain informal networks can easily use them in their favour. Secondly, tycoons do not have to capture state leaders, since these leaders were already interested in helping them.

According to recent findings, more time should be spent on examining informal networks to explain the negative consequences of transition. This, however, does not mean that the state capture model developed by the World Bank cannot be put to use. It should be applied in more developed democracies where an appropriate legal system is in force and where it is clear who sets the law and how one can influence those setting it.

In the end it needs to be stressed that with the highest forms of corruption, called state capture, prevention is even more necessary due to the nature of the phenomenon (it is hard to discover, even harder to prove). The two main mechanisms that need to be established to fight state capture are transparency and competition. Transparency means an environment in which information is clear and available to all, an environment where the public is regularly informed, and where an increased number of citizens participate in decision-making processes. It also means that the financing and operation of political parties needs to be transparent, and that civil society controls conflicts of interest and the connected provision of benefits. Competition denotes an environment in which monopolies are prevented, where competitiveness and market economy are encouraged, and where the environment is favourable for entrepreneurship.

In Slovenia the area of state capture has not yet been researched in detail. An attempt should be made to utilize the model suggested by the World Bank, since Slovenia is closer to Western countries, in which clear boundaries between public and private activities are set. Evidence shows that this model is better suited for researching the highest forms of corruption in developed than in transition countries.

REFERENCES

Anderson, J.H. & Gray, G.W. (2006). *Anticorruption in transition 3. Who is succeeding... and why?* Washington: The International Bank for Reconstruction and Development/The World Bank.

Anti-Corruption Resource Centre (2003). 'Measures addressing state capture in Russia/ Ukraine/Central Asia'. *Helpdesk Query in Helpdesk Reply,* at [http://www.u4.no/help-desk/helpdesk/queries/query18.cfm, accessed February 25, 2009.

Barlow, D. & Buckley, D. (2004). *Reform dynamics and state capture.* EPRIEE project, July 2004, at http://www.epriee.ncl.ac.uk/Statecapture1.pdf, accessed May 15, 2009.

Barret, L. (2004). 'The role of informal networks in the privatisation process in Croatia'. In *Integrating the Balkans in the European Union: Functional borders and sustainable security.* Work package 3: The Informal Sector. Working Paper, no. 3, at http://www.eliamep.gr/old-site/eliame-old/eliamep/www.eliamep.gr/eliamep/files/Informality_&_Privatisation_ Croatia.pdf, accessed February 25, 2009.

Beck, U. (2003). *What is globalisation?* Blackwell.

Derleth, J. W. (2000). *The transition in Central and Eastern European politics.* New Jersey: Prentice Hall.

Dobovšek, B. (2005). *Korupcija in politika.* Collection of scientific papers, foreword. Ljubljana: Government of the Republic of Slovenia, Ministry of the Interior.

EPRIEE Project (2002-2004). Newcastle University, Newcastle Upon Tyne Department of Economics, at http://www.ncl.ac.uk/search/advanced.php?q=state+capture&qq=&nq=&collection=&within=&go=Search, accessed May 15, 2009.

Freedom House (2004). http://www.freedomhouse.org, accessed March 15, 2005.

Hellman, J., Jones, G. & Kaufmann, D. (2000). *Size the state, seize the day – state capture, corruption, and influence in transition.* The World Bank, at http://www.worldbank.org/ wbi/governance/pdf/seize_synth.pdf, accessed February 25, 2009.

Hellman, J., Jones, G., Kaufmann, D. & Schankerman, M. (2000). *Measuring governance corruption and state capture: how firms and bureaucrats shape the business environment in transition economies.* The World Bank, at http://129.3.20.41/eps/dev/papers/0308/ 0308004.pdf, accessed 25.2.2009.

Hellman, J. & Kaufmann, D. (2001). *Confronting the challenge of state capture in transition economics,* at http://www.imf.org/external/pubs/ft/fandd/2001/09/hellman.htm, accessed February 25, 2009.

Hellman, J., Jones, G. & Kaufmann, D. (2002). *Far from home: Do foreign investors import higher standards of governance in transition economies.* The World Bank, at http:// papers.ssrn.com/sol3/papers.cfm?abstract_id=386900, accessed February 25, 2009

Igliar, A. (1996). 'Vpliv lobiranja na parlamentarno odloanje', *Drugo strokovno sreanje pravnikov.* Ljubljana: Institute of Public Administration, University of Ljubljana.

Kandu, Z. (2003). 'Kriminaliteta, lovekove pravice in varnost v po(zno)modernem svetu'. *Revija za kriminalistiko in kriminologijo,* 2, Ljubljana.

Knack, S. (2006). *Measuring Corruption in Eastern Europe and Central Asia: A Critique of the Cross-Country indicators.* World Bank Policy Research Working Paper 3968, at http:// www-wds.worldbank.org/external/default/WDSContentServer/IW3P/IB/2006/07/13/ 000016406_20060713140304/Rendered/PDF/wps3968.pdf, accessed February 27, 2009.

Lambsdorff, J.G. (2007). *The institutional economics of corruption and reform. Theory, evidence, and policy.* New York: Cambridge University Press.

Meško, G. (2004). 'Partnerschaftliche Sicherheitsgewährleistung: Wünsche, Ideale, Hindernisse'. *Kriminalistik*, 58(12): 768-773.

Philip, M. (2001). *Corruption and state capture: An analytical framework.* Oxford: Department of Politics and International Relations, University of Oxford, accessed February 25, 2009.

Rose-Ackermann, S. (1999). *Corruption and government – causes, consequences, and reform.* Cambridge: Cambridge University Press, at http://www.worldbank.org/wbi/governance/pdf/prague_corrupt_capture.pdf.

Švob-Dokič, N. (2000). *Tranzicijski procesi i meunarodni položaj novih europskih država.* Zagreb: Barbat.

Synovate (2005). The business environment and enterprise performance survey (BEEPS) 2005: A brief report on observation, experiences and methodology from the survey, at http://www.ebrd.com/country/sector/econo/surveys/beeps05r.pdf, accessed February 27, 2009.

Political-criminal-business nexus and state capture in Georgia, Ukraine and Kyrgyzstan: a comparative analysis

Alexander Kupatadze

INTRODUCTION

The political-criminal-business nexus[96] is a relatively new concept that has attracted much scholarly and policy attention over the past few years. This discussion of a 'nexus' is especially relevant in the post-Soviet context where the transition processes since the early 1990s have resulted in an 'unholy alliance' between politicians, businessmen and criminals in a number of newly independent states. The alliance is based on a web of affiliations of 'underworld' and 'upperworld' societal participants (Liddick, 1999: 1) with complex reciprocal relationships.

This article concentrates on Georgia, Ukraine and Kyrgyzstan, three countries with similar backgrounds of having been part of the Soviet Union and having experienced similar trajectories of post-Soviet transition, although being quite different in terms of their culture and history. Recently all three countries witnessed large-scale public upheavals resulting in regime transitions, events frequently referred to as revolutions (the Rose revolution in Georgia, 2003; the Orange revolution in Ukraine, 2004; the 'Tulip Revolution' in Kyrgyzstan, 2005). The very existence of powerful criminalized informal networks that lived off the state budgets of these countries was among the variables of explanatory power as to why the revolutions happened in these countries. All three events have been called 'anti-corruption movements' or 'anti-crime revolutions',[97] sparked by a popular rejection of rampant corruption, clan structures and well-established organized crime which led to the mobilization of the masses against the ruling regimes. 'Sending bandits to prison' was most salient in Ukraine's Orange Revolution. Therefore corruption and crime were supposed to have suffered a major setback in the post-revolutionary period, considering the public pressure on the elites. The implicit contract between the masses and the elites crafted during the public uprising is in itself the source of legitimacy for the new regime, which, on

---

96. In the literature the nexus is referred to in different ways: Williams ((2001: 113) calls it a triangle of business, crime and politics; Los (2003:145) refers to it as a state-market-crime nexus.

97. On the Rose Revolution, see for example Shelley and Scot (2003), Kandelaki (2006: 3); on the Orange Revolution, Yuryi Lutsenko repeated several times that it was primarily an anti-criminal revolution; see, for example, Lutsenko quoted in Kuzio (2006), Kuzio (2008); on the Tulip Revolution, see Aslund (2005), Radnitz (2006: 141).

its side was expected to narrow the possibilities and willingness of incoming elites to engage in rent-seeking. The fight against corruption can be thought of as a political good deliverable by the state, as 'indigenous expectation, conceivably obligation that gave content to the social contract between ruler and ruled' (Rotberg, 2004: 2-3). However the expectations did not materialize, especially in the cases of Ukraine and Kyrgyzstan.

This chapter is based on extensive field research in the three countries in the period 2005-2008. Overall roughly 100 individuals from the government structures, especially law enforcement, academia, NGOs and the media were interviewed. The three countries selected for the study demonstrate well the different forms of state capture in post-Soviet Eurasia. All three of them have been identified as 'highly captured states'.[98] Furthermore all three countries experienced so-called coloured revolutions, the events that were closely related to corruption and crime in terms of both causation and impact.

To summarise the situation and the problem: the state in Ukraine, Kyrgyzstan and Georgia has been captured in different forms in the post-Soviet period. Former Soviet Union countries provide ample empirical data to look at various forms of state capture, being the different practices used by informal networks for neutralizing state power or the use of state power for personal interest. Georgia, a country notorious for its contribution to the world of professional criminals (*vory-v-zakone*) was most affected by this form of traditional organized crime. The presence and consequently the influence of the *vory* was much less in the two other countries. In Kyrgyzstan sportsmen became main actors in organized crime activities, which matured from street gangs to fully fledged mafia groups in the late 1990s. On the other hand, the ruling families have always played a key role in licit and illicit markets in Kyrgyzstan. In Ukraine which, unlike the two other countries had a large industrial base, the state was mainly captured by large oligarchic capital. Almost all of these oligarchs were to various degrees related to shady privatisation deals and have been involved in illegal or semi-legal activities, such as loan sharking in the early 1990s and later corporate raiding. It was also alleged that some of the oligarchs were related to organized crime groups, or at least were using their protection in the immediate aftermath of the Soviet Union's breakup.

Thus state capture in three countries displays diverse, albeit attention-grabbing, trends. Hereby the revolutions are regarded as a variable that changed the patterns of relationships between underworld and upperworld and therefore the patterns of state capture. In Georgia, the professional criminals have lost money and influence. In Kyrgyzstan organized crime groups became very influential and capitalized on collapsing state institutions, so managing to wield power at the central government level – although the incoming elites have re-asserted themselves and the new ruling family is playing increasingly an important role in licit

---

98. See for instance EBRD (1999); Hellman et al. (2000).

and illicit markets. In Ukraine the division of the political elites contributed to the increasing professionalization of organized crime groups trying to project influence, however the patterns of state capture did not change much and oligarchic capital still plays a major role. The discussion which follows stresses these trends and provides an explanation of the diverging patterns.

First a theoretical perspective on the political-criminal-business nexus is offered and its relationship with state capture considered. Second, the specific post-soviet context is discussed and three case studies demonstrating different trajectories of state capture are outlined. In conclusion an explanation of the post-soviet nature of state capture is offered. The informal economies in these countries are closely intertwined with the criminal economies and show the involvement of various actors including elites and organized criminals. The 'captor agents' profit from state resources as well, diverting substantial public assets for private gains thus 'living off politics' and making the state a permanent source of income (Weber, 1919) – to put it in Weberian terms.

THE POLITICAL-CRIMINAL-BUSINESS NEXUS AND STATE CAPTURE

In order to fully understand organized crime, one needs to appreciate the importance of the 'traditional network of collusive relationships with members of external, licit groups – social, political or entrepreneurial' (Armao, 2003: 27). In weak states the political elites would need a partnership with crime groups (Schulte-Bockholt, 2006: 25-26), since the formal institutions are underdeveloped and inefficient. The collusion may result in organized crime assuming a quasi-governmental role, developing and assuming power where and when government cannot do (Finckenauer, 2005: 74) and thus becoming an 'informal or alternate government and policing agency' (Kelly, 2004: 110). This would equate to state capture by organized crime groups.

In this chapter, the World Bank's (2000: 1) definition of state capture will be adopted: 'the actions of individuals, groups, or firms in both the public and private sector to influence the legislative process of laws, regulations, decrees, and other government policies (i.e. the basic rules of the game) to their own advantage by means of the illicit and non-transparent provision of private benefits to public officials'. Two elements are crucial here: 'all forms of state capture are directed towards extracting rents' and state agencies are captured when they operate for private as opposed to public interest (World Bank, 2000: 2-3). Private here necessarily implies the detriment of the common good (Kotkin and Sajo, 2002: 16), although it does not necessarily mean outright personal benefit. Rather it can be interpreted as favouring one's own clients (supporters, allies) or one's own organisation (for instance political party). Dobovšek (2008: 685) argues that state capture always contains three entities: first, the private/public person/organiza-tion who exerts influence for the sake of private interests, second the person/institution which is influenced (through regulation) and third, the effect on the public which is impaired, although not usually obviously and directly.

Here the state can be thought of as 'a heap of loosely connected parts or fragments, frequently with ill-defined boundaries between them and other groupings inside and outside the official state borders and often promoting conflicting sets of rules with one another and with 'official' Law'' (Migdal, 2001: 22). This struggle for domination between various groupings, such as organized crime groups and ruling cliques, is basically the process of state-making, two crucial elements of which are the fight over the monopolization of violence and over providing protection, according to Tilly (1985: 169-191) This definition is directly related to the organized crime model presented below, the baseline of which is determining who dominates. Godson (2003: 1-5) thinks that 'in some areas the problem of the political-criminal nexus is chronic... only the forms and balance of power among the players change. Sometimes the politicians dominate, sometimes the criminals. Regardless of who is dominant, the coalition of forces influences many aspects of government.'

Distinctions are drawn between the types of institutions that are captured—the legislature, the executive, the judiciary or regulatory bodies (World Bank, 2000: 2) however the main focus here is on the types of actors that capture the state. It is argued that state capture or criminalization of the state happens in three ways. State capture *by criminal interests* is present in all three forms, however a distinction is made between state capture by organized crime groups, state capture by criminalized elites and a mixture of both. In the first case organized crime groups co-opt and establish control over state institutions or 'obtain preferential treatment from public servants through extortion' – what Lambsdorff (2002: 2) calls an 'extreme example'. In the second case, elites monopolize control over organized criminal activity and in the third case there are signs of both processes. Corruption, especially 'grand', high-level corruption, as opposed to petty corruption, is an important variable here, based on which of the various groups project power. Corruption is defined as behaviour which deviates from the formal duties of a public role because of private (personal, close family, private clique) financial or status gains (Nye, 1967: 419).

State capture by organized crime groups means the dominance of the underworld. Hence the state is criminalized through the efforts of powerful organized crime groups aimed at co-opting and hijacking state institutions. In this case organized crime groups are more powerful than the ruling regime and political elites. Armao (2003: 30) would call it a Mafia State in which organized criminals 'assume both the political leadership and the monopoly of the economic and financial resources of the State'. Here organized crime groups can be regarded as an 'illicit authority' that 'enjoy legitimate social recognition to the extent that they step into a power vacuum left by a weak state and provide public goods that the state fails to provide' (Hall and Biersteker, 2002: 16). In a criminalized state the organized crime leaders set the rules of the game and directly participate in state policy making. The political and business elites are dependent on them, although they maintain some kind of autonomy. The extent of the dominance by organized crime groups can vary from case to case.

In the second category the state is criminalized through co-opting organized crime leaders or by the incorporation of protectors and perpetrators of organized crime into political and business elites that monopolize control over organized criminal activity. In this case the ruling elites are strong and organized crime groups are weak. Larry Diamond (2008) is insightful: 'the natural tendency of elites everywhere has been to monopolize power rather than to restrain it... and once they have succeeded in restricting political access, these elites use their con-solidated power to limit economic competitions so as to generate profits that ben-efit them rather than society at large'. Thus in this kind of state the rulers' aim is to maximize their own take and to act like a protection racket (Moselle and Polak, 2001: 4). In this case the power of the rulers over the populace may come from a greater capacity for violence (Olson, 1993: 567) and normally the rulers maintain large police force thus having considerable capacity to harm bandits (Moselle and Polak, 2001: 5, 17). This kind of state meets the definition of Marxist state theo-rists who would view the state as a 'neutral instrument to be manipulated and steered in the interests of the ruling elite' (Hay, 2006: 71) as well as the argu-ments of elitist state theorists who would posit that the 'power elite comprised of politicians, military and corporate bosses mould public policy to suit their own ends' (Evans, 2006: 45).

In the case of divided elites and a weak state dominance is shared between under-world and upperworld or the informal networks comprise the representatives of both. Here we can speak about a symbiotic balance model where the state is frag-mented by competing political and business groups that are fighting each other, sometimes through the help of criminals. It shows the signs of both predatory and criminalized state. In this case the distinction between the political and busi-ness elite and organized crime groups is extremely blurred. Wedel (2001: 4-5) calls it a *partially appropriated state*, where 'informal groups privatize certain state functions. Individual clans, each of which controls property and resources, are so closely identified with particular ministries or institutional segments of govern-ment that the respective agendas of the state and the clan sometimes seem identi-cal. ... These clans are ambiguous groups, entities, and institutions, situated somewhere between the state and private spheres.'

As a result of continuous competition for resources the state is manipulated by various interests – criminal, business and political. Reforms are constantly pushed forward and then reversed back. Powerful firms distort the reform agenda for their narrow private gains (Hellman and Schankerman, 2000: 3). The net winners in a malfunctioning state (such as former Communist *nomenclatura* or 'new entrepreneurs-cum-mafiosi') are trying 'to stall the economy in a *partial reform equilibrium* that generates concentrated rents' and try to preserve the status quo as long as possible 'by blocking any measures to eliminate these distortions' (Hellman, 1998: 23-25).

The distinctions between the three models outlined above is at best simplification for the sake of analysis, since it is very difficult to draw a line, especially in the post-communist context, between public and private, legal and illegal, public official and organized criminal. The following chart sums up the discussion on state capture by criminal interests.

Figure 1 The political criminal continuum and state capture

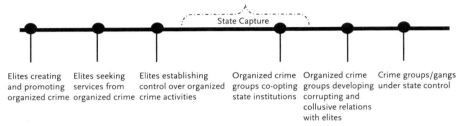

Elites creating and promoting organized crime | Elites seeking services from organized crime | Elites establishing control over organized crime activities | Organized crime groups co-opting state institutions | Organized crime groups developing corrupting and collusive relations with elites | Crime groups/gangs under state control

Over time crime groups from the gangs become highly sophisticated criminal networks with transnational connections. The organized crime continuum proposed by Frank Hagan (1983: 54; 2006: 135-136) differentiated between three levels in crime groups' development, moving from street gangs up to semi-organized crime groups and next to full-fledged groups. The more groups develop the less dependent they become on legal entities (Rawlinson, 2002: 296) and organized crime goes beyond being a law enforcement problem and becomes 'a state within a state' (Lupsha, 1996: 32).

In a similar fashion to thinking about a continuum of crime groups, the involvement of political and business elites in organized crime can be thought of as a continuum having the sporadic involvement of individual elite members in organized criminal activities at one extreme, and the takeover and monopolization of organized criminal activities by licit actors at the other. After all, elites should not always be presented as the honest ones corrupted by 'evil' organized crime. They can be viewed as 'the people who are corruptible – those people who chose to act as criminals' instead (Beare, 2007: 3)

A transformation in society, especially such an abrupt one as the coloured revolutions in the three countries, moves states along the continuum. Frequently these events serve as windows of opportunity for crime groups or factions of criminalized elites to obtain new resources. Capitalizing on chaos and collapsing state institutions, organized crime groups may become stronger and dictate their conditions to the state: what happened in the case of Kyrgyzstan since the Tulip Revolution. On the other hand organized crime groups may be put on the defensive since incoming elites try to establish control and hence eliminate any competition from non-state rivals.

THE POST-SOVIET TRANSITION AND THE POLITICAL-BUSINESS-CRIMINAL NEXUS

State capture has been a prevalent problem in newly independent states since the breakup of the Soviet Union. The transition to a free market economy has resulted in the emergence of powerful political-criminal clans that have greatly benefited from the privatisation process in the early 1990s. Privatisation here refers specifically to the transfer of Soviet state assets to private ownership. The Soviet *nomenklatura* largely retained its power in the majority of Soviet Union successor states through trading political power for economic benefits and stakes in the privatisation of major enterprises of their respective countries (Kornai, 1990). Many of the privatisation deals were implemented through insider dealing and other forms of shady takeovers of the enterprises. In some countries state weakness resulting from institutional collapse in the transition process left the political elites weak and thus dependent on a newly emerging class of criminals or quasi-legal entrepreneurs. Much of the literature on state capture has concentrated on the captor firms[99] and their role in influencing state policies. Importantly the boundaries between business and organized crime groups were very difficult to discern initially. Given the state was weak and incapable of guaranteeing private property rights and enforcement of contracts business sought protection from powerful organized crime groups that were acting unrestrained by the state. This collaboration frequently grew into full mergers and takeover of the businesses by the criminal protectors. Stakes in various businesses across many countries of the former Soviet Union are owned by dummy individuals or organisations that are controlled by influential criminals, such as *vory-v-zakone*.

The process of state formation has been ongoing, however. The political elites have consolidated power through first amassing personal wealth through corruption and rent-seeking and second through strengthening the state apparatus and law enforcement structures for potential use for private purposes against non-state competitors. The efforts of the political elites in some cases led to stronger states, for instance in Putin's Russia or Nazarbayev's Kazakhstan, although in other cases the state remained weak and captured by the vested interests of criminalized elites, for instance in Kyrgyzstan under Akaev or Georgia under Shevardnadze.

Disagreements over the division of licit and illicit markets have resulted in numerous clashes, assassinations and kidnappings in the early 1990s. In this period many of the traditional organised crime figures, such as professional criminals (*vory-v-zakone*) have been killed or lost power. Those who survived had to adapt to new circumstances and abandon the traditional codes of behaviour that included a ban on cooperation with the authorities or living lavish lives. At the same time the state was strengthening. The period 1997-1998 was a breaking point in terms of the balance between the upperworld and the underworld. More

---

99. See Hellman et al. (2000; 2001), Fries et al. (2003).

efficient law enforcement structures confronted criminal leaders and many illicit organisations were destroyed through concerted government efforts. Again those who survived were co-opted into the elites or the opposite – were obliged to keep a low profile.

In line with the three categories distinguished above the case of Georgia in the period of mid and late 1990s shows clear signs of state capture by professional criminals. The situation has changed after the Rose Revolution when the new government under US-educated lawyer Mikheil Saakashvili launched a campaign against crime and corruption. However the political-criminal nexus is coming back after the incumbent elites were weakened in November 2007.

The Kyrgyz case shows the dominance of ruling families although with varying degrees. The revolution has brought changes to Kyrgyzstan as well, when organized crime groups became stronger initially, although the new ruling family has managed to re-assert control.

The case of Ukraine indicates how the oligarchs have captured the state. The effect of the Orange Revolution was to weaken the position of some oligarchs and strengthen that of others (Aslund, 2005b: 13), although the nature of state capture itself did not change.

This is not to imply that other groups are weak and do not influence state policies to various extents, however the distinction is made to demonstrate the patterns of state capture in the former Soviet Union. Hence organized crime groups wield power, especially on the regional level in Ukraine and Kyrgyzstan for instance, although they have lost the capacity to influence the political domain at the central level. In Georgia the relatives and family members of the incumbent Presidents were always influential but certainly the ruling family's dominance and interference in licit and illicit markets is more clear-cut in Kyrgyzstan.

STATE CAPTURE BY ORGANIZED CRIME: PROFESSIONAL CRIMINALS IN GEORGIA

Vory-v-zakone are senior criminal figures in the former Soviet Union who 'maintain, interpret and enforce the thieves' code' (Galeotti, 1998: 429). Such criminal leaders first developed in the Soviet Union during the 1920s in Soviet prison camps, the Gulags (Varese, 2001: 145-146). Reportedly the *vory* were first created by the Soviet authorities to establish control over the criminal community in and outside the prisons. *Vory* share similarities with the early Sicilian mafia godfathers in that they provided an alternative power structure to the state, operated within a defined honour code and maintained strict secrecy. *Vor* had no right to work either in prison or in the community, serve in the army or collaborate with state representatives (Afanasyev, 1994: 438). However later on some of the rules have been changed and the *vory* penetrated legal economies and political elites, initially through contacts made in Soviet prisons with other criminals, underground entrepreneurs and Soviet dissidents.[100]

Two gatherings (*skhodka* in criminal slang) of the major *vory v zakone* in Russia, one at the end of the 1970s and one in the mid-1980s, had a significant influence on the development of the nexus between professional criminals and the *nomenklatura* and red directors of state-owned Soviet factories. At the first meeting in Kislovodsk, agreements with the *tsekhaviki*, a Russian slang word denoting Russian private entrepreneurs banned by Soviet law, were forged to assist their activities in return for payments of roughly 10 per cent of their income (Serio and Razinkin, 1995: 76). This working relationship across the black economy would be 'repugnant to any right-thinking *vor*' (Handelman, 1995: 42). The deal was mainly advocated by Georgian professional criminals, commonly referred to as *Lavrushniki*[101] in Russia. As a result, well-entrenched illicit networks developed comprising professional criminals and banned businesses. The flourishing corruption in the party structures of the Soviet Union (Galeotti, 2002: xii) and the paralysis of the command-administrative economy, which gave birth to free economic agents (Handelman, 1995: 29) in the 1970s facilitated the process. Another meeting in Tbilisi in 1982 was convened to discuss the future of the criminal world. Two views dominated the meeting: several influential thieves wanted to remain loyal to the traditional rules of the Soviet underworld and stay away from politics, but another faction advocated a path of penetrating the political and economic life of the Soviet Union (Serio and Razinkin, 1995: 76). The supporters of the latter view were in the majority. Hence during the period of the Soviet Union the *vory* controlled a large part of the underground trade in spare parts, automobiles, timber, caviar and gems. In the final years of the Soviet Union's existence, this black economy was estimated to have a value of 110 billion roubles (Handelman, 1995: 28).

In 1991-1993, there were 600 *vory v zakone* operating in the former Soviet Union, according to Russian Ministry of the Interior estimates (Varese, 2001: 167; Handelman, 1995: 28). Roughly one-third of these were ethnic Russians and another third were ethnic Georgians. The remainder was of various nationalities such as Armenian, Azerbaijani and Uzbek among others (Serio and Razinkin, 1995: 77). There are now an estimated 400 Georgian *vory v zakone* (the figure almost doubled after the break-up of the Soviet Union).

Thus in Georgia, infamous with its large contribution to the world of Soviet professional criminals, *vory v zakone* took the lead, while there was no significant presence of professional criminals in Ukraine and Kyrgyzstan where sportsmen became the main actors in criminal groups. Hence *vory* were already established and their influence was significant in Georgia which also means that the thieves' code was widely followed and accepted in the underworld. Importantly Georgian

---

100.Chalidze (1977: 310) has estimated that more than one million individuals are convicted in Soviet Union annually.
101. Meaning bay leaves, which are grown in the Caucasus.

thieves were mainly trying to infiltrate the 'upper world' (i.e. politics and legal business) from the very beginning, i.e. since the break-up of Soviet Union. For instance Jaba Ioseliani, professional criminal and leader of the paramilitary group *Mkhedrioni* became President Shevardnadze's deputy in the early 1990s. This explains the diverging patterns of state capture in Georgia compared to Ukraine and Kyrgyzstan where initially criminals mostly relied on physical intimidation since their main activity was racketeering and they gradually developed into crime groups with political connections.

In fact the professional criminals were ruling the country. They enjoyed a near monopoly over the racketeering and extortion businesses, participated in human kidnapping and owned stakes or provided protection for major businesses in the country. The high level of collusion allowed them to participate in decision-making processes at the government level. They were linked with high officials of the government and law enforcement structures. For instance Tariel Oniani enjoyed extensive links with bureaucrats in Shevardnadze's government, among them the representatives of local governments, Members of Parliament, high-ranking officials of the Ministry of the Interior,[102] including two former Ministers of the Interior and Aslan Abashidze, head of the Adjaria autonomous republic. The collusion was evident at every level of the government, including executive and legislative branches of power. In 2000 police discovered two professional criminals in the car belonging to Rudik Tsatava, the deputy chairman of the Ministerial council of the Abkhaz government in exile (newspaper *Rezonansi*, August 22, 2000). Jemal Mikeladze, an influential professional criminal in Moscow was arrested in 2000 together with a former official of the Adjarian Ministry of Interior (Newspaper *Rezonansi*, 25 April 2000).

Oniani was possibly the most influential among the *vory*. Allegedly he had shares in private businesses, among them 'Airzena', one of the leading aviation companies in Georgia.[103] Oniani has helped the Georgian government in solving internal and external problems *quid pro quo* increasing the extent of dependency of authorities on the criminal world. Sources in the police have reported that Oniani participated in releasing hostages, for instance in the case of UN observers abducted in the Kodori Gorge back in 2003.[104] Oniani frequently acted as a mediator between large businesses in Georgia. For instance allegedly he was involved in the dispute between two major beer-producing companies in late 1990s (newspaper *Rezonansi*, 22 August 2000). This mediation by criminals was not confined to single isolated cases. The businesses and citizens were reluctant to turn to the inefficient and corrupt courts and instead were seeking justice through the *vory*,

102. In 2005 Mikheil Saakashvili, President of Georgia claimed that Koba Narchemashvili, the former Minster of Internal Affairs of Georgia, would meet Tariel Oniani in Tbilisi airport whenever he visited Georgia. Oniani would even be escorted by the police. See Address by President Saakashvili at charity dinner with businessmen, December 28, 2005, available online at www.president.gov.ge, retrieved 14 January 2006
103. Interview with former deputy Minister of Interior, Tbilisi, Georgia, 30 August 2008.
104. For more information on the case see Devdariani (2003).

turning to them to solve disputes. In general professional criminals were widely popular and even became role models for young people. In 1995 more than 25 percent of school children surveyed in Georgia said they aspired to be *vory v zakone* (Serio and Razinkin, 1995: 76).

Police data on the various businesses of professional criminals indicate that the *vory* were trying to penetrate every business that was yielding any significant income. Their business interests ranged from restaurants and bars to the micro-bus services (so-called *marshutka*). Their involvement also varied from direct ownership to protection although, as already mentioned, sometimes the two forms of involvement overlapped. The case of Bondo Shalikiani, MP-elect during Shevardnadze's time shows how much wealth the criminal leaders managed to amass as a result of the 10 years long post-Soviet transition. Shalikiani was arrested in March 2004. While the legal grounds for his arrest raised many questions, his assets proved to be vast. He had shares in electrical-mechanical and transport factories, a meat factory, the TV channel Kutaisi, sanatoriums and about 20 gas stations. Certainly all these assets have been confiscated and Shalikiani paid 140,000 US dollars as a fine (Khorbaladze, 2004).

Thus such people were offering protection to private businesses and controlled a significant part of the informal and formal economy of the country. The new legislation adopted in 2005 modelled after the American RICO (Racketeer Influenced and Corrupt Organizations Act) and Italian anti-mafia legislation criminalized the fact of being a 'thief in law' per se and involved sanctions including the confiscation of property. Simultaneously police reform has been implemented that significantly increased public trust in the police and the Ministry of the Interior became a much more efficient structure.[105] The police service reliability indicator[106] as measured by World Economic Forum in its annual Global Competitiveness Report has increased from 2.6 points in 2004 (one of the lowest among over 130 countries) to 4.6 points in 2007, at the level of Slovenia and Turkey and the second highest indicator in the former Soviet Union countries after Estonia. All these efforts that have resulted in a strengthened state have curbed the influence of professional criminals. They have been transferred to prison No 7 thus isolating them from the rest of the inmates and from the outside world. Therefore they lost the capability to exert influence in the prisons as well as being able to coordinate various criminal activities from prison. The side effect of strengthening the police, however, was the numerous alleged violations of human rights in the post-revolutionary period including police abuses and the use of excessive force.[107]

---

105. For more information on police reform see Kupatadze (2007).
106. 'Police services (1= cannot be relied upon to protect businesses from criminals, 7=can be relied upon to protect businesses from criminals)'.
107. See for instance US State Department country reports on human rights practices in Georgia (2006) and Amnesty International Report, Georgia profile (2007).

However, some reports suggest the political-criminal nexus is re-emerging. The Saakashvili government lost much of its legitimacy since its election in 2004 due to unpopular reforms, the adverse socio-economic situation and high unemployment rates. The public anger was shown by large anti-government demonstrations in November 2007 after which Saakashvili called for a snap presidential election. Since then the use of criminals for political purposes has been reported by some local observers. For instance during the parliamentary election of 2008 a number of criminals were set free in exchange for their active involvement in the election campaign of the ruling party (Mtivlishvili 2008). Thus weakened elites were obliged to re-establish relationships with criminals although to a lesser extent compared to the pre-revolutionary period.

STATE CAPTURED BY BUSINESS ELITES: OLIGARCHS IN THE UKRAINE

Ukraine has what Georgia and Kyrgyzstan lack: a developed industrial base and a large natural resource base. In general the country is rich in mineral resources – the principal ones being iron, magnesium and coal. Ukraine is the 6th largest producer of iron in the world. Its manufacturing sector is dominated by heavy industries like iron and steel (30% of industrial production), coal mining, chemical, mechanical engineering and shipbuilding. Manufactured goods include airplanes, turbines, metallurgical equipment, diesel locomotives and tractors (FITA, Ukraine profile). The groups and individuals related to the Soviet *nomenklatura* have benefited enormously from initial privatisation of these vast resources. As a result a class of super-rich individuals emerged that are commonly referred as oligarchs.

An oligarchy was first discussed in Plato's *Republic* and Aristotle's *Politics* and was defined as a form of government by a small group (Guriev and Rachinsky, 2005: 132). The oligarchs in the post-soviet context are the prototypes of the robber barons of the United States[108] and DeLong's description of the latter applies well to post-Soviet oligarchs:

> 'those lucky enough to be in the right place at the right time, driven and smart enough to see particular economic opportunities and seize them, foresighted enough to have gathered a large share of the equity of a highly-profitable enterprise into their hands, and well-connected enough to fend off political attempts to curb their wealth (or well-connected enough to make political favours the foundation of their wealth).' (DeLong 2005)

Some of the practices used by the oligarchs for the control of resources have included conflicts of interest (at the very least), such as insider privatisation or illegal means, such as loans-for-shares.[109] In general, four types of groups bene-

---

108. For the analogy see Aslund (2007).
109. For more on Russian privatisation see Black et al. (2000); Lieberman and Veimetra (1996).

fited mainly from the post-Soviet economic transition process. The first group was based on 'old school ties', i.e. former communist *nomenklatura* and police/ KGB networks; the second was a shadow economic elite comprising red directors of Soviet factories, so-called *tsekhaviki* and *deltsi*;[110] the third, new emerging businessmen, usually young people with a strong entrepreneurial instinct and fourth, traditional organized crime that would comprise *vory v zakone*. The first two groups were the main benefactors from shady privatisation deals (Los and Zybertowicz, 2000; Glinkina, 1994), although stakes in newly privatised companies also fell into the hands of professional criminals in those countries where they had a strong presence, such as in Georgia. More functionally based crime groups with a background in sports or a common experience in Soviet prisons first emerged as violent racketeer groupings then gradually developed into mafia-like structures with business ownership interests. The younger entrepreneurs who started from scratch in the late 1980s also benefited, taking advantage of 'the co-existence of regulated and quasi-market prices' and then investing this money in industrial enterprises (Guriev and Rachinsky, 2005: 138-139).

Hence the origin of initial accumulations of capital is frequently criminal and this is not characteristic of the post-soviet context only. DeLong (2005) maintains that not only the American robber barons, but also the system in which they were embedded were completely corrupt. In general, allegedly almost all Ukrainian oligarchs have earned their fortunes through various semi-legal or illegal activities, such as commodity trading that involved several elements of fraud and rent seeking, or skimming. This usually involved such activities as non-payment of taxes to the state, extracting discounts on barter deals, having illegal monopolies acquired through shady deals, extensive lobbying etc. (Aslund and McFaul, 2006: 10).

The relationship between oligarchs and the state shows different patterns across different countries of the former Soviet Union. Unlike Russia where oligarchs were kept at bay after Putin's advance to power, in Ukraine the oligarchs captured the state and now control the main direction of state policies. Kalman found that 350 of the 450 Rada deputies have some kind of economic interest in over 700 Ukrainian business enterprises in 2001 (Kalman quoted in Williams and Picarelli, 2002). 300 of the Rada deputies were dollar millionaires (Wilson, 2005: 149) and more than half of Ukraine's richest men have been or are now active in politics (*Kyiv Post,* 2006a) and the rest are indirectly involved supporting various political groupings. Some oligarchs switch from party to party depending on who is in power, for instance Vasyl Khmelnytsky and Andryi Ivanov.

Two opposing views are discussed in the literature on the implications of oligarchic control of capital on the rule of law and property rights. On the one hand oligarchs, as private owners, should be interested in the establishment of private property rights and contract enforcement, on the other hand, given the immaturity of the political system, the incentive to use political influence for redistribu-

---

110. Russian slang words denoting private entrepreneurs banned by Soviet law.

tion from other economic agents is great (Hoff and Stiglitz, 2004; Guriev and Rachinsky, 2005: 146). The latter process, referred to as King John redistribution, involves redistribution from the have-nots to the haves by subverting legal, political and regulatory institutions to work in favour of the haves through political contributions, bribes, or just deployment of legal and political resources to get their way (Glaesera et al., 2003: 210). Thus this involves state capture by wealthy businessmen. It is argued that the wealthy businessmen favour the establishment of the rule of law and private property only to the extent that it remains ineffective enough to counteract their interests. The interest of oligarchs would be in lowering their own costs of safeguarding businesses through advancing more efficient law enforcement structures as long as they remain open to outside interference and vulnerable to manipulation by powerful informal networks.

The process of privatisation in the early 1990s earned an unpopular nickname of *prikhvatizatsia* meaning the grabbing of state resources. The methods of re-division of resources have now changed to a more 'formal' and 'legal' manner – corporate raiding, the new form of *prikhvatizatsia*. Frequently the same groups that were initially involved in shady privatisation deals in the early 1990s are now involved in raiding activities. Ukraine is still far from the universal application of rule of law principles, although the legal system is much more developed compared to what it was in the immediate aftermath of the breakup of the Soviet Union. Therefore the stakeholders striving for re-division of scarce resources are now more likely to stick to semi-legal means rather than purely illicit methods. After all, as Kuzio argues 'it would be unreasonable to expect re-privatization to be more corrupt than initial privatization'. The main problem was and still remains corruptibility and unfairness due to corruption in the courts (Kuzio, 2006).

Since the Orange Revolution the main apologist for re-privatisation was the former Prime Minister Yulia Tymoshenko. She has voiced support for investigating 3,000 privatizations undertaken since 1992, while Yushchenko has supported a list of 29 companies (Kuzio, 2005: 6). Yushchenko's main focus was the renationalization of Ukraine's biggest steel mill, Kryvorizhstal and Nikopol Ferroalloy Plant (*Kyiv Post*, 2006b). The latter was co-owned by Viktor Pinchuk, son-in-law of former President Kuchma and Rinat Akhmetov, the wealthiest man in the Ukraine and the main financier of Yuschenko's rival Party of Regions political party. Ultimately only Kryvorizhstal was re-privatized and, though initially bought for 800 million USD dollars by Ukrainian oligarchs, has been sold for 4.8 billion USD to Mittal Steel (Forbes, 2005).

However apart from government initiatives towards re-privatization, the main re-division of resources since the Orange Revolution has been implemented through raiding, which is interesting for this study since it involves elements of capture of the judiciary and executive systems. Raiding is a form of re-distribution of spoils; it basically means seizing a property object. The experts differentiate between 'white' and 'black' raiding. In the former case the raiders usually use legal forms of merger and acquisition. The latter is an almost completely illegal takeover of the business (Zerkalov, 2007: 6-9) and involves counterfeiting of documents, registration of companies through dummy individuals, bribing law enforcement structures and 'buying' court decisions. Usually raiders purchase a small share of stock, then file a lawsuit in a lower-level court in a remote town, bribe the court for a favorable decision and then take the possession of the property usually through using force, involving various private security companies or state law enforcement structures. The pervasive rent-seeking in the criminal justice system creates incentives for raiding. The courts in the Ukraine are rated as one of the most corrupt, being in the top five tier together with the state auto inspection, the police and healthcare services, according to the USAID study (2007: 19). In general, raiding and courts corruption are mutually reinforcing in post-Orange Revolution Ukraine.

There is a strong correlation between raiding activities and regime transition. The centres of power have multiplied and instead of a strictly centralized governance system under Kuchma, now several opposing factions of political-business elites are vying for power, none of them being in full control. In fact, raiding has increased after the Orange revolution, which is a clear indication of semi-legal redistribution of spoils accompanying regime transition. 60 percent of the respondents interviewed by Corporate Relations Research Center (CRRC) think that raiding has increased in Ukraine since 2005. Around 2,500 enterprises have been raided in the last 2-3 years. CRRC data show that the biggest raiders are usually the oligarchs, I. Kolomoyskyi (the group *Privat*), Konstantin Jevago (the group *Finansi i kredit*) and Rinat Akhmetov (the group System Capital Management) (Corporativ.info, 2006).

Some raiders use different actors in a forceful takeover of enterprises. Frequently private security companies or organized crime groups are also involved, for instance one of the sides in conflict used the Kyiv crime group in the dispute over a steel factory in 2006[111] and another entrepreneur-cum politician in Kharkiv, Eastern Ukraine used the crime group of Arthur Marabian, aka *Sviatoi* or *Papa*, the head of a sport organization, in a raiding attack on a meat-processing factory in Dergachevo.[112] However, most frequently the detachments of the Ministry of the Interior, such as the special purpose unit Berkut, are involved. These cases involve large payoffs to the law enforcement officials and are implemented by larger financial groups having extensive ties with the political elites.[113] The process of spoils redistribution through raiding clearly shows that the oligarchs still have an interest in maintaining a weak state with an inefficient criminal justice system that is vulnerable to manipulation because these conditions would allow them to obtain an additional stake in the economy.

---

111. Interview with Andrey Semidedko, head of anti-raiding association, 11 November 2007, Kiev Ukraine.
112. See for instance Ukraina Kriminalnaya (2007) and Komitet prativadeistvyi organizovannoi prestupnosty i korupcii (2007).
113. Author's field research in Ukraine, October-December 2007.

STATE CAPTURE BY POLITICAL ELITES: RULING FAMILIES IN KYRGYZSTAN

The more than decade-long rule of Akaev resulted in rampant corruption in every sector of the political and economic life of the country. The rent-seeking of Akaev's regime was reinforced by the role of the 'ruling family' in corruption schemes. Many of the lucrative business activities in Kyrgyzstan had to have endorsement from Akaev's family – Aidar, Akaev's son and Adil Toigonbaev, Akaev's son in law.[114] Aslund (2005) indicates that the ruling family enjoyed a monopoly on medium and large enterprises and Collins reports that Akaev's relatives controlled the businesses of sugar, cooking oil, bars and minibuses (2006: 234). The family also controlled many of the media sources. For instance Adil Toigonbaev's holdings allegedly included daily *Vecherniy Bishkek*, the television station KOORT, the weekly *Avtoradio*, and the Kyrgyzinfo website (Ibraev, 2004). Aidar owned Bitel, the country's largest mobile phone operator (Sydykov, 2007) and together with Adil controlled the jet fuel supplies to American military bases in Kyrgyzstan and Manas international airport.[115]

Hence the ruling family directly owned shares in a number of enterprises or frequently used to sell protection to the businesses extorting illegal shares from the companies. If the businesses refused protection, they would receive tax inspections and law enforcement squads who would threaten them in the case of continued disobedience (Aslund, 2005). Kyrgyz prosecutors raised five criminal cases against Aidar Akaev re-embezzling a total of US$4.5 million (AKIpress, 30 September 2008).

Mairam Akaeva, the president's wife, appeared to be informally in charge of staffing policy in the state organizations.[116] Reportedly foreign companies planning to do business in Kyrgyzstan, for instance in the gold mining sector, were also paying in order to obtain a favourable decision from the government.[117] The fund 'Meerim' run by Akaev's wife was repeatedly accused of diverting budgetary funds and money laundering (Marat 2006: 83). The fund was alleged to be a legal cover for human trafficking to the United States (RFERL, 2009). In a study conducted by the Kyrgyz origination *Sotsinformburo* Mairam Akaeva was ranked by an expert opinion survey in 2003 as the most influential figure in Kyrgyzstan (AKIpress, 21 May 2004).

As a result, Akaev's family amassed huge property. As Anders Aslund (2005) argues 'the assessments of the family's wealth vary, but a few hundred million U.S. dollars seems plausible'. Allegedly some of the criminal leaders were also supported by ruling family representatives, in order to have some kind of leverage over organized crime groups in the country. However, over time these criminals

---

114. Interviews with Kyrgyz experts, March-May 2007 Bishkek, Kyrgyzstan.
115. See for instance, International Oil Daily (2005) and Energy Intelligence Group (2003).
116. Interview with Elena Avdeeva, Chief editor, Newspaper *Belyi Parakhod*, 28 March, 2007, Bishkek, Kyrgyzstan.
117. See for instance the account of former government official Isaev (2006: 41).

got out of the control of their patrons and later on even contributed to their ouster in what has been called the Tulip Revolution.[118]

The informal channels of illegal payments have largely been institutionalized. Immediately after the Tulip Revolution these channels were temporarily disrupted and businessmen were confused to whom, how much and when they should pay the regular illegal amounts.[119] Engvall (2007: 37) mentions that there was 'no actor in a position to define the rules of the game'. The chaos and uncertainty after the 'revolution' left the legal and illegal markets in limbo, with the defining and widely accepted boundaries no longer clear. With Akaev's family and its operatives removed from informal control, it became vague where the centre of power would lie. However, since then it appears that the corruption pyramids have been restored in Kyrgyzstan and, as some analysts have put it, 'simply one family has been substituted by another'.[120] Azimbek Beknazarov, the Prosecutor General, acknowledged in 2005 that most of Akaev's property and companies had been transferred to the new powerbrokers (Sydykov, 2007).

The process of redistribution itself was a violent process in Kyrgyzstan resulting in a number of contract killings in the immediate aftermath of the Tulip Revolution. The process remained outside the control of legitimate public institutions and the political elites, acting in their private and not the state's interests and a number of non-state actors, among them criminal groups, were involved in property redistribution. Reportedly some representatives of the political elites used non-state actors, or more importantly, the state itself to obtain their share of the spoils (Kupatadze, 2008). Additionally, the analysis of post-revolutionary appointments to high ranking positions, especially in the law enforcement system leads to a conclusion that the state in Kyrgyzstan has been captured by a small clique of powerful individuals related through blood kinship.

CONCLUSIONS

More than a decade of post-Soviet transition has resulted in the emergence of political-criminal clans and corrupt, half-criminalized economies in many newly independent states in post-Soviet Eurasia. State capture by various actors ranging from organized crime groups to semi-criminalized elites has been a prevalent problem.

The different patterns of state capture have been delineated by the political economy of a particular country. The industrially developed Ukraine with its large resource base has produced a number of powerful and super-rich individuals who

---

118. Author's field research in Kyrgyzstan, March-May 2007.
119. Interview with Nur Amorov, a lecturer in political science, Kyrgyz-Slavic University, 18 April Bishkek, Kyrgyzstan.
120. Interviews with Kyrgyz experts, March-May 2007, Bishkek, Kyrgyzstan. See also Kupatadze (2008: 287).

influence state policies. The state in Georgia and Kyrgyzstan on the other hand has been less impacted by oligarchic capital and rather has been hijacked by other agents. The professional criminals in Georgia and ruling families in Kyrgyzstan have or have had a great impact on the state domain, either neutralizing state power or directing state resources. In countries where the informal networks are built more along blood kinship lines such as in Georgia and Kyrgyzstan, rather than money-based functional cooperation as in Ukraine, the state is more likely to be captured by groups based on close relative linkages. Certainly the explanation of diverging patterns in state capture needs to be situated in political-economic and social structures of their respective societies. The historical context of post-Soviet transition is also important. The ethnic conflicts in Abkhazia and South Ossetia of Georgia in the early 1990s directly contributed to the strengthening of the underworld through illicit revenue-generating opportunities based on the war economy. These criminal networks successfully hijacked the weakened central authority that lost control over more than twenty percent of the country's territory.

The process of state formation in the aftermath of the Soviet Union's breakup was basically the struggle for domination between various groups, such as organized crime groups, ruling cliques and large business groupings. The means of coercion and providing protection were the two contested areas. In every instance the rival factions have been gaining power at the expense of a weakening state. State structures have been manipulated depending on the interests of those who dominate.

In general elites always try to limit the influence of competitors and monopolize resources from licit as well as illicit activities. Their involvement in illicit activities may range from utilizing illegal methods, such as in the case of 'black raiding' to ripping money from illicit activities, such as human trafficking. The rent-seeking of elites makes the criminal justice system weak and corrupt, which directly translates into the preconditions for state capture and a resilient political-criminal nexus. Under the elite dominance model, organized crime groups keep a low profile and mainly act as auxiliaries to elite activities. In the conditions of weakly developed formal institutions, the elites may use informal methods of negotiation, which may include the use of criminals in the process. The political-criminal nexus does not go away easily and may re-emerge in the case of a weakening incumbent regime or a failing state.

On the other hand, organized crime groups may use the momentum developed by abrupt transitions, such as the coloured revolutions described above, as window of opportunity to co-opt state institutions. If incoming elites are united and do not lack resources such as financial means, they would not succumb to organized crime's blackmail, while divided and under-resourced elites may start collaborating with crime groups that may further develop to dependency on them. In the case of multiple centres of power that are more situated in the upper world and stronger state institutions the main goal of organized crime groups is *profit* rather than capturing state institutions. However, if the state institutions are collapsing, state capture becomes a goal in itself as happened in Kyrgyzstan in the immediate aftermath of the Tulip Revolution. The existence of multiple centres of power in elites also further corrupts the system since the organized crime groups are diversifying their links with upper world agents to survive and continue their smooth functioning.

This pattern of behaviour can be generalized to business groups. In many post-Soviet countries the distinction between political and business elites is lost. Powerful companies have an interest in a stronger state although not one strong enough to counteract their interests. The oligarchs need to keep the state institutions vulnerable to manipulation since this allows them to obtain a further stake in the economy.

The extent to which the elites are cohesive affects the pattern of state capture in another way. When political elites are consolidated as in the case of Georgia after the Rose Revolution, the capture of one branch of power, for instance, the legislature, automatically translates into the capture of two other branches. Conversely, in the case of divided elites, state capture may not cover all three branches, since power is divided among various factions of the elites that usually have diverging interests. This is the case with Ukraine in the post-Orange Revolution period.

REFERENCES

Afanasyev, V. (1994). 'Organized crime and society'. *Demokratizatsiya*, 2(3).

AKIpress (news agency) 2004. 21 May.

AKIpress (news agency) 2008. 30 September.

Amnesty International Report (2007). *Georgia profile*, available online at http://report2007.amnesty.org/eng/Regions/Europe-and-Central-Asia/Georgia.

Armao, F. (2003). 'Why is organized crime so successful?' In F. Allum & R. Siebert, *Organized crime and the challenge to democracy*. Routledge.

Aslund, A. (2005a). 'Economic reform after the revolution in the Kyrgyz Republic'. *Demokratizatsiya*, 13(4): 469-483.

Aslund, A. (2005b). 'Comparative oligarchy: Russia, Ukraine and the United States'. *Studies & Analyses No. 296*, Center for Social and Economic Research, Warsaw, Poland.

Aslund, A. & McFaul, M. (2006). *Revolution in orange: the origins of Ukraine's democratic breakthrough*. Carnegie Endowment for International Peace.

Aslund, A. (2007). *How capitalism was built: the transformation of Central and Eastern Europe, Russia and Central Asia*. Cambridge University Press, pp. 257-272.

Beare, M.E. (2007). 'The devil made me do it: business partners in crime'. *Journal of Financial Crime*, 14(1): 34-48.

Black, B.S., Kraakman, R.H. & Tarassova, A. (2000) 'Russian privatization and corporate governance: What went wrong?' *Stanford Law Review*, 52: 1731-1808.

Chalidze, V. (1977). *Ugalovnaia Rassia*. New York: Khronika Press.

Collins, K. (2006). *Clan politics and regime transition in Central Asia.* Cambridge University Press.

Corporativ.info (2006). Reiderstvo v Ukraine, 13 December.

DeLong, J. B. (2005). 'Robber Barons'. Brad DeLong's Website, 1 Jan. 1998. University of California at Berkeley, and NBER.

Devdariani, J. (2003). 'Barbs over kidnapping reach dangerous pitch in Georgia in Eurasia Insight', available at http://www.eurasianet.org/departments/insight/articles/eavo62303.shtml.

Diamond, L.(2008). 'The democratic rollback: The resurgence of the predatory state'. *Foreign Affairs*, March/April, 36-48.

Dobovšek, B. (2008). 'Economic organized crime networks in emerging democracies'. *International Journal of Social Economics*, 35(9): 679-690.

EBRD (1999). *Transition report 1999*, Governance in transition abstract, available online at http://transitionreport.co.uk/TRO/c.abs/transition-report/volume1999/issue1/article93.

Economist (The) (2006). 'A dope dupe – Kyrgyzstan', 23 September.

Energy Intelligence Group (news contribution) (2003). 'American pie – Pentagon scours Central Asia to fuel US military'. NEFTE Compass.

Engvall, J. (2007). 'Kyrgyzstan: the anatomy of a state'. *Problems of Post-Communism*, 54(4): 33-45.

Evans, M. (2006). 'Elitism'. In C. Hay, M. Lister & D. Marsh (eds.), *The state, theories and issues.* Palgrave Macmillan.

Finckenauer, J.O. (2005), 'Problems of definition: What is organized crime?' *Trends in Organized Crime*, 8(3).

FITA (The Federation of International Trade Associations). 'Ukraine profile', available online at http://fita.org/countries/ukraine.html.

Forbes (2005). Available online at http://www.forbes.com/2005/10/24/mittal-ukraine-steel-cx_cn_1024autofacescano4.html, 24 October.

Fries, S., Lysenko, T. & Polanec, S.(2003). *The 2002 Business Environment and Enterprise Performance Survey: Results from a survey of 6,100 firms.* Working Paper 84. London: European Bank for Reconstruction and Development, available online at www.ebrd.com/pubs/econo/wp0084.pdf.

Galeotti, M. (1998). 'The Mafiya and the New Russia'. *Australian Journal of Politics and History*, 44: 415-429.

Galeotti, M. (2002). 'Introduction'. In *Russian and Post-soviet organized crime.* Ashgate.

Glaesera, E., Scheinkmanb, J. & Shleifer, A. (2003). 'The injustice of inequality'. *Journal of Monetary Economics*, 50:199-222.

Glinkina, S.P. (1994). 'Privatizatsiya and Kriminalizatsiya, how organized crime is hijacking privatization'. *Demokratizatsiya*, 2(1).

Godson, R. (2003). *Menace to society: political-criminal collaboration around the world.* Piscataway, NJ: Transaction Publishers.

Guriev, S. & Rachinsky, A. (2005). 'The role of oligarchs in Russian capitalism'. *Journal of Economic Perspective*, 19(1): 131-150.

Hagan, F.A. (1983). 'The organized crime continuum: a further specification of a new conceptual model'. *Criminal Justice Review*, 8(2): 52-57.

Hagan, F.A. (2006). 'Organized crime and organized crime: indeterminate problems of definition'. *Trends in Organized Crime*, 9(4): 127-137.

Hall, R.B. & Biersteker, T.J. (2002). 'The emergence of private authority in the international system'. In *The emergence of private authority in global governance*. Cambridge: Cambridge University Press.

Handelman, S. (1995). *Comrade criminal*. Yale University Press.

Hay, C. (2006). 'What's Marxist about Marxist state theory'. In C. Hay, M. Lister & D. Marsh (eds.), *The state, theories and issues*. Basingstoke: Palgrave Macmillan.

Hellman, J. (1998). 'Winners take all: The politics of partial reform in postcommunist transitions'. *World Politics*, 50(2).

Hellman, J., Jones, G., Kaufmann, D. & Schankerman, M. (2000). *Measuring governance, corruption, and state capture: How firms and bureaucrats shape the business environment in transition economies*. World Bank Policy Research Working Paper 2312, Washington D.C., http://www.worldbank.org/wbi/governance/pubs/measuregov.htm

Hellman, J., Jones, G. & Kaufmann, D. (2001). *Seize the state, seize the day: State capture, corruption and influence in transition*. World Bank Policy Research Working Paper 2444, Washington. D.C., http://www.worldbank.org/wbi/governance/pdf/seize_synth.pdf

Hellman, J.S. & Schankerman, M. (2000). *Intervention, corruption and capture: the nexus between enterprises and the state*. Working paper No. 58, EBRD.

Hoff, K. & Stiglitz, J.E. (2004). 'After the Big Bang? Obstacles to the emergence of the rule of law in post-Communist societies'. *The American Economic Review*, 94(3), 753-763.

Ibraev, T. (2004). Pyramida Scheme, Transitions Online.

International Oil Daily (news contribution) (2005). US military faces threat in central Asia; fuel supplies restricted at some bases, 18 July.

Isaev, K. (2006). *Vastok dela tonkae ili litso kirgizskoi vlasti glazami achevidtsa*. Bishkek: TAS.

Kandelaki, G. (2006). 'Georgia's Rose Revolution. A participant's perspective, special report'. United State Institute of Peace, available online at http://www.usip.org/pubs/specialreports/sr167.pdf.

Kelly, R.J. (2004). 'An American way of crime and corruption'. In R. Godson (ed.), *Menace to society: political-criminal collaboration around the world*. National Strategy Information Center, US.

Khorbaladze, T. (2004). 'Anticorruption passions of the Georgian government: How is corruption fought in Georgia?' *South Caucasus. Monthly Analytical Magazine*, Caucasus Journalist Network, available online at http://caucasusjournalists.net/ENG/item.asp?id=131.

Komitet pradivadeistvyi organizovannoi prestupnosty i korupcii (2007). Available online at http://kpk.org.ua/2007/03/30/kharkov__gorod_mentovskijj.html, 30 March.

Kornai, J. (1990). *The road to a free economy: Shifting from a socialist system: The example of Hungary*. New York: Norton.

Kotkin, S. & Sajo, A. (eds.) (2002). *Political corruption in transition, a skeptic's handbook*. Central European University Press.

Kupatadze, A. et al. (2007). 'Policing and police reform in Georgia'. In L.I. Shelley, et al., *Organized crime and corruption in Georgia*. Routledge, pp. 93-111.

Kupatadze, A. (2008). 'Organized crime before and after the Tulip Revolution: The changing dynamics of upperworld-underworld networks'. *Central Asian Survey*, 27(3): 279-299.

Kuzio, T. (2005). Testimony to the Committee on International Relations, US House of Representatives, Washington D.C., 27 July.

Kuzio, T. (2006). 'Re-privatization and the revolution'. *Kyiv Post*, 23 February.

Kuzio, T. (2008). 'Leaders lack will to root out corruption'. *Kyiv Post*, 23 July.

Kyiv Post (2006a). 'The 30 richest Ukrainians'. Special insert, 29 June.

Kyiv Post (2006b). 8 March.

Lambsdorff, J.G. (2002). 'Corruption and rent-seeking'. *Public Choice*, 113: 116, 97-125.

Liddick, D.R. (1999). *An empirical, theoretical and historical overview of organized crime.* Edwin Mellen Press.

Lieberman, W. & Veimetra, R. (1996). 'The rush for state shares in the 'Klondyke' of Wild East capitalism: Loans-for-shares transactions in Russia'. *George Wash. J. Int. Law Econ.*, 29: 737-768.

Los, M. (2003). 'Crime in transition: The post-communist state, markets and crime'. *Crime, Law and Social Change*, 40.

Los, M. & Zybertowicz, A.(2000). *Privatizing the police-state: The case of Poland.* St. Martin's Press.

Lupsha, P.A.(1996). 'Transnational organized crime versus the nation-state. *Transnational Organized Crime*, 2(1).

Marat, E. (2006). *The state-crime nexus in Central Asia: State weakness, organized crime, and corruption in Kyrgyzstan and Tajikistan.* Silk Road Studies Program and Central Asia and Caucasus Institute.

Migdal, J.S. (2001). *State in society, studying how states and societies transform and constitute one another.* Cambridge: Cambridge University Press.

Moselle, A. & Polak, B. (2001). 'A model of predatory state'. *Journal of Law, Economics, and Organization*, 17(1): 1-33.

Mtivlishvili, G. (2008). Criminals freed in countdown to rampant election fraud, HRIDC, June 27, available online at http://www.humanrights.ge/index.php?a=article&id=2872&lang=en, Web port on Human Rights of Georgia.

Nye, S. (1967). 'Corruption and political development: A cost-benefit analysis'. *American Political Science Review*, 61(2): 417-427.

Olson, M. (1993). 'Dictatorship, democracy, and development'. *American Political Science Review*, 87(3).

Radnitz, S. (2006). 'What really happened in Kyrgyzstan?' *Journal of Democracy*, 17(2): 132-146.

Rawlinson, P. (2002). 'Capitalist, criminals and oligarchs – Sutherland and the new "robber barons"'. *Crime, law and social change*, 37: 293-307.

RFERL (Radio Free Europe Radio Liberty)(2009). 'Under the radar, migrants from Central Asia, Georgia head to U.S.'. Radio Free Europe Radio Liberty, available online at http://www.rferl.org/content/Under_the_Radar_Migrants_From_Central_Asia_Georgia_Head_To_US/1510350.html

Rotberg, R.I. (2004). 'The failure and collapse of nation-states, breakdown prevention and repair'. In *When States Fail, Causes and Consequences.* Princeton University Press.

Schulte-Bockholt, A. (2006). *The politics of organized crime and the organized crime of politics, a study in criminal power.* Lexington books.

Serio, J.D. & Razinkin, V. (1995). 'Thieves professing the code: The traditional role of vory v zakone in Russia's criminal world and adaptations to a new social reality'. *Low Intensity Conflict and Law Enforcement*, 4(1).

Shelley, L. & Scot, E. (2003). 'Georgia's "revolution of roses" can be transplanted'. *Washington Post*, 30 November, B05.

Sydykov, A. (2007). 'Taking our due'. Transitions Online, 9 March.

Tilly, Ch. (1985). 'War making and state making as organized crime'. In P. Evans, D. Rueschemeyer & Th. Skocpol (eds.), *Bringing the State Back In*. Cambridge: Cambridge University Press, pp. 169-191.

Ukraina Kriminalnaya (2007). Available online at http://www.cripo.com.ua/ ?sect_id=4&aid=37065, 25 June.

USAID (2007). *Corruption in Ukraine 2007 Baseline National Survey for the MCC Threshold Country Program*.

US State Department (2006). *Country reports on human rights practices Georgia, 2006*. Available online at http://www.state.gov/g/drl/rls/hrrpt/2006/78813.htm.

Varese, F. (2001). *The Russian mafia, private protection in a new market economy*. Oxford: Oxford University Press.

Weber, M. (1919). 'The profession and vocation of politics'. Reprinted in M. Weber (1994), *Political writings*, edited by P. Lassman & R. Speris. Cambridge: Cambridge University Press, pp. 309-369.

Wedel, J.R. (2001). 'Corruption and organized crime in post-Communist states: New ways of manifesting old patterns'. *Trends in Organized Crime*, 7(1).

Williams, Ph. (2001). 'Crime, Illicit Markets and Money laundering'. In P.J. Simmons & Ch. Oudraat (eds.), *Managing global issues: Lessons learned*. Carnegie Endowment for International Peace.

Williams, P. & Picarelli, J. (2002). 'Organized crime in Ukraine: Challenge and response, National Criminal Justice Referrence Service (NCJRS), available online at http://www.ncjrs.gov/pdffiles1/nij/grants/198321.pdf.

Wilson, A. (2005). *Ukraine's Orange Revolution*. Yale University Press.

World Bank (2000). *Anticorruption in transition, a contribution to the policy debate*.

Zerkalov, D.B. (2007). *Reideri pasobie*. KNT, Kiev.

Serbia on the routes of human trafficking

Sanja Copic and Biljana Simeunovic-Patic

INTRODUCTION

Trafficking in human beings, although not a new phenomenon (Picarelli, 2007), has become one of the most important issues put on the agenda of nternational and regional organizations during the past two decades. As observed by Kelly, 'at the beginning of the twenty-first century there is no doubt that migration, especially its illegal/irregular forms of trafficking in persons and smuggling of migrants, has become a major international policy issue' (2007: 73). Thousands of migrants are crossing borders each year in 'search for work opportunities, increased incomes or the possibilities to start a new and better life' (Brunovskis and Tyldum, 2004: 19). Unfortunately, in such circumstances many of them, particularly women and children, end up in trafficking rings, being exploited in different fields of the informal economy, and essentially becoming goods for this transnational industry (Ramcharan, 2002: 161). Consequently, human trafficking has become 'one of the fastest growing criminal businesses in the world, generating massive profits for international criminal organizations' (Europol, 2006: 8).

Human trafficking is a complex and dynamic social phenomenon, whose mobility and organization in their international dimensions (Zamfiresku, 2001: 15) increase the degree of its gravity and danger. It is very often considered a modern-day form of slavery (Bales, 1999: 19), but also'one of economic survival strategies on the part of both traffickers and those being trafficked' (Baldwin-Edwards, 2006: 9) or, as observed by Lindstrom (2004: 46), a 'manifestation of the wider structural changes brought about by globalization and regionalization'. As a matter of fact, the processes of globalization, the development of the market economy, political instabilities and economic crises, civil wars, social inequalities, and gender discrimination as well as 'wider processes of global social transformation' (Lee, 2007: 7), have contributed to huge migration flows worldwide, particularly to its irregular forms – human trafficking and smuggling in migrants, but also to the occurrence of different forms of illegal businesses, the informal economy and illegal markets in general. That was particularly visible at the end of the twentieth century in some parts of Europe, such as the Eastern and Central European countries. Social changes in this part of the world which emerged as the result of political and economic transition contributed to 'favorable conditions for development of illegal markets', while human trafficking became 'one of the most profitable illegal markets' (Nikolic-Ristanovic, 2003: 7, 9). Or, as noted by Tyldam et al., (2005: 9):

'Trafficking in human beings (re-)appeared on the political agenda in Western Europe in the early 1990s, when the political transitions in Eastern Europe and the wars in the former Yugoslavia led to mass migration of persons from Eastern Europe and the Balkans.'

Consequently, human trafficking as an illegal market, a market in which people are treated as goods, is necessarily connected to other forms of illegal markets and the informal (grey) economy (Ely-Raphel, 2002: 173).

Being located in the Balkans and the South Eastern European region, it was not possible for Serbia to resist these global and regional trends and turbulences. Serbia became one of the main transit countries for (economic) migration from the East to the West. While being mainly a transit country, it is also becoming a country of origin, since it has recently experienced huge political and economic instability, and is still in the process of social and economic transition, which has brought a rise in unemployment, economic insecurity and social marginalization – which have become important push factors for labour emigration. From this departure point, in this paper we will try to emphasize the current position of Serbia on the routes of human trafficking, particularly within Europe, and point out some changes and challenges that have emerged recently. For the purpose of this paper human trafficking will be positioned and analyzed primarily within the context of broader migration flows and migration policy (Lee, 2007: 3-10). The paper is based on data obtained from different sources: reports of state institutions, non-governmental organizations, and surveys on human trafficking in Serbia conducted by the Victimology Society of Serbia in 2003, and during 2008 and the beginning of 2009.[121]

SERBIA: A CROSSROAD OF HUMAN TRAFFICKING ROUTES

Global human trafficking reflects global (labour) migration flows in general, or as noted by Morawska (2007: 95), human trafficking is flowing in a 'compass' pattern from (semi)peripheral or economically less- and underdeveloped areas (the South-East) to core or more developed areas (the North-West) of the world'. By positioning human trafficking within the concept of broader migration flows and migration policy, we can, as does Chuang (2004: 140), consider human trafficking 'as "an opportunistic response" to the tension between the economic necessity to migrate, on the one hand, and the politically motivated restrictions on migration, on the other'. That was more than obvious in Europe at the very end of the twentieth century.

---

121. The survey presents a central part of the currently running research project on 'Male victims of human trafficking in Serbia'. The aim of the survey conducted in 2008 and first two months of 2009 was to gain knowledge about the scope, structure and characteristics of trafficking in human beings in Serbia, with particular emphasis on male trafficking, as well as about the response of state agencies and the NGO sector to this phenomenon. The project is being conducted by the Victimology Society of Serbia and is financed by the US Department of State, Office to Monitor and Combat Trafficking in Persons.

Due to the period of political transition in the late 1980s and the beginning of the 1990s there was an opening of Eastern and Central European borders, through which passed a big wave of trafficked victims entering the West.[122] In that period trafficking in human beings benefited from the restrictive immigration policies of Western countries, which stopped chances of legal migration, turning under-privileged and marginalized social groups towards irregular forms of migration (Salt, 2000: 32, Mrvic-Petrovic, 2002: 14). Or, as quoted by Goodey, '[b]y closing virtually all legal methods of entry, Europe has ensured that outsiders have no choice but to try the trafficker...' (2002: 139). A little bit later, a second big wave of human trafficking emerged, moving the 'human beings market' to the Balkan countries, at first, and then to other South Eastern European countries: Romania, Moldova, Bulgaria, and Albania. Finally, some new trends in human trafficking, particularly in women, can be noticed in Europe: an expansion of trafficking in human beings from the countries of the former Soviet Union towards Asia and other destinations outside the European continent (Morawska, 2007: 97). Conse-quently, different routes of human trafficking are crossing Europe, maintaining several directions: the Balkan route, the Central-European route, the East route, the Mediterranean route, the Baltic route, and the North-African route (Europol, 2006: 18).

From a historical point of view, the Balkan Peninsula has always been and still is an important crossroad in the routes going from the East to the West. However, the Balkan region became particularly relevant to the development of different forms of illegal trafficking during the 1990s, benefiting from both global trends, and regional turbulences (Hajdinjak, 2002, Europol, 2006: 5, Arsovska, 2008). At the end of the 1990s, the Balkans, earlier mostly a transit zone, increasingly became the destination for numerous victims. This situation was because of the lack of adequate legal regulation, inadequate implementation and use of existing laws, corruption, porosity of state borders, restricted control of migration flows, as well as the war and militarization of the region, the concentration of foreign (peacekeeping) forces in Kosovo and Bosnia and Herzegovina, and political insta-bility (Kolakovi et al., 2002, Lehti, 2003: 22, Arsovska, 2008). These factors resulted in an increased demand for sexual services, a pull factor that led to a huge number of victims, primarily women form the East, ending up in forced prostitution in the region. On the other hand, poverty, masses of refugees, unem-ployment, and a lack of vision for the future in general, resulting from the war in the territory of the former Yugoslavia contributed as push factors to an increased number of victims from the Balkans ending up in trafficking rings in the West (Nikolic-Ristanovic, 2002: 133).

---

122. The largest number of victims from Eastern Europe (around 80%) ended up in Western European countries – in Germany, Italy, Switzerland, the Netherlands, Austria, and England. Some 15% reached the Middle East (Israel, Saudi Arab) or the Far East (Japan, Thailand), while 3% came to the USA and Canada, and the rest ended up in Central European countries, mainly in Poland, Hun-gary and the Czech Republic. (Milivojevi and Vukobratovi, 1999: 53; US Congres 2000: 8).

The Balkan route either crosses the Balkans or begins in the countries of the Balkan Peninsula, moving further in three directions: towards the North, via Hungary to the Western European countries; to Slovenia and then to the West; and, thirdly, to the South, i.e. to Greece, then to Italy and other EU countries. This last route is increasingly used for the transfer of victims from Turkey, some Asian countries, the Middle East in particular, and Africa towards Western and Central European countries, mainly across the territory of Kosovo and Bosnia and Herzegovina (IOM, 2004: 9). Consequently, as correctly observed by some authors, 'from the late 1990s onwards, the western Balkan countries have been singled out as one of the main hotbeds of organized crime', including trafficking in human beings (Arsovska, 2008: 50).

Being positioned on the Balkan Peninsula, Serbia is certainly an important part of the Balkan route for human trafficking. At the beginning of the 1990s Serbia was predominantly a destination country, particularly for women from the former Soviet Union. During the 1990s, with the worsening of the economic situation, it gradually turned into a transit country. At the beginning of the twenty-first century it was estimated that most victims of human trafficking, particularly women, who ended up in Western European countries came to one of the destination countries via the Balkans, including Serbia (Limanowska, 2002: 4). Finally, Serbia is also turning into a country of origin, as well as into a country with internal trafficking (Nikolic-Ristanovic et al., 2004; Surtees, 2005: 12-17).

In the course of 2002 and the first half of 2003, as suggested by the data obtained in the survey on trafficking in human beings in Serbia (Nikolic-Ristanovic et al., 2004), trafficking in foreign women usually began in the countries of Eastern Europe, mainly the countries of the former Soviet Union, heading towards the West. The majority of victims came from the Ukraine, Moldova, and Romania, with some from Russia and Bulgaria. Trafficking channels started from the Ukraine and Moldova, passing through Romania, Bulgaria, and, less frequently, through Hungary. After entering, at that time, Serbia and Montenegro the routes maintained the East-West and North-South direction, although some routes led to the North (to Hungary). Routes from the East to the West went towards Republika Srpska (a part of Bosnia and Herzegovina) or Croatia, with one part heading north towards Hungary. The North-South channels went through Belgrade towards Kosovo, Macedonia or Albania, or towards Montenegro and then to Kosovo, Albania, or Italy, or other countries in Western Europe.

For male victims of trafficking, Serbia was predominantly a transit country. However, there were also some indications that it was a country of origin as well, and a few anecdotal indications that it might be a country of destination for the trafficking for the purpose of labour exploitation as well (Nikolic-Ristanovic et al., 2004).[123] During 2002 and the first half of 2003, 100 adult men were acknowledged as victims of trafficking by respondents to the previously mentioned survey. They originated from China, Afghanistan, Romania, Iraq, Iran, Turkey, Pakistan, Bangladesh, and Serbia. The routes of trafficking for these people went from Eastern Europe, the Far and the Middle East via Bulgaria and Romania to Serbia, forming a network of trafficking routes primarily in the central and northern parts of Serbia. After entering Serbia, trafficking routes went to the North – to Hungary, and to the West, i.e. to Croatia and then to EU countries. Germany, Italy and Great Britain were identified as the main destination countries for male victims.

Finally, concerning trafficking in children, Serbia used to be a country of origin as well as a country of transit and temporary destination for girls who were included in organized sex-trafficking, together with adult women. There are also data referring to the internal trafficking of Roma and non-Roma children (Serbian children trafficked from small towns to bigger cities e.g. Belgrade, Nis, Novi Pazar etc.). Recent data on trafficking in children in Serbia shows an increasing trend (Jovanovic, 2006), particularly those concerning trafficking in Roma children (Mihic, 2006).

Recent changes in trafficking patterns

Findings from the 2008-2009 survey on human trafficking in Serbia suggest some changes in trafficking routes. In comparison to the end of the 1990s and the beginning of the 2000s, a decrease in the number of victims entering from Romania and Bulgaria is noted. This trend became particularly visible during 2006 and 2007. Generally speaking, trafficking routes in Serbia today primarily go from the South to the North or West, and, to a more limited degree, from the North-East to the West.

Two main directions can be identified today: the first is via Moldova and Romania to Serbia, while the second is from the South to the North and West, i.e. from the territory of Kosovo, leading through the central part of Serbia to Hungary or Croatia, moving on to Western Europe. It seems that the enlargement of the EU and particularly the entry of Romania and Bulgaria into the EU has contributed to changes in trafficking routes which cross Serbia, particularly in terms of entry points. Namely, if a victim is transferred from the source country to Romania or Bulgaria, it seems fairly likely that he/she will be directly transported/transferred to other EU countries (via Hungary, Austria etc.), rather than exiting the EU by entering Serbia, and then trying to reenter EU in Hungary, for example. This change may possibly be due to the enhancement of border controls in these two EU countries that find themselves on the boundaries of the EU towards the East – on the edge of the 'gated walls' or the 'Fortress EU' (Goodey, 2002) – which certainly diminishes possible entries to Serbia from these directions.

---

123. According to research on trafficking in human beings in Serbia conducted by NGO Victimology Society in Serbia in 2003 (Nikolic-Ristanovic et al., 2004), Chinese citizens and men from Eastern European countries (Moldova etc.) are often used as illegal workers. However, there was insufficient information on whether these were trafficking cases or not.

On the other hand, in comparison to the beginning of the 2000s, a route towards Hungary became much more interesting, as far as it enables direct entry into the EU, which certainly makes further movement towards the West much easier. Besides, this route became interesting for traffickers and smugglers after the sea routes going from Albania directly to Italy had been cut off by police intervention (Lindstrom, 2004: 46; Arsovska, 2008). Finally, as observed above, at the end of the 1990s and the beginning of the twenty-first century, one of the main routes for human trafficking, particularly in women, went to Kosovo. However, as stated by some respondents, recently there were fewer victims, or at least those who were identified as victims, who had been found on their way to Kosovo or who had been exploited on the territory of Kosovo. Today we may, actually, notice a reverse direction of human trafficking, but also of illegal/irregular migration in general, coming from Kosovo and going through central Serbia to the North. Based on these findings we may conclude that the political, economy, and social circumstances of a country and the region contribute to changes in human trafficking routes and patterns (Arsovska, 2008).

Kosovo, as stated by some of our respondents, presents a 'black hole' for this part of Europe: a variety of routes for smuggling and illegal trafficking, including human trafficking, cross in the territory of Kosovo. This route is primarily used for trafficking in and smuggling of people from Asia, Albania, and those coming via Turkey. This can be explained by a number of factors: the weak legal and political system, the non-existence of visa regimes, free entrance and stay in the territory of Kosovo, as well as the weakness of Kosovo borders, particularly with Albania. This situation provides fertile soil for traffickers and smugglers to develop their 'businesses'. However, due to the political instability in this territory, one might expect Kosovo to remain an interesting area for different forms of illegal trafficking, including human trafficking, at least in the near future.

All these changes certainly contribute to the changes in the structure of those being victimized by trafficking in human beings. To consider this, we need first to look at the question of who the victims of human trafficking in Serbia are.

WHO ARE THE VICTIMS OF HUMAN TRAFFICKING IN SERBIA?

Numbers and characteristics of victims seem to be one of the important bases from which to try to understand trends in human trafficking in order to obtain a better assessment of the total number of persons involved in trafficking rings (Aromaa, 2005: 6). Unfortunately, there is as yet no unified system for monitoring and analysis of the data on human trafficking in Serbia: the data from various sources (governmental, non-governmental or international agencies/organizations), particularly those concerning victims, differ widely (Copic and Nikolic-Ristanovic, 2006). In addition, the available data on trafficking in children and men are particularly insufficient. Bearing in mind the probable very large dark figure of victimization by human trafficking in general and victimization of male

victims in particular, as well as the unknown numbers of victims of human trafficking that does not include sexual exploitation, it is unfeasible to draw any accu-
rate general conclusions on the phenomenon of trafficking in human beings in
Serbia. Additionally, it is very difficult to portray accurately the exact scope and
other characteristics of the issue of human trafficking in Serbia, particularly if we
bear in mind the fact that only a small number of persons are recognized and
identified as victims of trafficking in human beings by the relevant authorities.

On the other hand, just after the political changes in 2000, numerous anti-trafficking initiatives and campaigns were launched in Serbia, primarily with the
support of and pressure from the international organizations active in the field of
anti-trafficking activities in the Balkans (Lindstrom, 2004). Upon ratification of
the *UN Convention against Transnational Organized Crime and the United Nations
Protocol to Prevent, Suppress and Punish Trafficking in Persons, especially Women and
Children* in 2001, significant improvements in all aspects of the response to the
problem of trafficking in human beings were attained. That is probably one of the
reasons why there are no data on this phenomenon before the beginning of the
twenty first century. Namely, as pointed out by Limanowska, '[d]uring the period
from January 2000 to July 2001, the police stopped and questioned approximately 600 women. Three hundred of them were judged to be trafficked' (2002:
78-79). However, in practice, these cases were prosecuted under 'other criminal
offences' (procurement, kidnapping, bodily injuries, rape etc.). Consequently, this
kind of treatment presented 'fragmentarily criminal prosecution for specific
criminal offences, i.e. for one or more minor criminal offences, which are not
considered as a whole or in their interconnection, so there is no possibility for
pronouncing sanctions, which are adequate for this social threat' (Nikolic-
Ristanovic, 2005: 7).

According to the Second Annual Report on Victims of Trafficking in South-Eastern Europe (Surtees, 2005), 214 victims of human trafficking were identified and
assisted in Serbia during a four-year period, i.e. between 1 January 2001 and 31
December 2004. Most of the victims were foreigners – 169 (primarily originating
from Moldova, Ukraine and Romania), while 45 were Serbian citizens; the majority of identified and assisted victims were females.

The data provided by the Ministry of Interior of the Republic of Serbia shows that
Serbian police officers identified 223 victims of human trafficking in the five-year
period, i.e. from 2002 to 2006. Most of the victims identified were Serbian citizens (63), followed primarily by citizens of Romania, Moldova and the Ukraine,
and, to a much lesser extent by citizens of Russia, Bulgaria, Bosnia and Herzegovina, Georgia, Albania, Croatia, Iraq, Congo and Macedonia.[124] However, it can
be noticed that during 2002 and 2003 all the recognized victims were foreigners;

---

124. Source: Ministry of Interior, *Trgovina ljudima* (*Trafficking in people*), report. Retrieved from:
    www.mup.sr.gov.yu/domino/saveti.nsf/traffickingl.pdf (January 30, 2009).

since 2004, the situation has changed and Serbian citizens have formed a significant part of the victims identified by police officers.

As to the data of the Agency for Coordination of the Protection of Victims of Trafficking,[125] 214 victims of human trafficking were identified from 1 March 2004 up to the end of 2007: in 2004 the Agency identified 38 victims, in 2005 – 54 victims, in 2006 – 62 victims, and in 2007 – 60 victims of human trafficking. Most of the identified victims were women. What can be noticed from the data from the Agency is a continuing increase in the number of domestic victims being identified (primarily in terms of those being internally trafficked), but also an increase in child victims, particularly during 2006 and 2007.

According to the biannual report of NGO ASTRA,[126] in the course of 2004-2005 this organization assisted 135 victims of trafficking in human beings, most of whom were female victims, while more than two thirds were citizens of Serbia. Foreign victims were primarily from Romania, Moldova and the Ukraine. Serbia was the country of destination for more than 50% of victims; for 14.81% the destination country was Italy, while 3.7% were in transit to each of the following countries: Greece, Sweden, Croatia and Bosnia.

NGO Atina[127] assisted 16 women victims of trafficking in 2005 and 44 in 2006. In 2005, 14 victims were adults and 2 were children, while in 2006, 27 adult victims of trafficking were assisted and 17 children. In relation to nationality: in 2005 there were 10 Serbian citizens and 6 foreigners, while in 2006 this organization assisted 34 domestic victims and 10 foreigners. In 2006 most of the foreign victims were from the Ukraine, followed by Moldova and Romania.

Finally, the report of the NGO Counseling against family violence,[128] which manages one of the shelters for women victims of trafficking, indicates that 181 women victims of human trafficking were assisted by this organization and accommodated in the shelter from 1 January 2002 until the middle of 2005. During this period there were 49 women from Moldova, 33 from Ukraine, 38 from Romania, and 47 from Serbia (including Montenegro as well), while there were several victims from other countries, such as Russia, Albania, Iraq, Georgia, and Bulgaria. During the three-year period (2002-2004), 29 children went through the shelter, who were mainly from Serbia.

---

125. The Agency was established in 2004. Since mid 2005 it is a part of the Ministry of Labour and Social Policy. Its main duties include: receiving information on possible trafficked persons from all other bodies; going into the field to rescue possible victims; referring victims to the proper assistance providers; keeping victims fully informed on their options and rights; avoiding secondary victimization; providing assistance in all administrative proceedings; coordinating assistance during legal proceedings; transporting victims; gathering data on available assistance providers and services; and overseeing the reintegration of victims in Serbia.
126. Biannual Report 2004/5, ASTRA – Anti Trafficking Action, p. 35-38.
127. Annual Report 2005-2006 http://www.atina.org.yu/index.php?option=com_content&task=view&id=10&Itemid=2
128. Activity report 2001-2005, Counselling against family violence, Belgrade. 2005.

To conclude, it can be seen that in Serbia, as probably in other countries:

> '"[V]ictims of trafficking" are identified and sampled based not on definitional attributes, but rather identification by law enforcement or NGO personnel working in shelters. Identification is thereby contingent on the identifiers' understanding of trafficking.' (Tyldum et al., 2005: 25)

Unfortunately, the image of human trafficking in the academic and professional literature in Serbia is still rather simple and stereotypical, which results in a lack of understanding of the complexities of this form of crime (Nikolic-Ristanovic, 2005: 5). This is mostly a consequence of an inadequate level of information and education of professionals, but also a result of the lack of clear operational terms for the trafficking in human beings that would enable prompt and adequate identification of victims in practice (Nikolic-Ristanovic, 2005: 13; Tyldum et. al., 2005: 12-19, Kelly, 2007: 86-87).

While there is basic agreement that trafficking involves often violent abuses of the basic human rights of its victims in the course of exploitative practices, there are in fact diverging views as to the nature, extent, and resolution of the 'trafficking problem' (Ascola, 2007: 205).

Consequently, as correctly observed by Richard Danziger, a strong distinction between state institutions and non-governmental organizations still remains in terms of understanding who the victims of human trafficking are (Danziger, 2006: 10).

On the other hand, there are data on victims of human trafficking presented in the reports of different organizations in Serbia. However, some authors emphasize that the data are collected in various ways, using different methodologies, and very often are not followed with appropriate explanation on how the data were obtained (Kangaspunta, 2005: 1; Copic and Nikolic-Ristanovic, 2006). In addition, the data on specific victims are presented in the records of two or more organizations, which makes for data 'duplication'/overlapping, resulting in a lack of ability to compare data from different sources, even difficulties in summation to find total numbers of victims. Furthermore, as some authors have noticed, in the regions where there are more non-governmental organizations dealing with human trafficking and the regions where people are more informed about available forms of assistance and support, rehabilitation programs, etc., the number of identified victims will be higher (Tyldum et al., 2005: 29). Consequently, the data regarding victims of trafficking in human beings are not reliable and they are often used or, more precisely, abused for various campaigns, fund raising etc. (Copic and Nikolic-Ristanovic, 2006). Or, as noted by some authors:

> 'By uncritically using or constructing estimates that are not based on sound methodological techniques and hard data, we may assist in misleading more than informing, and hinder the creation of relevant policies.' (Tyldum et al, 2005: 23)

At the same time, as observed by Ascola (2007: 205):

> '[E]stimates of the true number of trafficked persons remain "guesstimates", as do any claims of "increased trafficking", in part because trafficking is typically an underground practice that involves illegal activities (and because its victims are often too scared to stand up to their exploiters).'

Nevertheless, if we take into consideration that the number of women who were not recognized as victims of trafficking and referred to appropriate victim support services is at least ten times bigger than the number of those assisted (Counter Trafficking Regional Point, 2003: 189), we could argue that the human trafficking problem is obviously bigger. Or, as observed by Morawska (2007: 94) 'the estimated numbers of trafficked persons more than double every 10 years'. Consequently, there is a need to conduct surveys as 'unambiguous classifications of victims of human trafficking are most easily obtained through survey data' (Tyldum et al., 2005: 25). To illustrate this: in the course of 2002 and the first half of 2003, more than 1,000 victims of trafficking were identified, or rather, recognized as victims of trafficking in Serbia (Nikolic-Ristanovic et al., 2004): 960 were women, 94 children, and 100 men. Although we are aware that it is hard to give a precise estimate of the extent of human trafficking, we could conclude from the Victimology Society of Serbia's 2003 survey data that human trafficking has a broader scope than that seen from the reports of relevant stakeholders.

Characteristics of human trafficking victims

The available data, in terms of both reports on identified victims and those obtained through the surveys discussed above, show that most female victims recognized in recent years in Serbia were citizens of Moldova, Ukraine, Romania, and Serbia. However, there is a noticeable trend towards Serbia being a country of origin as well (Commission of the European Communities, 2007). Serbian women are victims both of internal and transnational trafficking, usually ending up in Bosnia and Herzegovina and Italy. Internal sex-trafficking of Serbian women is relatively increasing in recent years, comprising around three-quarters of trafficking victimization in 2007. The main temporary or permanent destination points for internal sex-trafficking are big cities (i.e. Belgrade and Novi Sad), as well as border cities, e.g. Novi Pazar.

Women victims of human trafficking are usually between 18 and 30 years of age, with a lower level of education, mainly facing unemployment, poverty, and economic inequality. They usually originate from a difficult family milieu: dysfunctional families, domestic violence, alcoholism etc. Due to that, it is obvious that 'gender discrimination and structural disadvantages faced by women' (Tyldum et al., 2005: 38) are important push factors for trafficking in women. Sex-trafficking was, and still is a predominant form of trafficking in women, while in the cases of labour exploitation women are exploited primarily in hotels, restaurants, and domestic work.

On the other hand, as the findings of the Victimology Society's survey on human trafficking (which has an emphasis on male victims of human trafficking in Serbia, see footnote 2) suggest, for adult men, victims are mainly between 20 and 50 years of age, equally from Serbia and abroad. Foreigners primarily originate from China and Turkey, followed by those from Afghanistan, Albania, India, Kazakhstan, Pakistan, Moldova, and Romania. They have a low level of education, tending to be facing unemployment and poverty. Transnational trafficking is dominant, so Serbia is primarily a transit country (to Italy or other EU countries), but also a country of origin (to Russia, Ukraine, the UAE, Malta), while rarely being a country of destination. Labour exploitation is the most frequent form of trafficking in men: male victims are exposed to longer working hours, lower payment then promised/agreed, or even to non-payment. Even if the trafficking chain was cut-off in Serbia, it could be presumed that men would be exposed to some forms of (labour) exploitation, becoming a part of the informal economy. For example, in a conviction for human trafficking pronounced by the municipal court in Kursumlija in 2006 (K 186/06), it was stated that victims (Albanians from Kosovo) 'did not have appropriate documents for border crossing and they did not have passports... nor residence permits for any country of the Western Europe; due to that these persons would be engaged with the work in black ecomony in the EU countries and in that way their manpower would be exploited, because they wouldn't receive adequate payment for their work nor would be registered for the social insurance [...]'.

The main way to recruit both men and women is by offering/promising a job, which is obvious if we consider their poverty, bad financial situation, and non-employment as main push factors, on the one hand, and myths about the West, looking for better jobs, incomes, and future as pull factors, on the other hand (Europol, 2006). If we connect that to some of the core mitigating factors, such as the demand for cheaper manpower and prostitution, organized crime, restricted immigration policy, corruption etc. we may see how traffickers can easily 'profit' from this 'business'. In that context it becomes obvious, as noted by Tyldam et al. (2005: 48), that 'economic inequalities have always been a trigger for migration', including human trafficking as well. Traffickers use various mechanisms for controlling their victims: violence, threats, keeping passports (in the case of foreign victims), while victims are exposed to bad living and working conditions. This all emphasizes the fact that human trafficking should be considered a form of human rights violation.

Both men and women are transported or transferred from one place/country to another by different means (by car, plain, train, boat), but also on foot (particularly during illegal crossing of the border). In the case of transnational trafficking, which assumes crossing one or more borders, victims are transported both legally and illegally – outside the official border crossing points, or through official border crossing points but with forged documents or hidden in cars, trains, buses or other means of transportation. As stated in a conviction pronounced by the district court in Vranje in 2004 (K 55/04), whilst being transported victims were placed 'in a small space – a secret compartment under the floor of the back part of the car [...] there was a lack of oxygen, they were breathing heavily and even started to choke [...].'

Finally, we can note the increasing numbers of children identified as victims of human trafficking in Serbia.[129] As mentioned above, it is girls rather than boys who tend to become victims. They were mainly between 15 and 18 years of age, exposed to sexual exploitation, begging and (forced) marriage (see also Zegarac, 2005). However, the latest survey on human trafficking in Serbia also suggests an increase in the number of boys identified as victims of human trafficking, particularly those between 14 and 17. They were mostly Serbian citizens, with some from Georgia, Albania, and Turkey. Internal trafficking was predominant, while in the cases of transnational trafficking; Serbia appears to be a country of origin or transit (but primarily to some neighboring countries, such as Bosnia and Herzegovina (including Republika Srpska), Croatia, Macedonia, and Montenegro). The main forms of child exploitation, particularly for boys, include begging, labour exploitation, pressure to commit crimes, and, to a lesser extent, sexual exploitation. Child victims are also placed under the control of the trafficker by using coercion and all forms of violence (physical, sexual and psychological).

Nevertheless, when speaking about children as victims of trafficking in human beings, it is important to emphasize that there are several risk factors which increase the vulnerability of this population to human trafficking. As some authors have pointed out (such as Nikolic-Ristanovic et al., 2008: 396-400) these risk factors include poverty, belonging to a marginalized ethnic group (in particular the Roma population), direct or indirect victimization by domestic violence, gender discrimination, having no parents or being separated from parents or guardians, families with a lot of children, exclusion from education, being disabled, being a child 'worker', street children, unaccompanied minors, children placed in social welfare institutions, refugees, displaced persons and persons affected by war, children of illegal migrants, and children with social or behavioral problems. Identifying these risk factors starts to create a basis for further development of state policy on the protection of children not only from human trafficking, but rather from all other forms of discrimination, violence, abuse, and exclusion.

Hence, these preliminary research findings suggest the existence of two important trends in recent years in Serbia, which need to be taken into account in formulating anti-trafficking policy: a permanent increase in the numbers of Serbian citizens recognized as victims of human trafficking by relevant state agencies, institutions and organizations that are offering assistance and support; and a greater extent of internal trafficking, particularly in women and children, which

---

129. According to the data from the Serbian Agency for Coordination of Protection to victims of trafficking in human beings there were 60 identified victims in 2007. Of these, 26 were minors, 9 were male and 51 female; 48 were from Serbia, four from China, two from FYR Macedonia and Bulgaria, and one each from Moldova, Ukraine, Croatia and Romania.

provides better earnings for the traffickers and minimizes the risk of them being caught.

New migration flows: a challenge for human trafficking

The analysis of the data obtained in the 2008-2009 survey on human trafficking in Serbia shows that since 2006 there has been a considerable increase in the numbers of Albanians transiting through Serbia. These are both adults and children (mostly those between 14 and 17 years), coming from rural areas of Northern Albania. They usually have a low level of education and are impoverished. In the absence of opportunities to work and to earn enough to live, they are turning to migration. However, legal entry to EU countries is restricted with few visas. Most have some relatives abroad (mostly in Italy, Germany, and Switzerland) and they try to reach the West, often with the help and support of these relatives or with support from their families living in Albania who collect together money for their illegal travel to the West. In such circumstances they become 'easy accessible victims' of traffickers and smugglers who are offer them transit to EU countries for a certain amount of money, usually between 3,000 and 5,000 euros.

People from Kosovo, particularly Albanians living in the territory of Kosovo, are almost in the same situation, as are the Roma population and some of those coming from Turkey, in particular Kurdish people. Illustrative of this are parts of the statements given by adult male Kurds from Turkey before the district court in Nis as witnesses (statements contained in the conviction pronounced in 2005 by the district court in Nis for trafficking in human beings, K 205/05):

> 'I wanted to get a job in France and to do anything. Namely, in the village I am living in, which is rather isolated, the situation in my family is very bad... Seven of us are living together and only my father and brother are working as day labourers. During the last 3-4 years I have been working as a day labourer and I have saved 3,000 euros, the money I gave to a man in Istanbul to transfer me to France. I intended to enter France illegally...'

> 'I wanted to go to France and work there as a repairman, because my family is in hard financial situation as far as no one is working. I just wanted to earn money for my family and my two young daughters.'

> 'I wanted to go to France and work there with the hoe and shovel, to work in agriculture and earn money, because the life in Turkey is very hard. The financial situation in my family is very bad, because there are twenty seven members of the family. I have been working as a day labourer in Turkey.'

From this perspective, there appears to be almost no difference between persons identified as victims of human trafficking and those willing to migrate illegally (illegal migrants, smuggled people). As observed by Morowska (2007: 95):

'As in the case of labour migration, the micro-level 'push' forces that move the trafficking victims to accept offers to travel abroad supposedly to earn better money or a better life [...] are poverty and lack of prospects at home.'

As mentioned above, both smuggling in people and human trafficking can be considered within the context of (illegal) economic migration. If we assume that a smuggled person reaches the destination country, we can hardly imagine that he would be able to obtain valid documents for staying and working in that country. Rather, illegal migrants, willingly or unwillingly, are turning to other illegal markets and the informal economy (Ely-Raphel, 2002: 173): black markets for documents (passports, visas, stay and work permits), black markets for work (manpower), as well as trafficking in narcotics, arms, cigarette smuggling etc. (Nikolic-Ristanovic, 2003: 10). Surely that means that at some stage they are likely to be exposed to some forms of victimization, control, and exploitation? In other words, illegal migrants are vulnerable to victimisation by human trafficking.

This raises the question of whether we can we treat illegal migrants during the transit phase as, at least, potential victims of human trafficking and offer them support, assistance, and protection? If not, they are likely to be approached and treated in a completely different way: as 'criminals' or 'willing violators of immigration laws and undeserving of protection' (Lee, 2007: 11). To illustrate: in the case of Serbia, those considered illegal migrants or smuggled persons are arrested, punished for the misdemeanor of illegal crossing of the state border or illegal staying in the country and usually sentenced to imprisonment for 7 to 15 days (but not more then 30 days). Afterwards, they are sent to the Shelter for foreigners (a form of detention centre, run by the Ministry of the Interior) and will wait to be deported to their home country. This is not the shelter which supports victims, provides assistance, and protects victims of human trafficking. It is just temporary accommodation for those foreigners that do not have passports and have not applied for asylum. However, if a foreigner who was sentenced for illegal staying in Serbia or illegal crossing of the state border has a passport, after release from the prison, he would be left to exit the country by himself. In both these situations, the people involved are rather vulnerable and could be and often are exposed to new forms of victimization, new arrangements for illegal migration etc.

Keeping this in mind, we should note the observation by Kelly (2007: 87) that trafficking in human beings should be viewed as a process, i.e. a continuum that includes different levels of abuse, exploitation, and positions of vulnerability of victims:

'There are both overlaps and transitions from smuggling to trafficking, with the movement almost always in the direction of increased exploitation. These are more likely where the journey is lengthier and more expensive, since it increases the opportunities for exploitation and the size of debt on arrival.'

Due to that, 'a discrete categorization of "trafficking" and "smuggling" may be artificial and unhelpful, and may draw attention away from the broader context of exploitation and complex causes of irregular migration' (Lee, 2007: 11). Or, as stated by Chuang (2004: 140): 'The problem of trafficking begins not with the traffickers themselves, but with the conditions that caused their victims to migrate under circumstances rendering them vulnerable to exploitation.'

This leads us to the conclusion that, at least in Serbia, we need to reconsider the context of trafficking and try to put more emphasis on trafficking within the broader context of migration flows and migration policy, as well as improving the identification of victims of human trafficking or potential victims, particularly those within the broader target population – migrants (Tyldum et al., 2005: 27). That approach may result in better prevention strategies: if we provide support and assistance to illegal migrants we could possibly prevent their further turning into victims of trafficking. Otherwise, we could be trapped in the concept of the 'ideal victim' (Spalek, 2006: 22) or the tendency to distinguish between 'inno-cent' and 'willing/guilty' victims (Tyldum et al., 2005: 53), even treating migrants as 'others' and 'outsiders' (Goody, 2002) which is liable to divert state policy towards these problems.

CONCLUSION

Human trafficking has still not been eradicated, not even more then half a cen-tury after the establishment of legislation banning the retaining of persons in conditions of enslavement or other forms of slavery, trafficking in human beings, and forced and mandatory labour. Human trafficking presents a global problem equally affecting countries of origin, transit and destination. However, it is more visible in societies with more vulnerable populations: economic migrants, politi-cal asylum seekers, large numbers of unemployed, people who are homeless due to wars or other conflicts, where political instability is present etc. (Ely-Raphel, 2002: 173). This is also the case for Serbia. It is therefore impossible to eradicate human trafficking as well as other forms of irregular migration from contempo-rary society, given social and economical inequalities, which are very obvious, and particularly the gaps between source and destination countries.

Illegal migrants, including victims or potential victims of human trafficking, are exposed to social marginalization and exclusion, which result in their turning to different forms of illegal markets and the informal economy. They are not pro-tected and are often in a position of having no choice, other than to accept 'dirty, dangerous and difficult jobs' (Kelly, 2005: 54). Due to this, as stated by Lee (2007: 8) 'promoting transparent legal channels of labour migration, ending the use of trafficked labour by employers, and protecting workers' rights in the context of internal and cross-border migration, may be crucial to tackling the trafficking trade'.

In terms of the routes of (illegal) labour migration flows, including human trafficking, although some changes and new trends are visible in Europe with the broadening of the EU and its shift towards the east, Serbia is still a significant area, particularly in terms of transit towards the EU and the West in general. This leads us to the conclusion that there is still a need to create and improve existing anti-trafficking polices in Serbia, which should try to focus more on creating adequate (non-repressive) forms of migration control, as well as developing comprehensive systems for support and protection of victims and potential victims, and their identification. In other words, it seems that only adequate and prompt identification of victims and potential victims (particularly in the sub-population of migrants) and their inclusion in systems of support and protection, could contribute to cut off trafficking channels and suppress this form of organized crime. However, there is still a need to put more attention on a human rights approach to the phenomenon of human trafficking, because it is first and foremost defined as a violation of individual human rights, and to integrate this approach into the control of illegal migration.

REFERENCES

Aromaa, K. (2005). *Trafficking in human beings: uniform definitions for better measuring and for effective counter-measures*. Paper presented at the International Conference 'Measuring trafficking in human beings: complexities and difficulties', Courmayeur Mont Blanc, Italy, 1-4. December 2005.

Arsovska, J. (2008), 'Decline, change or denial: human trafficking and EU response in the Balkan Triangle'. *Policing*, 2(1): 50-62.

Ascola, N. (2007). 'Violence against women, trafficking, and migration in the European Union. *European Law Journal*, 14(2): 204-217.

Baldwin-Edwards, M. (2006). *Patterns of migration in the Balkans*. Mediterranean Migration Observatory working paper, 9.

Bales, K. (1999). *Disposable people*. Berkeley, Los Angeles, London: University of California Press.

Brunovskis, A. & Tyldum, G. (2004). *Crossing borders – an empirical study of transnational prostitution and trafficking in human beings*. Oslo: Fafo-report 426.

Chuang, J. (2004). 'Beyond a snapshot: Preventing human trafficking in the global economy'. *History and Memory*, 16(2): 137-163.

Commission of the European Communities (2007). *Serbia 2007 Progress Report accompanying the Communication from the Commission to the European Parliament and the Council, Enlargement Strategy and Main Challenges 2007-2008*. COM(2007) 663 final, Commission Staff Working Document, SEC(2007) 1435. Retrieved from: www.ec.europa.eu/enlargement/pdf/key_documents/2007/nov/serbia_progress_reports_en.pdf, January 30, 2009.

Copic, S. & Nikolic-Ristanovic, V. (2006). 'Mechanism for the monitoring of trafficking in human beings in Serbia'. In: J. Skrnjug (ed.), *Mechanism for the monitoring of trafficking in human beings phenomenon: Bosnia and Herzegovina, Croatia, Serbia*. Belgrade: IOM, pp. 69-101.

Counter-Trafficking Regional Clearing Point (2003). *First Annual Report on Victims of Trafficking in South-Eastern* Europe. Belgrade: IOM, Stability Pact for South Eastern Europe-Task Force on Trafficking in human beings and ICMC.

Danziger, R. (2006). 'Where are the victims of trafficking?' *Forced Migration Review,* 25: 10-12.

Ely-Raphel, N. (2002). 'Trafficking in human beings'. In D. Vlassis (ed.), *Trafficking networks and logistics of transnational crime and international terrorism.* ISPAC, pp: 173-175.

EUROPOL (2006). *Trafficking in women and children for sexual exploitation in the EU: the involvement of the Western Balkans organised crime 2006.*

Goodey, J. (2002). 'Whose insecurity? Organized crime, its victims and the EU'. In: A. Crawford (ed.), *Crime and insecurity –the governance of safety in Europe.* Devon: Willan Publishing, pp. 135-158.

Hajdinjak, M. (2002). *Smuggling in the Southeast Europe: The Yugoslav wars and the development of regional criminal networks in the Balkans.* Center for the study of democracy.

IOM (2004). *Changing patterns and trends of trafficking in persons in the Balkan region.*

Jovanovic, A. (2006). 'Trafficking in children – experience from practice'. In V. Dejanovic (ed.), *Child trafficking in Serbia – threats and reality.* Belgrade: Childs Rights Centre, pp. 45-51.

Kangaspunta, K. (2005). *Collecting data on human trafficking.* Paper presented at the International Conference 'Measuring trafficking in human beings: complexities and difficulties', Courmayeur Mont Blanc, Italy, 1-4. December 2005.

Kelly, L. (2005). *Fertile fields: Trafficking in persons in Central Asia.* IOM.

Kelly, L. (2007). 'A conductive context: Trafficking of persons in Central Asia'. In M. Lee (ed.), *Human trafficking.* Devon: Willan Publishing, pp. 73-91.

Kolakovic, P., Martens, J. & Long, L. (2002). 'Irregular migration through Bosnia and Herzegovina'. In F. Laczko, I. Stacher & A. Klekowski von Koppenfels (eds.), *New challenges for migration policy in Central and Eastern Europe.* Hag: IOM i ICMPD, pp. 119-152.

Lee, M. (2007). 'Introduction: Understanding human trafficking'. In *Human trafficking.* Devon: Willan Publishing, pp. 1-25.

Lehti, M. (2003). *Trafficking in women and children in Europe.* Helsinki: HEUNI, No. 18.

Limanowska, B. (2002). *Trafficking in human beings in Southeastern Europe.* UNICEF, UNOHCHR, OSCE-ODIHR.

Lindstrom, N. (2004) 'Regional sex trafficking in the Balkans transnational networks in an enlarged Europe', *Problems of Post-Communism,* 51(3): 45–52.

Mihic, B. (2006). 'Trafficking in Children in Serbia'. In V. Dejanovic (ed.), *Child trafficking in Serbia – threats and reality.* Belgrade: Childs Rights Centre, pp. 11-32.

Milivojevic, S. & Vukobratovic, T. (1999). Tribina 'Trgovina ženama i decom i savremeni društveno ekonomski kontekst u SRJ'. Beograd: *Temida,* 3-4.

Morawska, E. (2007). 'Trafficking into and from Eastern Europe'. In M. Lee (ed.), *Human trafficking.* Devon: Willan Publishing, pp. 92-115.

Mrvic-Petrovic, N. (2002). 'Trgovina ljudskim bicima kao specificna forma zenske migracije'. Beograd: *Temida,* 1: 25-32.

Nikolic-Ristanovic, V. (2002). *Social change, gender and violence: Post-communist and war-affected societies.* Dordrecht, Boston, London: Kluwer.

Nikolic-Ristanovic, V. (2003). 'Ilegalna trzista, trgovina ljudima i transnacionalni organizovani kriminalitet'. *Temida,* 4: 3-13.

Nikolic-Ristanovic, V. (2005). 'Trgovina ljudima u Srbiji: izmedju moralne panike i drustvene strategije'. *Temida*, 4: 5-14.

Nikolic-Ristanovic, V., Copic, S., Simeunovic-Patic, B., Milivojevic, S. & Mihic, B. (2004). *Trgovina ljudima u Srbij*. Beograd: OEBS.

Nikolic-Ristanovic, V., Dimitrijevic, J. & Kovacevic-Lepojevic, M. (2008). 'Rizici trgovine decom i inkuzija'. In D. Radovanovic(ed.), *Poremecaji ponasanja u sistemu obrazovanja*. Beograd: Fakultet za specijalnu edukaciju i rehabilitaciju, pp. 389-404.

Picarelli, J. (2007). 'Historical approaches to the trade in human beings'. In M. Lee (ed.), *Human trafficking*. Devon: Willan Publishing, pp. 26-48.

Ramcharan, B. (2002), 'Human rights and human trafficking'. In F. Laczko, I. Stacher & A. Klekowski von Koppenfels (eds.), *New challenges for migration policy in Central and Eastern Europe*. Hag: IOM i ICMPD, pp. 161-171.

Salt, J. (2000). 'Trafficking and human smuggling: a European perspective', *International Organization for Migration special issue*, 1: 31-54.

Spalek, B. (2006). *Crime victims – theory, policy and practice*. New York: Palgrave Macmillan.

Surtees, R. (2005). *Second Annual Report on Victims of Trafficking in South-Eastern Europe 2005*. IOM.

US Congress (2000). *Trafficking in women and children: The U.S. and international responses*. Congressional Research Service Report 98-649 C, 10th May 2000.

Tyldman, G., Tveit, M. & Brunovskis, A. (2005), 'Taking stock – a review of the existing research on trafficking for sexual exploitation'. Oslo: Fafo-report 493.

Zamfiresku, D.G. (2001), 'Harmonizacija nacionalnih zakonodavstava sa standardima Unije u vezi sa trgovinom ljudima' ('Harmonizing national legislatures with the standards of the EU in regard to trafficking in human beings'). In *Krijumarenje ljudi – krijumarenje žena i dece*. Beograd: Centar za unapreenje pravnih studija, Ministarstvo unutrašnjih poslova Rumunije i Centar za pravna pitanja.

Zegarac, N. (2005). *Niija deca – trgovina decom u Srbiji i Crnoj Gori*. Beograd: Save the Children.

Authors' brief biographies

Hartmut Aden
Hartmut Aden is Professor at the Berlin School of Economics and Law (Hochschule für Wirtschaft und Recht) and was previously Senior Audit Manager at the German Federal Court of Auditors (Bundesrechnungshof, Bonn, 2005-2009) and Lecturer/Assistant Professor at the Leibniz University Hanover (1997-2005). He studied law and social sciences at Göttingen, Hannover and Paris. He has published *Polizeipolitik in Europa. Eine interdisziplinäre Studie über die Polizeiarbeit in Europa am Beispiel Deutschlands, Frankreichs und der Niederlande* (Westdeutscher Verlag, Wiesbaden 1998), *Herrschaftstheorien und Herrschaftsphänomene* (editor, Verlag für Sozialwissenschaften, Wiesbaden 2004) and numerous journal articles and chapters in books.

Sanja Copic
Sanja Copic is a researcher at the Institute for Criminological and Sociological Research in Belgrade, Serbia, as well as a researcher and President of the Executive Board of the Victimology Society of Serbia. Her main research interests are in trafficking in human beings, domestic violence, juvenile delinquency, the position of crime victims in the criminal justice system and restorative justice.

Bojan Dobovšek
Bojan Dobovšek is Assistant Professor in Criminology and Criminal Investigation and Vice Dean of the Faculty of Criminal Justice, University of Maribor, Slovenia. He is a Member of the Commission for the Prevention of Corruption, as a representative of the judiciary. He has been on the Board of Trustees of ARCA (the Association for Research into Crimes against Art), since its formation, and is an associate of the Institute fur Politikwissenschaft und Socialforschunf, University of Würzburg, Germany.

Nicholas Dorn
Nicholas Dorn is Professor of International Safety and Governance in the School of Law, Erasmus University Rotterdam. His overarching research interest is the (im)balance between public and private interests, as found in public regulation and market self-regulation. His 2008-9 work covers administrative regulation of licit markets including financial markets; private-public security; strategic intelligence; corruption and governance; and cosmopolitan currents in international law (see publications at http://ssrn.com/author=821888).

Valeria Ferraris
Valeria Ferraris obtained her doctorate at the Catholic University in Milan and is currently working in the Social Sciences Department at the University of Turin. She has conducted several pieces of research on immigration and trafficking in

human beings. Due to her previous work as a lawyer, her present key research interest is in legal policies and immigration.

Alexander Kupatadze

Alexander Kupatadze is a PhD candidate at the School of International Relations of the University of St Andrews, UK. He holds a MA degree in International Relations from Tbilisi State University, Georgia and a MA degree in International Studies from Uppsala University, Sweden. Before starting his doctoral studies, he has extensively researched organized crime as an Associate Research Fellow at the Georgia Office of American University's Transnational Crime and Corruption Center (TraCCC). He has authored several articles and book chapters on criminality, smuggling and policing.

Clarissa Meerts

Clarissa Meerts is a Junior Teacher within the Department of Criminology, School of Law, Erasmus University Rotterdam, where she is completing her masters research. Her research interest include corporate security within companies and within public sectors organisations and the question of private settlements.

Paul Ponsaers

Paul Ponsaers is a full time professor at the Department of Penal Law and Criminology of the Faculty of Law, University of Ghent, Belgium. He has a Licentiate degree in Sociology and a Doctoral degree in Criminology. He is co-director of the inter-university 'Research Unit Social Analysis of Security Research' and promotor of the associated research unit 'Governance of Security'. He is President of the Association 'vzw Panopticon' and an editorial board member of the journal with the same name (Maklu), editor of the series 'Cahiers Police Studies' (Maklu), member of the Editorial Board of 'Orde van de Dag' (Kluwer) and President of the Editorial Board of the series *Het groene gras* (Boom Legal Publishers). He specialises in the fields of community policing, financial-economic crime, crime analysis and security policy, about which he has published extensively.

Pietro Saitta

Pietro Saitta obtained his PhD in sociology from the University of Urbino, Italy. He has researched and taught in the field of immigration at the Graduate Center of the City University of New York and at the Center for the Study of Ethnicity and Race of Columbia University, USA. He is now a senior researcher and lecturer at the University of Messina in Italy. His areas of interest include ethnicity, social policies, environment and qualitative methodologies. He has published, in particular, *Economie del sospetto. Le comunità maghrebine in Centro e Sud Italia e gli italiani* (Rubbettino, 2007).

Joanna Shapland

Joanna Shapland is Professor of Criminal Justice in the School of Law, University of Sheffield, UK and Director of the University of Sheffield Centre for Criminological Research. She has been at Sheffield University since 1988, and was previously at King's College London and at Oxford University. She is currently finalising work on a major research grant evaluating the use of restorative justice with adult offenders within criminal justice, as well as a longitudinal study of desistance from crime in young adult men. She has researched and published very widely in the fields of victimisation and victimology, desistance from crime, criminal justice, the informal economy and business and crime. She is the UK representative on the governing council of GERN and the Executive Editor of the *International Review of Victimology*.

Biljana Simeunovic-Patic

Biljana Simeunovic-Patic works as a researcher at the Institute of Criminological and Sociological Research in Belgrade, Serbia. Since completing her LL.M. degree at Belgrade University, she has been working on various national and international research projects run by the Institute as well as various non-governmental and international organizations, in the fields of criminology, victimology, criminal justice and trafficking in human beings. She has recently completed her PhD thesis at the University of Kragujevac on juvenile crime and justice in Serbia.

Antoinette Verhage

Antoinette Verhage has a Masters degree in Criminological Sciences and an Advanced Masters degree in European Criminology and Criminal Justice Systems. Since 2001, she has been working as a researcher for the research group Social Analysis of Security at the Department of Criminal Law and Criminology, Ghent University, Belgium. She is currently finalising her PhD research: 'The anti-money laundering complex and its interactions with the compliance industry. An empirical researchinto private actors in the battle against money laundering'.

Index